Hans Denck

No one may truly know Christ
except he follow him in life.

"FOLLOW ME"

NML NEW MONASTIC LIBRARY
Resources for Radical Discipleship

For over a millennium, if Christians wanted to read theology, practice Christian spirituality, or study the Bible, they went to the monastery to do so. There, people who inhabited the tradition and prayed the prayers of the church also copied manuscripts and offered fresh reflections about living the gospel in a new era. Two thousand years after the birth of the church, a new monastic movement is stirring in North America. In keeping with ancient tradition, new monastics study the classics of Christian reflection and are beginning to offer some reflections for a new era. The New Monastic Library includes reflections from new monastics as well as classic monastic resources unavailable elsewhere.

Series Editor: Jonathan Wilson-Hartgrove

"FOLLOW ME"

A History of Christian Intentionality

IVAN J. KAUFFMAN

EASTERN
MENNONITE
UNIVERSITY
Lancaster Programs
Library

CASCADE *Books* • Eugene, Oregon

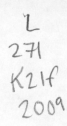
"FOLLOW ME"
A History of Christian Intentionality

New Monastic Library: Resources for Radical Discipleship 4

Cascade Books
A Division of Wipf and Stock Publishers
199 W. 8th Ave., Suite 3
Eugene, OR 97401

www.wipfandstock.com

ISBN 13: 978-1-55635-258-4

Cataloging-in-Publication data:

Kauffman, Ivan J.

"Follow me" : a history of Christian intentionality / Ivan J. Kauffman.

xxii + 252 p. ; 23 cm. —Includes bibliographical references.

New Monastic Library: Resources for Radical Discipleship 4

ISBN 13: 978-1-55635-258-4

1. Christian life. 2. Spirituality—History. 3. Monasticism and religious orders. 4. Monas-tic and religious life. I. Wilson-Hartgrove, Jonathan, 1980–. II. Anthony, Saint, c. 251–c. 350. III. Benedict, Saint, ca. 480–543. IV. Martin, Saint, Bishop of Tours, ca. 316–397. V. Bernard, of Clairvaux, Saint, 1090 or 91–1153. VI. Luther, Martin, 1483–1546. VII. Title. VIII. Series.

BX2432 K38 2009

Manufactured in the U.S.A.

Dedicated to the memory of my parents

Jess and Viola Winn Kauffman

and my parents-in-law

Orie Martin and Eda Zehr Conrad

They said "Yes"

and lived it to the end.

CONTENTS

PREFACE

This is a work of ecumenical history, an effort to view the Christian Church's story as a single whole. It has grown out of the Mennonite Catholic ecumenical dialogue in which the author has been deeply involved, but it has become something much broader—a history of all the movements which over the past two millennia have sought to follow Christ with complete intentionality.

As my research has progressed over the past decade it has become increasingly clear that the Mennonite Catholic story is only one chapter in a much larger story—the estrangement between those who view Christian faith in institutional terms, and those who view it primarily in personal terms.

And as the dialogue between North American Mennonites and the Benedictine monks of Saint John's Abbey in Collegeville, MN has progressed over this same period it has become equally clear that two distinct forms of Christian intentionality have emerged over the past 2,000 years, one celibate and monastic, the other non-celibate and evangelical.

My personal history is deeply rooted in these movements, and it would be dishonest not to disclose it. My paternal family has been Amish or Mennonite since the seventeenth century, and my parents were Mennonite pastors. I grew up in a community that was both Mennonite and evangelical, and I was formed by both traditions. I fully expected to live out my life in the Mennonite community, but in the 1960s a rather surprising series of events brought me into membership in the Roman Catholic Church and that is where I have spent the past forty years.

I have deep commitments to both my Mennonite heritage and to the Catholic faith which I now practice with great devotion, and I do not find

ix

them exclusive. I have referred to myself as a Mennonite Catholic. I do so in much the same way that others refer to themselves as Polish Catholics, or Hispanic Catholics or Black Catholics.

But my fundamental commitment is to the unity of the Church. I have come to believe that the disunity of the Churches is not only unfortunate but unacceptable, and that the unity of the Church is not something we can attend to when other more important things have been dealt with. I am deeply convinced there is nothing more important than the unity of the Church and nothing that can justify our continued acceptance of our disunity.

Having said that I hasten to add that I do not share the view of those who believe the unity of the Church can only be achieved by all Christians submitting to Roman authority—at least in its present forms. That may be what the Spirit is leading us toward, but recent events do not appear to indicate that. I do not know how we will eventually be brought into greater unity, but I do know from our experience in the Mennonite Catholic dialogue that a shared study of history will necessarily play a key part in that process.

We are not disunited because those of us now living have chosen to be divided into several major traditions and dozens of autonomous denominations. We are members of disunited churches because they are the ones which existed when we came on the scene, and we had either to join one of the disunited Churches that exist or else belong to no Church at all.

There is no Christian tradition, no denomination that does not share some responsibility for the disunity of the Church. Pope John Paul II has clearly stated his conviction that the Roman Church bears some responsibility for the Church's present divisions and that is a point of view which the research reported in this book supports.

Looking to the past will never by itself heal our divisions, but until we understand how we have come to be divided we will be powerless to deal with them. And we will never understand our divisions until we have together looked at their causes—not in an attempt to assess blame or to defend the status quo, but in a common charitable search for new perspectives that will enable us to relate to each other in new ways.

It is in that spirit that I offer this book to my fellow Christians.

"Follow Me"

Two fishermen are at work beside a lake, preparing their nets to fish. They are brothers, working alongside their father in the family business. It is a successful one; the family owns its own boat and employs other fishermen.

There was nothing unique about this day. As they did every day the fishermen planned to rest when they finished mending the nets, and then sail into the lake at night when the fishing is best, hoping to bring back food for their families and the other people in their village. This is the way fishermen on the Lake of Galilee had always lived. It was the way their fathers and grandfathers had lived, and their great-grandfathers, and it was the way their children would live.

These were ordinary people, living as ordinary people everywhere live—then and now. But this particular day something happened that would completely transform their lives, and which would eventually transform the world. A rabbi from a neighboring village walked up to the two brothers and said to them, "Follow me." He did not explain why the fishermen should follow him, or even what it meant to follow him. He simply said "Follow me." And they said "Yes."

The suddenness of their "Yes" is remarkable. They must have known the rabbi, but had he ever before asked them to forsake everything and follow him—to share his life, to live as he did? And what was so attractive about his invitation that it caused two sensible and prudent fishermen, men whose survival depended on making good decisions, to suddenly drop everything and embark on an entirely new life?

But this is what happened. And it happened not only to these two brothers but to many others as well. Immediately after the first fishermen began following Jesus he went up to two other brothers who were also preparing to go fishing and said to them, "Follow me." They also said "Yes."

Throughout Jesus' subsequent public career the words "Follow me" would recur like the refrain in a hymn. He would walk up to a man named Matthew who worked for the Roman occupation army as a tax collector and say to him, "Follow me," and he too would immediately follow. When a wealthy young man came to Jesus asking what he could do to be saved Jesus answered, in effect, "You must live as I do."

To be a Christian during Jesus' lifetime meant literally following him as he traveled about in the places where the ordinary people of his time lived. Some people accepted his invitation, but most did not—and for good reason. It was a costly decision; it meant keeping nothing for oneself. And it was a risky one. What if Jesus was not the person they believed him to be, the Messiah promised long ago by the prophets? Jesus constantly warned his followers that following him would involve immense sacrifice.

But despite the cost many of those who knew Jesus face to face would choose to follow him and their choices would ultimately affect all humanity. Along with the four fishermen who were called first, and the eight disciples who Jesus later chose to continue his ministry after his death, all those who followed him received an education unlike any which previous humans had ever received. It involved not only their minds, but their very being; not only what they did, but why they did it; not only what they felt obligated to do, but what they wanted to do.

These original followers of Christ were taught to see the world in a fundamentally new way. It was, they learned, a friendly place that did not need to be conquered by violence in order for humans to survive. They learned to view God as a benevolent and loving parent, not an angry and vengeful judge. They were taught to address God as "Abba," their word for "Daddy".

They learned how to heal, how to feed the hungry, how to serve others. Most important they learned the power of love at Golgotha and Gethsemane, and they saw this new way's power confirmed by the Resurrection. And finally they received this power themselves at Pentecost—and again at the lake in Galilee where it had all begun. And

with that power they were transformed from fishermen and other ordinary people into missionaries and preachers and administrators, the
founders of the great global religion we now call Christianity.

What caused this almost incredible change? What transformed these
fishermen into world-changing religious leaders, and their followers into
people able to create a new religion?

They have left us their answers to these questions in the accounts
they left behind, the books we now call the Gospels. They tell us their
abilities came from their decision to follow Christ, and from the power
they were given when they acted on that decision, even before they knew
what it meant. This new way was costly, not only for themselves but also
for their families, but it brought them such joy, such deeply meaningful
lives, they risked everything to tell their story to the world.

Their "Yes" has rippled through human history for twenty centuries
now, affecting a constantly growing number of people everywhere. There
is no one living today who has not been affected by it in some way.

One such person was the twentieth-century Swedish diplomat Dag
Hammarskjöld who led the United Nations in its formative years. At his
death this great leader left behind a spiritual testament which includes
this passage:

> I don't know Who—or what—put the question, I don't know
> when it was put. I don't even remember answering. But at some
> moment I did answer *Yes* to Someone—or Something—and from
> that hour I was certain that existence is meaningful and that
> therefore, my life, in self-surrender, had a goal. From that mo-
> ment I have known what it means 'not to look back,' and 'to take
> no thought for the morrow.'

This call comes to each of us in different ways, but it always comes.
And when it comes we must answer. And how we answer changes
history.

INTENTIONALITY IN EARLY CHRISTIANITY

In Jesus' lifetime people followed him in varying ways, and to varying degrees. At the core were the Twelve, men who had given up everything—
their businesses, their family's security, their personal freedom—to follow

Jesus. These are the people who traveled with Jesus, who shared his daily life, and who continued his mission after his death and resurrection.

There were also the Seventy, about which we know much less—but obviously persons willing to devote a period of time to proclaiming Jesus' message full time, but who returned to their usual lives once that time had ended.

There were also the women from Galilee who traveled with Jesus and the Twelve. They could not be part of the Seventy because they were women, but they provided the financial means for their male colleagues to teach, preach and heal. These women made substantial contributions to Jesus' ministry, likely at considerable personal sacrifice, but at some point they also appear to have returned to their homes, judging from the silence about them which we find in the subsequent tradition.

In addition to these two groups other disciples are mentioned in the Gospels and in Acts. These were the people who listened to Jesus, who took his words seriously and who tried to put them into practice, but who maintained the daily existence they had inherited from their ancestors and which everyone in their culture maintained.

Beyond these circles of committed followers was another larger group. These were those who had heard Jesus speak and had been moved by his teachings but who only observed him. Some had seen the miraculous healings Jesus performed and others had heard about them, in some cases from the healed persons themselves. Still others had heard about the miraculous feedings, and some had even participated in them.

This larger group had a commitment to Jesus, but it was a conditional one. Jesus had attracted their attention, but he would retain it only so long as it benefited them. There was as yet no irreversible commitment—no commitment to follow Jesus whatever the cost.

Still further from Jesus were persons in the leadership elite. People in this group followed Jesus only in the sense that they were attempting to determine whether he was a threat to their privileged positions. In the end they would decide that he was and they would decide to kill him, but even in viewing Jesus as a threat their lives became centered on him.

Jesus himself appears to have accepted all these varying degrees of commitment, even to the point of regarding those in leadership who were opposing him as playing an essential role in the new religious tradition he was forming. When Jesus appears in human history everyone is measured by their reaction to him.

Early Christianity

In the first decades of Christianity we find a pattern that is quite similar to the one that existed during Jesus' life.

At the highest level of intentionality were the Twelve—now called Apostles, and now joined by Paul—men whose lives were devoted entirely to disseminating the amazing story of Jesus' life as widely as possible. As this preaching mission succeeded they were increasingly required to devote their attention to leading and administering the communities of believers which had formed as the result of their preaching and teaching. Consequently they soon realized they needed to ordain other believers to take responsibility for the Church's charitable activities. These new ministers were called deacons, after the Greek word for service.

Surrounding the apostles and the deacons in Jerusalem was a third small group whose level of commitment was very close to theirs. These were lay people, men and women, who had made an unqualified commitment to the Christian community, selling their personal property and living in economic community with the Apostles and with each other.

This early example of intentional Christian community seems not to have survived the persecution which dispersed the Jerusalem Church a few decades after it was founded, but this early post-Resurrection community would be the first in a long line of evangelical lay communities which would spring up in the Christian Churches, continuing to the present.

Clearly the vast majority of first-century Christians did not live at the same level of commitment as the Jerusalem community, nor were they expected to. When one couple in the Jerusalem Church announced they wanted to join the community, and so had sold their property and were donating the proceeds to the Apostles—when in fact they had secretly kept a portion for themselves—Peter condemned them for lying to the community, not for having kept some property for themselves.

In the early centuries of Christianity communal property did not become the norm, but persecution, and even more the constant threat of persecution, did become the norm. This situation of sustained adversity, which lasted for nearly three centuries, virtually required all Christians to live at very high levels of commitment and intentionality.

During these centuries when their survival, both individually and as a group, was constantly under threat the early Christians adopted quite high standards of membership. In at least some places only fully committed Christians, i.e., those willing to die under persecution, were allowed to attend Sunday worship.

When some Christians failed the test of persecution, as inevitably happened, it produced a major controversy within the Church. A fierce division arose between those who believed anyone who had lapsed under persecution should never be allowed back into Church membership, and a more forgiving group who were willing to allow them back after a period of penance. Eventually the non-rigorists prevailed, but the tensions which produced these early schisms would recur in Church history, up to the present.

Persecution ended rather suddenly early in the 300s, and in the decades and centuries which followed Christians would gradually divide into two major groups. The first group slowly but surely became the civil religion of the former Roman Empire. The second formed small lay-initiated communities that sought to live out the Gospel without compromise, whatever the cost.

The clearest example of this second development is St. Anthony, the founder of Christian monasticism. As a young Christian in Egypt in the mid-200s he heard the story of the rich young ruler being read one Sunday in his local church and immediately determined to follow Jesus' advice to that earlier young man who had lived only 200 years earlier, and in a place nearby. He proceeded to sell the estate he had inherited from his parents, distributing the proceeds to charity, and devoting the rest of his life to prayer and spiritual development.

There were also small communities of married Christians throughout the Mediterranean area in the early centuries of the Church who had been inspired by the example of the Jerusalem community.

The faith and daily life of these groups, both monastic and lay, contrasted sharply with the large numbers of people who had only recently converted to Christianity, and who tended to regard their new faith as merely another religion, rather than a new way of life.

In many cases these recent converts had entered the Church under political or social pressure, and even when their conversion was voluntary it was often shallow. The Christian Church grew quite rapidly in the 300s, and there were simply not enough pastors and teachers to instruct and form the new Christians.

Institutional Christianity and Intentional Christians

In the centuries following persecution Christianity continued to evolve in two quite different ways. One produced a highly institutionalized civil religion. The other produced loose networks of intentional Christians, usually but not always living in self-governing voluntary communities.

The growth of institutional Christianity is easy for us to see and study because it played a prominent role in the historical events of its time, and because it developed the rituals and doctrines which have come to define Christianity for most people. The numerous buildings which institutional Christians have erected throughout the world are vivid evidence of its importance. Since the 300s the vast majority of those who consider themselves Christian, probably in the range of 85 to 90%, have been institutional Christians.

Intentional Christianity on the other hand is much harder for us to recognize and to study. That is because it is fundamentally personal and non-institutional, and because it has involved fewer people. But despite its smaller numbers and its institutional weakness this portion of Christianity has had a profound impact on both the Church and on western civilization, an impact completely out of proportion to its size. Because intentional Christians have, until recently, been forced to exist at the margins of society where they were heavily persecuted and regarded as heretics their influence has often been overlooked.

The differences between these two groups are substantial. For the majority of institutional Christians their religion is largely synonymous with affiliating with a particular religious organization. For such people this membership is a part of their life—very often an important part—but it is only a part of their life. Intentional Christians by contrast view their Christian faith as much more than a religion. For them it is a way of life, something that defines their entire existence. Everything they do—mentally or physically, politically or personally—is done because they believe being a Christian requires that action. Their religion is not a part of their life, it is their life.

Intentional Christians are the people who throughout history have read or heard the stories of Jesus from the Gospels, and have found themselves wanting, often passionately, to follow the example of the first generation Christians. These original Christians, the ones who had first said "Yes" to Jesus, had held nothing back, as Jesus had held nothing back for himself, and if they were to follow him these persons could hold nothing back for themselves.

Whereas institutional Christians struggle to reconcile the demands of living in their particular culture and society with the ideals presented by their religion, intentional Christians struggle to differentiate themselves from the societies they live in because they believe many practices of their society are incompatible with following Christ.

Always for these intentional Christians following Jesus means taking action, not at some distant time in the future, but *now*, in the time that actually exists. Many of the first Christians emphasized that this is how they came to follow Christ, dropping what they were doing on a particular day and from that moment beginning to live life in a new way. That is what those who have intentionally followed Jesus in subsequent centuries have sought to do.

Of course not everyone who heard Jesus say, "Follow me," during his lifetime had answered, "Yes". Some had said "I'll think about it." Others had said, "I'll do it when it's convenient." Still others had simply declined, saying "It's too hard." It has been the same every year since. But those who did say "Yes" to Jesus came to live their lives in fundamentally different ways, ways that were quite different than the way they would have chosen for themselves.

Their "Yes" necessarily occurred before they knew what it meant to accept Jesus' invitation, but that did not deter them. They learned to follow by following—often learning the most from the mistakes they made, as the stories they tell about themselves make quite clear.

Those who have answered Jesus' invitation with an intentional "Yes" in the centuries since have had a deep and long-lasting impact on our entire civilization. They are the people who have given their lives as martyrs. They are the people who have devoted their lives to spiritual development, often at the cost of great poverty and distress. They are the ones who have left the security and comfort of the communities and families they had grown up in to go into the wilderness and create new communities of the spirit.

They are the people who throughout the medieval period endured social ostracism and intense persecution in their struggle for social justice, eventually laying the foundations for democracy. They are the ones who in the 1500s died as martyrs for religious liberty, for separation of church and state, and for the right of voluntary assembly. They are the people who in the 1600s left their homes in England to establish a new nation in North America, a nation that would provide the seedbed for the global democracy that would transform the entire world in the twentieth century.

They are the people who in the 1700s devoted themselves to evangelizing the ordinary people of Europe and America, and who created local congregations where poor and working class people could be comfortable. They are the people who in the 1800s volunteered their best leaders and who contributed vast sums to send missionaries to Asia and Africa. They are the people who in the same period forced society to confront the shameful institution of slavery and to abolish it.

They are the people who in the twentieth century forced their fellow Christians to confront the legacy of religiously legitimated warfare and to enact laws recognizing the right of conscientious objection to military service. These are the people who are forcing us today to confront the massive number of abortions taking place throughout the world.

Without these people and their courageous actions throughout the centuries the world would be a very different place. They are the intentional Christians. They are the ones who have asked not "What *must* I do to be a Christian?" but "How can I be *more* Christian?"

The River of Grace

There is a river of grace flowing through human history, a river which like all rivers has two banks. On one bank the Church's institutions have thrived and developed, and Christians devoted to these institutions have built homes there.

On the other bank live those Christians called to uncompromised intentionality. There they have built their homes, and have created a different set of institutions.

Both banks are part of Christianity, but the people who live there have developed two quite different ways of being Christians. These two lists suggest the contrast between these two ways—and the importance of both.

The River of Grace

INTENTIONAL	INSTITUTIONAL
Creating the new which the river makes possible	Preserving the old which the river has produced
Prophetic	Priestly
City of God	City of Man
Monasticism	Diocesan Church
Radical innovation	Evolutionary change
Perfectionist ideals	Acceptance of evil as inevitable
Tightly bounded voluntary communities	Inclusive biological-based communities
Emphasis on the spiritual	Emphasis on the historical
Individuals are primary	Institutions are primary
Bible as authority	Tradition as authority
Evangelical	Catholic
Believer	Church
Freedom	Continuity

Communal [handwritten note next to "Individuals are primary"]

Isn't there always a third way? [handwritten note]

Monastic Intentionality and Evangelical Intentionality

Just as Christianity has developed in two distinct ways, one institutional and the other intentional, intentional Christianity has developed in two distinct ways, one monastic and the other evangelical.

Of these two forms the evangelical form is the oldest, appearing in Christianity's first decade in the Jerusalem Church. Monasticism by contrast would not appear in Christianity until some two hundred years later, and would not become a major force in the Church until several centuries later.

But the evangelical lay movements, even though part of Christianity in its earliest years, never found a secure place in the Church's institutions until after the Reformation. In the 1,500 years before the Reformation an antagonistic relationship between the institutional Church and the lay movements developed, in contrast to monastic intentionality which developed in a positive relationship to the institutional Churches.

The primary distinction between these two forms of Christian intentionality is the monastic requirement of celibacy. Evangelical intentionality by contrast has always assumed its members would be married and have families.

Both the evangelical and monastic strands of intentional Christianity have generated numerous movements and institutions over the centuries. This book's purpose is to provide an overview of both monastic intentionality and lay evangelical intentionality over the entire two-thousand-year history of Christianity. It will note both their similarities and their differences, and analyze the ways both have influenced the development of western civilization.

PART ONE

Monastic Intentionality

Christians now living are largely unaware of the major contributions which the first millennium monastic movement made to forming both the Christian tradition and western civilization. They are only slightly more aware of the role which the religious orders have played in the second millennium in shaping the world we now live in.

This section of the book is a summary history which recounts the major developments in monasticism. The story begins in Egypt in the 200s and continues through the twentieth century.

ONE

From Anthony to Benedict

The monastic movement began in Egypt in the 200s, when Christians were still being persecuted by the Roman imperial authorities. This movement grew rapidly within the Christian community and by the 300s had spread throughout the Christian world. By the 500s it had become so widely accepted that one of the monks at a monastery in Rome was elected pope, and as Pope Gregory the Great he in turn made the monastic rule created by an earlier Italian monk, St. Benedict, normative for all western monasticism.

EGYPTIAN MONASTICISM

Christianity came to Egypt almost immediately, and by the third century was established throughout that nation. The bishop of Alexandria, one of the largest and most powerful cities in the world at the time, was regarded as one of the Church's major leaders, on a par with the bishop of Rome. There were parishes and bishops throughout the Nile Valley and large numbers of Christians everywhere.

But Egypt also had a long and significant pre-Christian past, and had formed a culture that viewed the physical and the spiritual as completely intertwined. Egypt also occupied one of the world's most unique geographic locations—a fertile river valley stretching north and south for hundreds of miles, but bordered on both sides by a barren and dangerous desert. It would be in this unique situation that Christian monasticism would emerge.

St. Anthony of the Desert

One Sunday morning in the year 251 a young man from a Christian family was walking to church in Egypt. He came from a prominent and prosperous family in his village but his parents had died a few months earlier, leaving him alone in the world at age 20, except for a younger sister.

As he walked along that morning the young man was thinking of the apostles and how they had given up everything to follow Christ. And he was also thinking about the original Christian believers described in the *Acts of the Apostles* who had sold everything and given the money to the apostles to be distributed to the poor.

When the young Anthony reached his village church the service had already begun, and the gospel was being read. That morning it was the story of Jesus' encounter with a wealthy young man who had asked, "What must I do to be saved?" Jesus had told the young man, "If you would be perfect go sell what you possess and give to the poor and you will have treasure in heaven."

These words struck the young Anthony to the roots of his being. He said afterwards that he felt this story was addressed to him personally. When he left the church he immediately proceeded to give the land he had inherited to his neighbors. He sold the other property he had inherited as soon as possible and gave the money to the poor.

At first he kept a small amount to support his sister, but when he went to church the next Sunday the gospel was from the Sermon on the Mount in which Jesus told his disciples, "Do not be anxious about tomorrow." Anthony again felt compelled to act at once on Jesus' words, and when he left the worship service he gave all his remaining possessions to the poor.

He put his sister, then a young girl, in the care of a group of unmarried Christian women who lived nearby, and proceeded to devote the rest of his life to prayer and spiritual development. It was a decision that would change the course of human history.

There were no monasteries at the time, but there were a few solitary monks living alone on the edge of society and Anthony apprenticed himself to one of them and began to imitate this monk's way of life. Later he would travel throughout the nearby area, living with other monks and learning from them.

Anthony's reputation as a holy man grew quickly, even in his 20s. He struggled mightily with the difficulties of the ascetic life, especially with renouncing sexual companionship, but his will was exceptionally strong and he prevailed. He often spent entire nights without sleeping, and when he did sleep it was either on a reed mat or on the bare ground. His only food was bread with a little salt, and he drank only water. He said "the soul's intensity is strongest when the pleasures of the body are weakest."

He spent his days trying to become a person who was "ready to appear before God"—someone whose heart was pure and who was prepared always to obey God's will, without compromise. He took the life of Elijah, the founder of the Hebrew prophetic tradition, as his model and judged himself each day by that great prophet's example.

After preparing in this way for about 15 years the young monk took a step that was to define his place in history. No longer content to struggle with his personal demons which he had largely conquered, he set out to defeat the demons that infected his society. He had his friends lock him in a tomb near his village, where he lived alone in the place where his culture believed the spirits who controlled society lived.

One day when a friend came to bring Anthony some food he found the young monk lying on the floor, apparently dead. The friend picked him up and carried him to the village church where Anthony's relatives and the townspeople gathered around him as they would a corpse.

But about midnight Anthony emerged from his coma. Looking around he saw that everyone else had gone to sleep. Anthony got up, woke his friend and asked him to take him back to the tomb and lock him in again. Anthony immediately resumed his combat with the demons, crying aloud, "Here I am—Anthony! I do not run from your blows, for even if you give me more, nothing shall separate me from the love of Christ."

The demons responded by shaking the walls of the tomb as though an earthquake was taking place. Anthony sensed the tomb was filled with reptiles and wild animals charging toward him. He was terrified and in severe pain, but he was able to respond rationally, telling the demons he was under Christ's protection and that therefore they had no power over him.

When this ordeal ended Anthony asked Christ, "Where were you? Why didn't you appear at the beginning, so that you could stop my distresses?" Anthony says a voice answered, "I was here, Anthony, but I waited to watch your struggle. And now, since you persevered and were not defeated, I will be your helper forever, and I will make you famous everywhere."

That promise would be kept. Anthony lived in the Egyptian desert for another 70 years, and by the time of his death at age 105 he would be famous throughout the Christian world.

St. Athanasius of Alexandria, the great Christian theologian and bishop, would become St. Anthony's friend and biographer, and through the book Athanasius wrote and published this illiterate Coptic farmer would become known throughout the Christian world. Athanasius' *Life of Anthony* was copied, translated and published for the next 1,700 years, and inspired generations of other Christians to become more intentional Christians, and many to become monks.

The Other Monks

There were Christian monks living in Egypt before Anthony and many living at the same time, and by the time he died there were thousands of other men and women living as monks in Egypt. Most are unknown to us but a few have survived in the historical record. We have only tantalizing fragments of their stories and would like to know much more about them, but what we do know makes it obvious that Egyptian monasticism was a substantial movement, not simply a few isolated figures living heroically in the desert.

Among the early Christian monks whose names have been passed down in history is St. Paul the Hermit, an Egyptian Christian who had fled into the desert to escape persecution some 20 years before Anthony began his monastic career. Paul lived in the desert for 90 years, and is the first Christian hermit known to us. Legend has it that he was fed each day by a raven who brought him bread.

There is also St. Thaïs, an Alexandrian courtesan who was converted by one of the desert monks and who is reported to have shut herself up in a cell in one of the women's monasteries for three years of penance. She is reported to have died only 15 days after her years of penance were finished.

And there is St. Moses the Black, an Ethiopian warrior who had for many years led a criminal gang which terrorized his area and whose strength and ferocity were legendary. He was converted by some monks who lived in the area and decided to follow their example. He eventually joined the monastery at Petra in the Desert of Scete, and under the guidance of its abbot gradually learned to control his violence. He was eventually ordained a priest. He is reported to have died defending his monastery against an attacking band of marauders, a band much like the one he had once led.

From Monk to Monastery

At first the early Egyptian monks formed informal groups around an experienced older monk who they referred to as their 'father', their 'Apa'. But a monastery is more than a group of monks, and it was the achievement of one of the early Egyptian monks, Pachomius, to establish the first Christian monastic institutions.

By the end of the 300s the institutionalization of the monastic movement in Egypt had reached the point that a monk from Palestine who came to visit the Egyptian monasteries in 388 found a monastic village in Nitria inhabited by some 5,000 monks. Most lived in individual huts, although some lived with one other monk.

They supported themselves by weaving flax. In this village of monks there was a bakery, and there were doctors. There was wine for sale. On Saturdays and Sundays the monks gathered for common worship and a few of their number had been ordained so they could serve as priests. Strangers were welcomed at the guest house and they could stay as long as they liked, but after a week they were expected to work.

There was no written monastic rule, but there were three whips hanging from palm trees. One was used to discipline monks guilty of prohibited behavior, a second was used to punish thieves who invaded the community, and a third was for strangers who behaved badly.

Our informant, a monk named Palladius, tells us that when he stood in the village in the evening and listened to the monks singing the Psalms together, each from his own cell, he imagined that he had been taken up to heaven.

Early Monasticism and the Church

One became a monk in the 200s and 300s by deciding to be one. It was monks who created monasticism, not monasticism that made monks. The early Church did not create monasteries and then invite individuals to live in them, as would later be the case. The early Christian communities accepted the relatively few of their numbers who became monks as good Christians, perhaps even as exceptionally good Christians, but they did not teach that only monks were good Christians, or that all good Christians should become monks.

The monks for their part did not seek ordination or any other mark of validation from the institutional Church. To the contrary, the monastic movement in the beginning was overwhelmingly a lay movement, and indeed often forbade its members to be ordained. The Egyptian monks created a set of institutions that had not existed before, but they did not do so in opposition to the Church's already existing institutions. The monks held ordained persons in great esteem and made constant efforts to support them.

The monks had withdrawn into the desert to find the silence needed for lives devoted entirely to prayer, but they had not withdrawn from the world. And the people who lived at the time—from the emperor Constantine to the common farmers of Egypt—clearly regarded the monks' lives as relevant to their own.

The Egyptian monks for their part were often engaged in the turbulent and violent politics of their time, and in the great religious debates which were intertwined with those politics. They distinguished the spiritual and the physical very clearly, and placed the spiritual first, but they did not believe the material did not matter.

THE IMPACT OF EGYPTIAN MONASTICISM

The impact which Egyptian monasticism had on the world of late antiquity can only be understood when this new movement is viewed against the background of the religious crisis then taking place throughout the Mediterranean world. It is this crisis which provided the opportunity for both the exceptionally rapid expansion of Christianity in its first 500 years, and the development of the monastic movement within the Christian community during that same period.

Truth

As the Roman Empire had increasingly achieved its goal of the political and economic integration of the entire Mediterranean world, it had brought the peoples of the ancient world into much closer contact with one another than had ever before been the case. The result was that throughout the Roman Empire people were discovering that people elsewhere were worshipping a bewildering array of gods, not all of them alike by any means. The beliefs which the various local cultures had regarded as essential for human survival and therefore beyond question were suddenly discovered to be completely ignored in other cultures.

The result was to subject all the existing belief systems to serious doubt, and the consequences of this were profound. Religious belief by its very nature involves that which is beyond doubt, and if beliefs that had been firmly fixed since time immemorial could now be questioned, what was there that could not be questioned?

At the same time rationality was becoming much more widely dispersed throughout society, thanks primarily to the Greek philosophers who had spread across the Mediterranean world, both in person and via their writings. Their new way of thinking and the questioning it inevitably produced greatly increased this dilemma.

Christian faith introduced yet another new challenge into this situation. ancient peoples were accustomed to new gods being introduced into the world. This had always happened with considerable frequency in the ancient world. But the new Christian God was different, for never before had the ancient world encountered a new god determined to replace all the old gods.

What this meant in practical terms was two things. The first was that all the previous religious traditions had to be abandoned—traditions which had formed over millennia. Elaborate mythologies and religious rituals which were embodied in temples and established priesthoods had grown up around these old traditions and entire cultures had in turn formed around them, but despite this Christianity insisted they be abandoned.

Even more important Christianity required those who adopted its beliefs to make a place in their minds for the concept *truth*. Polytheism as a theological system is endlessly elastic. It always has room for yet another god, representing yet another view of reality. A person might choose one god over another, but it had always been assumed, tacitly at least, that such choices didn't really matter—that one god is as good as another and that one's choices represented personal opinion, not objective reality.

The peoples of the ancient world appear not to have troubled their minds with questions about the relationship between the various gods being worshipped all around them. Nor do they seem to have asked themselves how it was possible for so many competing gods all to claim power. They appear to have simply accepted that there were many gods existing somewhere, gods which humans had to relate to as best they could. If human worship and religious practice were somewhat chaotic and irrational it was because reality itself was chaotic and irrational.

Into this ancient mental and theological environment Christianity came as a revolutionary force. It required its believers not only to accept the Christian God, but also to reject all the old gods as merely demonic forces pretending to be gods.

How could this new religion make such sweeping claims? It did so by asserting that in the spiritual realm some things are true and some are not, just as some things are true in the physical realm and some are not. And from this basis Christians argued that only what is true, what actually exists in the spiritual realm, deserves to be worshipped.

Those who rejected Christian beliefs, as most people at the time did, had to reject both its essential features—the belief that truth exists in the spiritual realm, and the belief that the life of Jesus reveals the ultimate truth about God.

But even to reject these beliefs one had to wrestle with questions that had never before been raised. The very boldness of Christianity's claims to truth, although they were profoundly counter-cultural, nonetheless represented the only real alternative to returning to the old religions with their increasingly discredited mythologies. The only other alternative was to decide that it doesn't matter what one believes—that people can believe contradictory things about the fundamental nature of human existence and still regard each other as reasonable.

The monks were the most visible and profound witness to the Christian belief in truth. They had risked their lives on it.

Social Equality

A second thing which made both this new religion and its monastic off-shoot fundamentally different was that it was not tribal. In fact to become a Christian was to give up ones tribal affiliation and to transfer his or her primary allegiance to a trans-national institution to which any person belonging to any tribe, any nationality, and of any social status, even females and infants, could belong.

For Christians what was primary was not one's social status, which was determined by the accidents of birth, but the existence of truth itself, a truth that had been revealed in a way everyone could understand—as a life lived by a person who was both fully human and fully divine. This ultimate-truth-embodied-in-a-life was both a great leveler, and a great connector.

Again the monks were living out this belief in a way that could not be ignored by their contemporaries.

Intentionality

For people living at the time perhaps the most conspicuous thing about the monastic way of life was that it demonstrated the power all human persons have to act intentionally. The monks achieved this in the most convincing way possible—by the example of actual lives lived in successful communities.

Fatalism was central to all the pre-Christian religions. Despite their many other differences they agreed in regarding humans as essentially powerless pawns, subject to the capricious whims of superhuman spirits who obeyed no law except their own self-interest and self-preservation. The most any human could hope for was to somehow placate these unpredictable super-humans so they would help you attain your personal goals, whatever they were, and so they did not cause you harm.

This view was directly challenged by the Christian monks. The monks were unanimous in insisting that what enabled their way of life was the reality of a benevolent and orderly God, whose actions were predictable and who always acted in ways that enhanced human life. This God was one that actually existed and that was all-powerful, not the product of human imagination. In their daily praying of the Psalms the monks both absorbed this belief and proclaimed it.

Furthermore the monks demonstrated by their way of life, maintained over decades and centuries, that ordinary human beings from any social class or any background could choose to live in ways that were not governed by the universal human passions—the desire for food, for sexual intimacy, for personal autonomy, for wealth, for physical comfort.

By means of what has been called "the prophecy of behavior" the monks taught the world that being religious entailed a substantial change in the way one lived his or her daily life. Even if one did not copy the monastic way of life, everyone was challenged by its example to evaluate their own behaviors and values, and to ask whether what had been long-standing custom in that person's culture could in fact be changed—and should be changed.

The monks demonstrated, as the martyrs before them had, that Christian faith makes it possible for ordinary people to live in an entirely new way, but they did so in a new way—by their lives rather than by their deaths.

MONASTICISM AFTER EGYPT

Christian monasticism emerged in Egypt, but that is not where it would grow to maturity. The reasons for this are not clear to present historians, but the fact itself is beyond dispute.

Almost immediately after Christian monasticism emerged in Egypt, other Christians began imitating the Egyptian monks, forming monastic communities throughout the Mediterranean world, and within 300 years the monastic movement's center would move across the Mediterranean, to its northern shores—to Greece and Italy and France—where it would take permanent root and develop into its final forms.

Palestine

Monasticism first spread to Palestine, where after persecution ended Christians increasingly began to visit the sites where the events recorded in Scripture had taken place. These pilgrimages to the holy places became an increasingly important part of Christian practice, and would remain so to the present.

As part of this development Christian monks began to establish residence in the Holy Land. St. Jerome, who moved from Rome to Bethlehem to carry out his lifetime of Biblical scholarship and translation, is the best known of these persons, but he was far from being the only one. When Jerome arrived in the Holy Land in the late 300s a monastery already existed on the Mount of Olives, and there were also two monasteries for women. During his lifetime there were at least three monasteries for women and two for men in Bethlehem, including the one he had founded.

Indeed by the year 400 Palestine had begun to replace Egypt as the center of Christian monasticism, and in the next century organized communities of monks began to form throughout Palestine. They were called lauras. One of them, founded by St. Euthymius in the valley of Cedron, included novices, newly professed monks, and the more experienced monks who lived alone as hermits. On Saturdays and Sundays the entire community, including the hermits, would gather for worship and communion, and bring their work to be sold.

Greek Monasticism

St. John Chrysostom reports that when he was growing up in Antioch in the mid-300s there were monks everywhere, both in the cities and in the mountains around them. The popularity of monasticism was so great that at one point a violent opposition against it developed, involving both Christians and non-Christians, an opposition so strong it verged on persecution. Chrysostom, who later became a monk, wrote a treatise defending the new movement and dealt with his own mother's opposition by living a monastic life in his parental home until his mother's death.

The monastic movement would take a different form in the Greek-speaking world, and has continued to have a different character there than in the West. The founder of eastern monasticism is Basil the Great, a person whose importance in the Eastern Church is as great as St. Benedict's in the western Church.

What is the same is that monasticism became an essential part of Christianity in the east. By 518 there were at least 54 monasteries in the city of Constantinople alone, and today the monastic community at Mount Athos is vivid evidence of the continued vitality and importance of the monastic movement in the Eastern Church.

Italy

In Italy the impact of Athanasius' *Life of Anthony* was substantial. The book was quickly translated from the original Greek into Latin, and within a few decades after Anthony's death it had become a Christian best seller.

We have a vivid picture of the impact this book had on Italian Christianity in St. Augustine's autobiography, the *Confessions.* Augustine had come to Milan as a young man in the 380s, seeking professional success as a teacher of rhetoric. He had become disillusioned with the Manichean religion—a dualistic and semi-Christian sect he had joined as a youth—but he was not yet a Catholic. Although unmarried, he had a long-term relationship with a woman and together they had a son.

Augustine had begun attending Mass at the cathedral in Milan, where he heard St. Ambrose preach, and this had brought him to becoming a catechumen—one who was affiliated with the Christian Church but who was not yet baptized. He had also begun reading St. Paul's letters. But what would bring Augustine into full Christian membership, and set him on the road to becoming one of the great intellectuals in western civilization, was reading the story of Anthony.

Augustine first heard about Anthony from a Christian colleague who was an official in the imperial civil service. This man had visited Augustine and a friend one afternoon and had told him about the monastic movement. Up to that point neither Augustine nor his friend had ever heard of Anthony, nor any of the other Christian monks.

When they first heard Anthony's story they "were amazed" Augustine says. That this unique life had occurred "so recently, almost in our own time" and that it had taken place in a Christian community which held orthodox Christian doctrines left them both astonished. When Augustine and his friend learned there were monastic communities everywhere in the Christian world—including one just outside the city walls in Milan which was supported by Ambrose himself—they were even more astonished. "We listened in rapt silence," Augustine says.

Their colleague told them he had learned of Anthony's life one day when he had been in Trier with the emperor, and had been walking around town with three other officials. They happened on a Christian family who owned a copy of Athanasius' *Life of Anthony,* and who invited them in to visit. One of the officials began reading the book, and was so taken by its story that he decided on the spot to resign his post in the civil service and become a monk.

This official had turned to his companion and said, "What do we hope to achieve with all our labors? What is our aim in life? What is the motive of our service to the state? Can we hope for any higher office in the palace than to be Friends of the Emperor? And in that position what is not fragile and full of dangers? How many hazards must one risk to attain a position of even greater danger? And when will we arrive there? Whereas, if I wish to become God's friend, in an instant I may become that now."

Visibly struggling within himself this man had finally turned to his friend and said, "I have broken away from our ambition, and have decided to serve God, and I propose to start doing that from this hour in this place." His friend replied that he would join him. The man telling the story said he had decided not to join his colleagues in becoming a monk, but that as a result he had parted with a heavy heart.

As the young Augustine listened to this account of radical conversion he was moved to the depths of his being. He began to compare his own undisciplined life with that of the monks, and he later wrote, "I stood naked to myself." When his visitor left Augustine turned to his friend and said, "What is wrong with us? What is this that you have heard? Uneducated people are rising up and capturing heaven, and we with our high culture without any heart—see where we roll in the mud of flesh and blood. Is it because they are ahead of us that we are ashamed to follow?"

Augustine went into the garden, making gestures which he said were like those which "men make when they want to achieve something and lack the strength." He knew what he wanted to do but could not do it. "From a hidden depth a profound self-examination had dredged up a heap of all my misery and set it in the sight of my heart," he says. "That precipitated a vast storm, bearing a massive downpour of tears."

At this point Augustine heard a child's voice saying, "Pick up and read, pick up and read." Remembering that Anthony's conversion had begun when he had heard the story of the rich young ruler read in his church, Augustine took his copy of Paul's letters and opened it at random. His eyes fell on these words: "Not in riots and drunken parties, not in eroticism and indecencies, not in strife and rivalry, but put on the Lord Jesus Christ and make no provision for the flesh and its lusts."

"I neither wished nor needed to read further," Augustine says. "All the shadows of doubt were dispelled." He went to his mother, who had followed him to Milan, and told her that he had decided to become a Christian and end his relationship with his female companion. "The effect of your converting me to yourself," he said to God, "was that I did not now seek a wife and had no ambition for success in this world."

Augustine would live that commitment for the remainder of his life, and the impact on western civilization of what he would write as a result would be massive. Augustine did not become a desert monk, as Anthony had, but he did live in a monastic community even after he was ordained a bishop. It was that community which enabled him to spend his life as an unusually productive writer—in many ways the founder of western Christian theology.

St. Benedict

By the 400s the ideal of monasticism was firmly implanted in western Christianity, but it had not yet been institutionalized. That crucial step would take place through the leadership of an Italian monk whose name would become synonymous with western monasticism, St. Benedict of Nursia.

Benedict's influence came from his ability to absorb what had taken place before he came on the scene, learning both from the successes and the failures of early monasticism. This enabled him to create a structured form of monastic life that would be sustainable over long periods, and which would be able to incorporate people from many different temperaments and backgrounds.

Benedict's life, important as it appears to us now, did not make any great impact on his contemporaries. It was only after his death, and in fact not until some centuries after his death, that its full impact would be felt.

Benedict's New Vision

Benedict's contribution was a new vision of what the monastic movement could become. He retained what the monastic movement had learned about self-discipline and prayer during the previous three centuries—both negative and positive—and he incorporated that experience and its accumulated wisdom into a written rule which guides the international Benedictine community to this day.

But Benedict also saw something no one before him had seen, and this new vision would have a profound impact, not only on monasticism but on western civilization as a whole, an impact so basic and long-lasting that Pope John Paul officially named him "the Father of Europe."

This new vision is summed up in the Latin phrase *"Ora et labora"*—prayer and work—the principle which still guides all Benedictine communities. After Benedict the monastery was no longer a place where one went simply to pray. Prayer and conversion still remained central to the monastic vision, but they were now no longer an end in themselves.

The work which the monks did in this new kind of monastery was not done merely to support the monks, as had previously been the case, and as is still the case in many monasteries. After Benedict the monastery became less a retreat from the world and more a place where people from the world went for spiritual guidance, healing, and education. Increasingly the new kind of person being created in the monasteries was called to serve the larger Church—first as bishops, then as missionaries, and finally with increasing frequency as teachers throughout Europe.

Each century since Benedict has seen a gradual increase in the extent to which the monastery has been a servant to the world, as contrasted to a retreat from the world. Mother Teresa of Calcutta in the late twentieth century represents the culmination of this process. She and St. Anthony stand at the end and the beginning of a vast culture-creating movement, and Benedict is the link between them.

Perhaps the best evidence that this rather radical transformation was intentional on Benedict's part is in Pope Gregory the Great's use of monks as missionaries. If there was anyone who understood and appreciated Benedict it was this great Roman administrator who first became a monk and then a pope. And so we may conclude that in sending out monks as missionaries—an action completely at odds with the original intent of the Egyptian monastic movement—Gregory saw himself acting in a way that Benedict would have approved. In any case it would be this vision that would increasingly motivate the monastic movement in succeeding centuries.

If we look for evidence of this transformation in Benedict's own writings we will find it in the sections on hospitality in the *Rule*. Whereas St. Anthony had been so determined to minimize the interruptions to his solitude caused by the many visitors he attracted in his later years that he moved to a virtually uninhabited place, St. Benedict viewed his monastic vocation as involving radical hospitality.

"Let all guests arriving at the monastery be received as Christ himself," he wrote. "Let the Abbot pour water on the hands of the guests; and both he and the whole community shall wash the feet of all guests." He added, "Let great care and solicitude be shown particularly in the reception of the poor and of travelers, because it is in them that Christ is more especially received."

What could more clearly mark the change Benedict initiated in the monastic tradition than his belief that Christians encounter Christ in the social realm—in the lives of other humans, especially strangers who come to us uninvited—as contrasted to finding Christ in the solitude of the desert?

Whereas in Egyptian monasticism the emphasis was on combat with the demons, which had to be faced in solitary encounters in the desert, Benedictine monasticism has always emphasized human relationships—first within the monastery, but then beyond the monastic community in an endless web of hospitality extending throughout the world.

Benedict and the Rule

Today Benedict's name is virtually synonymous with the *Rule* that he left us. But in fact large portions of the rule attributed to him were written by an earlier anonymous monk, and later adapted by Benedict. What is important about Benedict is not so much this particular *Rule*—although its significance can hardly be overestimated—but the idea of order itself.

It is evident from the rule dealing with *gyrovagues* that by Benedict's time the monastic movement had become in many cases a refuge for those who wished to live individualistic lives, unaccountable to other persons. Benedict had experienced the consequences of that individualism when he agreed to serve as abbot to a small group of monks who later turned on him and tried to poison him because he had held them accountable to monastic discipline. After this experience Benedict made certain that being a monk meant being accountable to other monks and to the leader of one's community, and that it meant living by a written rule.

Living by a rule means more than following orders. In the new communities which the Benedictine monks created across Europe nothing happened by chance. The primary weapon in the monk's battle against flesh and the devil was self-discipline, and discipline always took the form of order—an ordered day, an ordered community, an ordered life. By contrast life outside the monastery was a kind of loosely controlled chaos. People slept when they felt like it, and woke when they felt like it, or when circumstances demanded—when the baby woke up crying or the cattle demanded to be fed.

Time had a completely different meaning in the new communities which the monks were creating. No longer did time just happen. No longer was it an abstraction which one seldom thought about if at all. Monastic time was something very real, actually the essence of life, for it was time that permitted prayer and without prayer what was the purpose of life?

And so time was counted and its use carefully planned in advance. What occurred here occurred because of human choices, and became events through the combined voluntary actions of everyone in the community.

The Intentional Community

Yet another thing made the monastic communities fundamentally different from the communities which surrounded them. It was that membership in the monastic communities was voluntary. Everywhere else in the ancient world one's place in society was determined almost entirely by birth, but the monasteries by contrast were populated by people who had chosen to be there. It was their personal decision which had formed their communities, not their birthplaces which had determined the structure of their lives.

Some of the monks had been slaves, some had been belonged to wealthy families that owned slaves. Some came from peasant families, some from land-owning families. Some had been educated, some were still learning to read. Some were strong, some weak; some gifted, most of very ordinary abilities. But despite their great diversity the members of these monastic communities lived as a single family, each respecting and serving the others, each filling a meaningful place in the community's life.

Like all other institutions the monasteries were governed by a single leader who held office for life, but there was this great difference—the monasteries' leaders had been chosen in an open election by the people they governed. There was no precedent for this is the ancient world.

Benedict and Gregory the Great

Just as St. Anthony's popularity and influence owes as much to St. Athanasius' biography as it does to Anthony's own life, so also does Benedict's place in Church history owe as much to Pope Gregory the Great's biography—and to Gregory's own actions based on his study of Benedict's life—as it does to Benedict's own actions.

This is not in any way to detract from the significance of either Anthony's life or of Benedict's epochal accomplishments, but it is to recognize that both these lives were a part of the events of their time, and that their personal greatness rests very strongly on the greatness of their contemporaries. It is hard to imagine the history of western monasticism without the contributions of both Athanasius and Gregory the Great. Both of the biographies they wrote are unique literary documents which are in themselves as significant as the lives they portray, and which are filled with a profound spirituality that matches the great saints being described.

Furthermore in Gregory's case it was his formation in the Benedictine community in Rome, one of the first to be established, which shaped him as a Christian, and which in turn shaped his papacy—and which in turn has shaped the Christian Church in the centuries since. Gregory almost single-handedly created what we now call the papacy, and the fact that he did so on the foundations which the previously unknown Benedict had laid is an event of truly epochal significance. Whatever one's opinion of the papacy as an institution—or of the various bishops who have held that office—it is incontrovertible that as an institution the papacy has had a major impact on western civilization.

What were the effects which this combination of a new kind of monasticism and a new vision of the Catholic Church which Gregory brought into being have on the subsequent development of the Church? Among them are these major initiatives:

- Intentional mission sending, resulting in the conversion of England.

- A global Christian community governed by a rule, in the same way Benedict had envisioned monastic communities being governed.

- The integration of spirituality with civil politics.

In Gregory's papacy intentional Christianity and institutional Christianity were integrated, and the result was a burst of energy that still reverberates through human history. Gregory decisively moved the Church from the era of persecution, which had ended, into the era of evangelization which would be its future. And as a former high-level government official it was impossible for him to envision evangelization without corresponding changes in civic life.

But as a Benedictine monk Gregory's view of the future was based on law, not on military coercion, as had always been the case in previous Roman practice. His 'soldiers' would be the monks, who were sent out to convert the still non-Christian inhabitants of Europe—not only changing their religious practices but their entire way of life. His was a non-violent revolution, although he would not have used that word. But what other option did a dedicated son of Benedict have?

THE MONASTIC WITNESS IN LATE ANTIQUITY

We can only understand the impact which monasticism had in its early centuries to the extent that we understand how radically this new move-ment challenged the bedrock assumptions on which life was based at that time.

The monastic was one who lived alone—a single individual—and merely by adopting this life the individuals involved called into question several assumptions that were so basic to life in the ancient world they were regarded as beyond question. One such assumption was that hu-man survival requires individuals to subordinate their personal concerns to those of a larger social collective, most often an extended family or a clan.

Who you were in the ancient world depended almost entirely on the family you belonged to, and that of course was a matter of birth, not choice. Furthermore your standing in that family was also a matter of birth rather than choice. If you were a son your status was much higher than if you were a daughter. And if you were an eldest son your status was much higher than if you were a younger son.

If you had no family, either because your parents had died, or because your mother was unmarried, you had very little status at all. You might be adopted into an existing family, but even then your status would be lower than those who belonged to the family by birth. Unless you were part of an established family you could not survive, and unless you put the interests of the family before your own you could not be part of a family.

But the monks ignored all this. They voluntarily left their families and lived alone, not because they had to, but because they chose to. And despite breaking this most basic rule of the ancient social code they had survived, something which those who lived at the time would have assumed was impossible. Even more amazing to their contemporaries, these people without a family not only survived, they thrived. By all appearances they were happy and at peace in a way those who conformed to the traditional patterns were not. And they were healthy. People began coming to them for healing and for solutions to their problems.

Furthermore this new way of life was living proof that people could live in ways that were based on choice rather than determinism. The monks' ability to live without sexual companionship meant that sex was an option, not an obligation laid on humans by biological necessity. The monks' ability to choose what they ate, and how often they ate, meant that it was possible for humans to make eating an intentional activity in which human intelligence played a major role.

The monks' ability to order their days, to choose what to do and when, meant that other humans could do the same—that they did not need to live by impulse, that they too could make plans and act on them. The monks lived an intentional life. They had chosen to choose, and they had chosen to live lives modeled after the life they found in the Gospels.

What made the monks' intentionality possible was their constant attention to their inner lives, to prayer. Only those persons whose inner life is strong have the capacity to act intentionally, and only those who live intentionally can have a strong inner life. The human being is a unitary whole—mind and body, belief and action, sensation and choice. All these are bound together in a rich network of feedback loops, which together constitute human life.

All this would have a revolutionary impact on life at the time. By the year 400 it was obvious to any thoughtful person that the great Roman experiment, now some 500 years old, had both failed and succeeded. It had succeeded in bringing the entire Mediterranean world into a single economic and political unit, but it had failed to provide a way for all the numerous cultures and nations which it incorporated to live together in a sustainable way.

Caesar Augustus has obviously been one of the world's great political geniuses, but as the decades and centuries after him unfolded it became increasingly clear that he had created an empire that no one after him was able to govern. As things went from bad to worse in the 200s it became painfully obvious that something was very wrong, but nobody knew what it was. And so policies that had already failed were tried once again, failing yet again and producing steadily deepening despair throughout society. The Roman dream had collapsed into personal despair and political chaos.

But what was also becoming obvious was that the Christians were able to deal with this collapse much better than anyone else. They had no solution for the problems of the empire, and had little incentive to find one since the imperial authorities often tried to exterminate them. But they did have something to live for, something that did not depend on the empire's success, something so deeply meaningful they were prepared to die for it.

And so while the imperial government was crumbling the Christians were forming thriving local communities—communities able to shield their members from the worst impacts of the social and political disintegration taking place around them. What made this possible was the ability of local Christian communities to provide their members with a hope that no one else at the time had. And there was no witness to Christian hope that was more powerful than the lives of the monks.

Furthermore the new world which the Romans had made possible required a new kind of person. This new person had to be honest, committed to the common good rather than to personal gain. He had to be at peace with himself, so that he could be trusted to act prudently and rationally, rather than impulsively from frustration and anger. He had to be a realist, so that he could see things as they actually were, not blinded by prejudice, fear, or superstition. He had to be ethical, so that the rule of law, which was central to the Roman way could be carried out consistently.

What produced this new person in the Christian community was the belief that each individual has a direct, personal relationship with God—the God who "is love." This experience, especially when it is persisted in and reflected on over time, transforms and empowers the persons involved, giving them a sense of self-worth and dignity which no other experience does, and which at the same time makes people humble and motivates them to serve others.

Everywhere in late antiquity the results of this process of personal transformation were evident in local Christian communities, but nowhere was it more dramatically evident than in the lives of the Christian monks, and in the communities they formed.

underplays dimension of communal monasticism

TWO

From Martin of Tours to Cluny

Although Christian monasticism originated in Egypt and took institutional shape in Italy it would have its greatest growth and influence in northwest Europe, above all in the region we now call France. This would occur in the 500 years between about 500 and 1000, and the success of monasticism in the nations of northern Europe in this period would provide the foundations for what we today call western civilization.

The reasons for this great development in France and the adjacent nations are not entirely obvious. If we would have visited this area in the 500s and 600s we would have found an area populated largely by illiterate tribal peoples who possessed only the bare rudiments of civilization. The thought that within a few centuries this area would become the heartland for a new civilization would have seemed impossible, even laughable.

And if one would have suggested that Christian monasticism would play a central role in this civilization creating process it would have seemed even more unlikely. But that is what happened. It is one of the great untold stories of our past.

CREATING A NEW CIVILIZATION

How is it that a place that had always been on the edge of Mediterranean civilization came to be the heart of a new civilization? And why did the monastic movement, which until then had involved only a relatively few exceptionally religious individuals, come to play such a major role in this great process?

Certainly the collapse of the Roman Empire is a major part of the answer. This collapse was marked by two landmark events: first, moving the imperial capitol to Constantinople in the early 300s, followed by the sack of Rome by Barbarian warriors in 410. As the once all-powerful capital city slowly lost its power Roman military capacity declined with it, and as this process continued the tribes living on the empire's northern frontiers found themselves increasingly on their own.

For centuries these tribal peoples had lived in increasingly close contact with the Romans who had established colonies in their territories, but as the empire disintegrated the peoples of northwestern Europe could no longer define themselves as they previously had—as part of the Roman Empire, albeit an often unwilling part.

They surely rejoiced in the end of colonialism, but at the same time they could not forget they had once lived in a world that had a center. And so they had no choice but to create a new center. If they did not they would revert to the nomadic civilization they had left behind, something they were not willing to do.

The creation of a new civilization is a process that takes many centuries, and the creation of western civilization is a relatively recent event that is still unfinished. But slowly the idea of Europe, then of Christendom, then of the West would emerge to replace the old Roman ideal. And the monastic movement would play a central role in that epochal development.

The New Space

For a new civilization to emerge there must be a new geographical space, one large enough for a civilization to develop in and one without an already successful civilization. It must also be able to economically support a dense population. The area north and west of the Alps which we now call Western Europe met those criteria.

Previously this area had been regarded by both the Romans and the people who lived there as a wilderness that lay outside the civilized and cultivated world. Until the Roman Empire collapsed everything important had happened in the Mediterranean world. It had been the place where all technology, all political power, all trade and economic activity, all learning had originated. Nothing significant had happened in northern Europe except warfare with the Mediterranean nations.

But as it became clear that the Roman collapse was permanent, and that the new Byzantine Empire was too far away and too weak to govern northern Europe, those who lived there slowly but surely began to view themselves as occupying a place that had value in its own right.

The New People

Who were the peoples who populated this new space? As best historians can discern at this point they were an ethnic amalgam, a melting pot of tribal peoples who interbred with their neighbors to form constantly changing societies, both cultural and ethnic.

At this point we know little or nothing about most of these societies, but there are some which the surviving Roman records describe—the Celts, the Franks, the Goths, the Avars, the Slavs, the Huns, the Vandals, the Lombards, the Helvetes, the Magyrs. In recent decades some of these tribes have received attention from historians, although much more remains to be known. Those of us descended from the northern European tribes have only begun to understand the histories of our ancestors.

Many if not all these tribes appear to have belonged to what is now called the steppe civilization. These tribes occupied the prairie lands which stretch across Asia for thousands of miles, from the Danube to Mongolia. They were peoples who had learned to live wherever their agricultural and mechanical technologies—which centered on horses and livestock, and especially cattle—were appropriate.

These tribes had not developed the skills necessary to live in cities, and were neither literate nor politically sophisticated. Nor had they developed the skills needed to live in money-based economies. What they did know how to do was to live on the prairie. They were remarkably resourceful, especially in metallurgy, and were outstanding soldiers able to form effective military units, although limited to what could be organized by a single person to whom everyone in the army had some face-to-face relationship.

What is most striking about these peoples was their lack of fixed ties to a given territory. They would settle in a given place so long as it supplied their needs, but as soon as famine or other adversity arose, or some new opportunity appeared elsewhere, they were on the move, often vast communities numbering in the thousands. Needless to say such peoples had no time or inclination to build cities or to develop written languages.

They were defined by their movement, and by the technologies that enabled it.

For centuries these tribal peoples had been bunched up along the Roman Empire's northern border, roughly marked by the Danube River. They had been held in place by the Roman army, but they had also been pulled southward by the Empire's great wealth, and by the opportunity to serve in the Roman army. But when the Roman army collapsed in the 300s and 400s it was like a dike giving way. As many as several hundred thousand people eventually flooded southward and westward in search of a better way of life, much as people by the millions migrated west and north in the 1800s and 1900s.

This great migration and the eventual permanent settlement of the Northern tribal peoples would create modern Europe, both demographically and culturally. The civilization that came into being—a group of independent nations, each with its own language, culture and history—would be the result.

New Civilization

As this great migration continued it became increasingly clear that the cultures that had developed during the northern tribes' nomadic existence on the steppes were no longer viable. Now that they had settled more or less permanently and had adopted the rudiments of the Roman way of life they could not turn back. They had to create something new.

Furthermore the northern tribes were being stirred into a vast melting pot, created by their increasingly intense interaction with one another. None of their existing tribal cultures was strong enough to absorb the others, and so they had little choice but to give up the cultures they had developed in isolation in favor of a single new civilization that had room in it for both their varied pasts and their common aspirations for the future.

The magnitude of this change should not be underestimated. For a new civilization to emerge everything has to change, and that requires a great deal of time. People cannot adopt new languages, new social customs, new marriage practices, new political institutions in a single generation. And they certainly cannot do so when there is nothing to replace them. Humans simply cannot survive without the cultural traditions which structure their lives, both personally and socially.

This is especially true in the case of language, which is intensely conservative. All languages incorporate specific experiences and values—both in their vocabularies (we have words only for what we have experienced, and for what we regard as worth remembering), and in their grammars, which embody specific thought patterns and modes of perception. Languages of course do change, but they do so only very slowly. Even to change a language requires using the language which currently exists, since that is only one anyone understands.

So it was that the northern tribes when they set about forming a new civilization to replace both their old tribal civilization which no longer worked and the Roman civilization that had been imposed on them but which had now collapsed, had no choice but to retain many of their old ways. If there was to be a new civilization it would have to be built upon the old cultures, and incorporate many of their features.

The same was true of Roman civilization. The northern tribes did not want to destroy Roman civilization so much as to be a part of it. They wanted to share in its economic power, in its political stability and order, and in its law, literacy and business practices. It was obvious to everyone that their traditional practices were inferior to the Roman way in all these areas.

But at the same time it was obvious to them that their cultures were superior to the Roman culture in other ways. That is why the northern warriors had increasingly been able to defeat the Roman armies, and why the Romans increasingly depended on tribal soldiers to fill the ranks of their armies. There was a kind of raw vitality in the new civilization emerging in the north which the old Mediterranean civilization simply could not match.

New Religion

A second meta-event was taking place in northern Europe at the same time the Roman Empire was collapsing. This was the conversion of the northern European tribes to Christianity. Once again the reasons for this event are not immediately obvious, but the fact that it took place is beyond dispute, and the consequences are clearly far-reaching and substantial.

For the northern tribes adopting Christianity involved much more than simply changing religious rituals, or using a new name for the same gods which had always been worshipped by their tribes. Christianity was of course a new religion, with a new set of rituals, and it did introduce a new god into society, but this new Christian god was fundamentally different than any of the old gods.

And the rituals associated with this new religion were also fundamentally different than anything that had existed. Previous religious ritual had been fundamentally aristocratic. If people wanted to do something religious, something to placate the gods or ask their favor, they had to pay someone higher in the social pyramid to speak to the gods on their behalf. That was because the gods were viewed as residing at the very apex of the social pyramid, just above the kings and the high priests.

By contrast Christian ritual was astonishingly egalitarian. Anyone could be baptized, and anyone could participate in the Eucharist, which was essentially a meal rather than a sacrifice. This eliminated the religious advantage which wealthy people had previously enjoyed over poorer people. Since the rich had been able to afford more expensive sacrifices than the poor, they had previously enjoyed a more privileged access to the divine.

Another aspect of the new religion which would have been attractive to the northern European tribes was Christianity's insistence that what people did mattered. The connection between religion and morality which now seems so obvious to us was new at this point in human history. Prior to Christianity religion had largely been concerned with the behavior of the gods, not with human behavior. The gods were believed to act very much as humans typically do—lying, stealing, cheating, killing, quarreling, and being sexually promiscuous.

Christianity was different. It worshipped a god who was ethically rigorous and who kept the same divine laws that were imposed on humans. And if right and wrong exists at the divine level then surely it also exists at the human level, and that means some actions are to be encouraged and other are to be prohibited. This leads to the inescapable conclusion that human actions and human choices matter, not just for their immediate consequences but because God is watching and God cares.

The steppe cultures had evolved in an environment which required people to be intensely practical and resourceful. Unless what they did worked they simply would not survive the brutally cold winters. The feedback loop in the nomadic world is short and unforgiving. They had no long-established cities or political structures to fall back on, no reserves of capital built up over the generations to sustain them, no bountiful physical environment which would keep them alive no matter what they did. They knew that some things were true and others were not, that if the truth is ignored there were consequences.

Furthermore the new religion represented a new set of political values. For the northern tribes political relationships had been based on violence, and there was little in their experience which provided any reason to believe there was any alternative. The long conflict with the Romans, which had gone on for more than 500 years, had forced both sides to develop military technology to very high levels and to organize themselves into military societies in which everyone was increasingly involved in making weapons, engaging in combat, or in working to support those who did.

Over the long term such a way of life is never sustainable, and the result is always an eventual spiritual, economic, and political bankruptcy. Open-ended warfare extracts an immense cost from the societies involved, and in the end does not provide any benefits commensurate with the cost. This had happened throughout the Roman Empire by the year 400, and it happened in northern Europe a century or more later.

As a result people everywhere were open to something new, something which Christianity was able to provide. But the new Christian beliefs could not simply be inserted into the old cultures that had formed around very different beliefs, and so when the northern tribes began adopting the new religion which the Christian missionaries were proclaiming they had no viable option but to create a new civilization which embodied those new values. They did not realize that at the time, but it was true nevertheless.

New Monasticism in France

In France a new kind of monastic movement would emerge that would be characterized by a synthesis of five major strands, three of them inherited and two which were innovations. The three inherited ones were:

- The early Egyptian monastic tradition, initiated by Anthony and Pachomius, and brought to France by Martin of Tours, Cassian and others between 300 and 500.

- The Celtic Irish monastic tradition brought to France by Columban and other Irish missionary monks in the late 500s and early 600s.

- The Benedictine monastic tradition of rule by rational regulation developed in Italy and adopted throughout France between 500 and 700.

The two innovative strands were:

- The French pattern of close relationships between the monastic communities and the diocesan bishops, which rested on the frequent practice of selecting bishops from the monastic communities. This tradition had begun with Martin of Tours and became widespread in subsequent centuries.

- Charlemagne's practice of forming partnerships between the monastic communities and the local governing elites in the late 700s and early 800s. This practice was continued by his successors in the late 800s and 900s, and eventually resulted in the monastic federation centered at Cluny.

The monastic movement which came into being once this synthesis had formed in France in the 900s was quite different than the original monastic movement that had emerged in Egypt in the 200s and 300s. One need only compare St. Anthony's crude dwelling place hidden in the Egyptian desert to the wealth and architectural splendor of the Abbey of Cluny some 800 years later to appreciate how profound this transformation had been.

The crucial role monasticism would play in forming European civilization had not been apparent when this new monastic movement slowly emerged. It appears to have been the result of the two exceptional monks who came to France from elsewhere—not to found a new civilization but to evangelize its people.

Martin of Tours

A young soldier born into a military family in what is now Hungary came to France in the 330s. He had been born a few years after Constantine became the first Christian emperor, but the Roman army had remained much as it had been before Constantine's conversion and it was still his world—not by choice but by birth.

One bitterly cold day the young soldier encountered a poor man who was nearly freezing to death. In an effort to save the man's life Martin took his sword and cut his military cloak in half, in effect sharing his fate with the poor man's. Those who knew the young soldier were not surprised. He had been a catechumen ever since he was 10 years old even though his parents were not Christians, and as a soldier had lived such a disciplined life many considered him a monk.

That night in a dream Christ himself appeared to Martin, dressed in the half of his cloak which the young soldier had given to the poor man. Martin said later that he clearly heard Christ say to the angels standing near him, "Martin, who is still but a catechumen, clothed me with this robe." As a result of this experience the future saint, who was then about 20, quickly requested baptized.

Martin remained in the army for another two years, but then re-signed, saying to the emperor who had come to distribute bonuses to Martin's legion, "Hitherto I have served you as a soldier. Allow me now to become a soldier of God. Let the man who is to serve you receive your bo-nus. I am a soldier of Christ. It is not lawful for me to fight." The emperor flew into a rage, accusing Martin of cowardice, but Martin responded by offering to face the enemy the next day unarmed. He was spared this test when the enemy surrendered the next morning.

After leaving the army Martin became a student of St. Hilary, then France's leading bishop. Christianity in France was some 200 years old by that time, and was firmly established in the cities, although not in the countryside where traditional religious practices still prevailed.

Martin's life as a new Christian soon became entangled in the great battle between the Arians and the Niceans which dominated the Christian Church at that time. Hilary was the leading French defender of the trinitarian doctrines of Nicea, and when the more unitarian Arians came to power both he and Martin were forced into exile. Martin settled in Milan where he established a monastery, perhaps the one Augustine heard about when he lived there.

When the Niceans returned to power Martin returned to France with Hillary and there he established what is usually regarded as the first French monastery. When one of Martin's first monastic disciples died suddenly Martin was able to restore the young man to life, thus establishing his reputation as a powerful holy man. As a result the people of Tours made Martin their bishop in 371—despite some of the city's ruling class complaining that Martin "was a man of despicable countenance, that his clothing was mean, and his hair disgusting."

Martin would serve the people of Tours and the surrounding countryside for the next 26 years, but would continue to live as a monk. He established a new monastery across the river from Tours and by his death there were some 80 monks living there, conducting their lives much as the monks in the Egyptian desert were. Many of these French monks also became bishops.

Martin's biography is similar to Anthony's. He was a healer, a miracle worker, and he initiated a new way of life. But there was a significant difference as well. Martin regularly left his monastery to evangelize, something Anthony would not have done. "Before the times of Martin, almost no one in the regions around Tours had received the name of Christ," his biographer reports. "But through Martin's virtues and example Christ's name has prevailed to such an extent that now there is no place thereabouts which is not filled either with very crowded churches or monasteries. For wherever he destroyed heathen temples, there he used immediately to build either churches or monasteries."

Martin would leave behind three permanent legacies. The first was his example of being a person who was the equal of emperors and intellectuals even though he had no education and had refused military service. His biographer, a Latin intellectual of great ability, said of Martin, "I never heard from any other lips than those of Martin such exhibitions of knowledge and genius, or such specimens of good and pure speech. It is remarkable that in a man who had no claim to be called learned even this attribute of high intelligence was not wanting."

The second was Martin's example as a monk who served as a bishop. This would become a tradition in France and would do much to establish the tradition of celibate monastic practice for all clergy in western Christianity.

Martin's third legacy was his insistence that the Church and its leaders had an authority independent of civil government, another feature of western civilization that is unique and which would have enormous consequence in later centuries.

Columban

In the 590s, some 200 years after St. Martin's death, an Irish holy man appeared in northern France leading a small band of Irish monks who had come there as missionaries.

We know much about Columban's life because one of his contemporaries wrote his biography, but this otherwise informative biography tells us little about Columban's life in Ireland. However we know from other sources that a rich monastic life had already formed there, and that he was the product of it. We still do not know how Christianity first reached Ireland, so that already at this relatively early date Irish Christians were able to send missionaries to other nations. Irish monasticism is an important part of monastic history, but one which has not received the attention from historians that it deserves. It is clear that monasticism developed in a unique way in Ireland.

Columban and his monks were warmly welcomed by the young King Theudebert who provided royal protection for the new monastery because he viewed the presence of St. Columban and his monks as a great spiritual benefit to his realm. But when a few years later Columban began to criticize the king for his promiscuous sexual practices it produced a severe political crisis. On the surface the issue was whether the king's illegitimate offspring were members of the royal family and thus able to succeed him. But the real issue, as the king told Columban, was whether a group of persons could live in that society whose teachings departed "from the common customs".

Columban's refusal to compromise with the king forced the still tribal people of France in the early 600s to choose—either the old way represented by their warrior king, or the new way represented by St. Columban and his monks. King Theudebert and his grandmother expelled Columban and his monks from their territory, but this only provided St. Columban with an opportunity to demonstrate his courage and spiritual authority to even larger numbers of people.

Columban's expulsion would eventually produce two new monasteries—Sankt Gallen in Switzerland and Bobbio in Italy. Both institutions would become major centers of missionary activity and culture creation in the formative centuries of European civilization. Ultimately the king's attempt to assert the power of the old way was a great victory for the new way.

Columban's biographer was a near contemporary who had interviewed many of Columban's contemporaries. His conclusion was that this Irish missionary-saint—whose only concerns appeared to be prayer and personal conversion—presided over a political revolution in France. We can now see in retrospect that this revolution laid the foundations for Charlemagne's great work, which in turn would make possible everything which Charlemagne's achievement has produced up to the present.

The Monk as Holy Man

The fact that the people of France, Ireland, Britain and Germany invested enormous resources in building an inter-connected set of monasteries throughout their territories during the 500 years between 600 and 1100 is beyond dispute. The ruins of the buildings they erected are found throughout Europe, and the surviving documentary evidence refers to them constantly.

Nor is there any dispute that there was no precedent for institutions like these in the places where they were built. Archeologists have found nothing in the pre-Christian history of the northern tribes that would suggest the emergence of the monastic movement, and there is nothing in the Roman reports of the northern tribes that would offer the slightest hint such a thing would happen.

Nor is there any dispute that the northern tribes built monastic institutions on their territories in much greater numbers than did Mediterranean Christians. Nor would there be any serious dispute that the areas in which the medieval monasteries were built emerged as the heartland of what has come to be recognized as western civilization.

All this raises an important question: Why would a movement with no apparent precursors in the base culture, and one which required great personal sacrifice from its adherents, so suddenly achieve such great support throughout society, from the most lowly to the most powerful? Support of this extent—reaching across centuries of time and over a wide geographic area, involving several distinct cultures and supported by every social class—would appear to indicate that some basic need was being met. If so, what was it?

What we notice immediately about the area where the French monastic movement took root is that it lies on the fringes of the old Roman world. Here the independent tribal cultures, based on voluntary associations formed around charismatic leaders, had confronted the highly institutionalized Roman civilization, based on universal submission to clearly defined hierarchies.

Associated with this was the absence of strong religious institutions in the tribal societies. There were tribal shamans in the northern European tribes and there were ancestral and tribal gods, but we do not find temples being built here as they had been in the Mediterranean world for millennia. Mediterranean style religion would have seemed alien to the peoples of the northern tribes. The idea of a distant God, known through established rituals, and mediated through a divine institution was a viewpoint which the previous history and experience of the northern tribes gave them no capacity to understand.

But the presence of a charismatic holy man, like Columban, was something quite different, something they could understand. It was part of their cultural tradition. And so when charismatic holy men appeared in their midst and began preaching Christianity it had a great impact. Christianity as a vast system of doctrine was foreign to them, but Christianity as devotion to a specific human person—a person who lived or had lived in their locality and who had performed real miracles there—this they could understand and follow.

These local holy men fed the great religious hunger which appears to have existed throughout the northern tribes, judging from their actions in subsequent centuries. The combination of charismatic holy men and voluntary associations made perfect sense to tribal peoples.

The Mediterranean peoples who had adopted Christianity expected their old system of temples, priests and sacrifices to be replaced with a new system of similar institutions. In the same way the northern tribal people expected their new religion to provide them with a new supply of charismatic holy men who would replace their shamans, people able to communicate with the spiritual world in practical ways—healing illnesses, finding lost objects, ending droughts, winning wars, getting pregnant, succeeding in business, growing healthy crops.

We now refer to such events as miracles but people at that time viewed them very differently—not as events taking place outside normal causation but as part of normal reality, things that happened routinely and were to be expected. What made them unusual was only that certain persons with unique spiritual gifts could cause them to happen.

And so the Christian holy man or woman, virtually always a monk, replaced the tribal holy man—just as the Christian basilicas and cathedrals had replaced the pagan temples in the Mediterranean world. The ability of Christian holy men and women to perform miracles with greater frequency than their tribal predecessors surely played a major role in convincing the northern tribes it was reasonable to adopt Christianity.

The existence of these two very different cultural bases—one Mediterranean and the other northern tribal—meant that European Christianity would develop in two quite different ways. One base would produce a diocesan-based civil religion, headed by a hierarchy of bishops. The other would produce a monastic-based voluntary religion, headed by charismatic holy men. This division has persisted to the present time.

CHARLEMAGNE AND MONASTICISM

Beginning in the 700s the monastic movement entered an entirely new phase in France. That profoundly important development was an essential element in the new political culture which the great French king at the time, the towering figure now known as Charlemagne, would initiate.

Before Charlemagne monasticism had involved a few heroic individuals who lived outside the mainstream of society. Monastic life tended to be individualistic, and was almost completely counter-cultural. Even its connection to the Church was tenuous. But beginning in the 700s and continuing for the next 1,000 years, monasticism would be knit into the very fabric of both western civilization and the Christian Church.

This enormously important development took place in the new empire which Charlemagne would create and which in turn would provide the foundations for what is today called Europe.

Charlemagne's Achievement

Charlemagne's epochal achievement was made possible by the unique historical crucible which he had inherited from the past, and which we have already observed:

- There was a new place, created by the simultaneous collapse of the old Roman Empire, and the massive migrations which took the formerly nomadic northern tribes west and south.

- There was a new people, created by the intertwining of the indigenous peoples, the migrating tribes, and the Romans who had settled there as colonists and soldiers during the imperial era.

- And there was a new religion.

In this crucible a new civilization would gradually be formed. It would incorporate the best of all that had preceded it, but it would also change everything that had preceded it. There would be new languages and new forms of literature. There would be new economic practices and new political structures. There would also be new relationships between the genders and a new appreciation for children.

And there would be new ways of thinking, a new trust in reason, and a new emphasis on education and literacy. There would an endless flow of new technologies and a gradual expansion of this new civilization throughout the world based on those technologies. And there would be a vibrant, energetic new religion—constantly in ferment, constantly innovating and constantly evangelizing.

And at the center of all these developments would be the monastic communities which embodied and institutionalized the merging of the three great forces that Charlemagne was able to forge into a single whole, and which in turn laid the foundations for western civilization.

Romanitas was the most obvious of these forces. It was the combination of history, culture, politics and economics which had emerged in the 600 years between Rome's founding and its collapse. The Roman approach to empire had united the ancient world into a single political and economic unit, an utterly unprecedented event which stood in stark contrast to the petty warfare and political anarchy that had prevailed previously.

Even after the collapse of the empire the old Roman families who had come to southern France centuries earlier as colonists still considered themselves Romans and were still the de facto ruling elite. They had allied themselves with the Church of Rome, and members of their families dominated the Catholic hierarchy. These families frequently provided crucial support in establishing monasteries in their areas, and often sent their sons to be educated there, and often to become monks.

Even though the Roman Empire had collapsed in Europe by Charlemagne's time, it still controlled Greece and the Middle East, and there were many in the west who still remembered Rome's days of power with great fondness.

The second great force was the formerly nomadic tribal peoples who had settled in northern France. The Romans referred to them as 'barbarians', i.e. 'bearded ones', because their males had much heavier facial hair than Mediterranean males. The 'barbarians' themselves had no name for their cultural group, largely because those who belonged to these cultures had no sense of belonging to a culture. Their horizons extended only to the edges of their particular tribes, which they typically referred to as "the people."

These 'barbarian' cultures produced strong individuals but weak cultural traditions and political institutions. They consisted of constantly shifting warrior bands, with little or no sense of national identity. Whoever would be able to mold these strong, innovative, resourceful and adaptive individuals into a coherent culture, and create unified social and political institutions in which they could combine their resources and energies, would possess great power.

In practical terms that task involved convincing the indigenous peoples of northern Europe to voluntarily adopt Roman style institutions. The person who achieved this epochal result was Charlemagne.

The third great force which Charlemagne would combine into the new civilization he was forming was Christianity, and this force would provide the cohering center for his great process of civilization creation.

By the year 600 Christianity was some 500 years old—roughly the age of Protestantism at the end of the twentieth century. Christianity had by this time become the religion of the empire—to the extent that the empire still had a religion. Its power was clearly demonstrated by the large churches constructed at public expense at the center of most major cities. It had become organized into a single international institution centered in Rome, where the bishop of Rome had replaced the Roman emperor as the focus of unity in the west.

There were respected and influential bishops in every city, but a major part of their influence came from their relationships to the bishop of Rome. Local, national and international coherence all reinforced each other, and together they produced a kind of effective political power which had no real competition at this point in European history.

Religion in the ancient world had been a confusing maze of competing local gods, each with its own cult and its own set of myths and each seeking authority at the expense of the others. Christianity by contrast proclaimed a God who wanted the human family to be unified. Pre-Christian religion had divided people by its great diversity. The new religion united people, socially and nationally, by proclaiming a single God for all peoples—rich and poor, weak and powerful, old and young, female and male.

But this new religion had a decidedly Roman face and this produced a substantial problem for the northern European tribes. For centuries they had been at war with the Romans, struggling to preserve their way of life against Roman attempts to force them into cultural subjection. The northern tribes wanted what the Romans had, but they could not become Romans. The cultural gap was too great.

The challenge was to find a way to be Christian while retaining ones cultural roots. This would happen under Charlemagne's leadership, and once again the monastic movement would play a crucial role in bringing it about.

Charlemagne as the First Christian King

The rise of the northern tribes to international leadership began with two clearly marked events—the sack of Rome by northern European warriors in 410, and the coronation of a northern European king as emperor of the west in Rome in 800, almost 400 years later. Both events were the culmination of events before them, and they acquire their epoch-making significance from events that followed, but in retrospect they mark historical boundaries—times when changes of permanent importance occurred.

Charlemagne's coronation might have been just another attempt to recreate the ancient imperial ideal in Western Europe—and to the extent that it initiated the dream of a Holy Roman Empire it was that—but subsequent events would show that Charlemagne was much more the first Christian king than he was the last Roman emperor.

What distinguished the Christian kings from the emperors was not that they had any less authority than the emperors. Initially Christianity required no fundamental changes in political institutions. A king who was a Christian was still expected to lead in battle, to punish his enemies and to reward his friends, and to live in the manner kings had always lived, as Charlemagne did.

But despite these similarities, when a king adopted Christianity something fundamental changed. One could not claim to be a Christian, whether king or the poorest of the poor, without acknowledging his or her relationship to a higher authority. The belief that a single God reigns omnipotent over all human activity and holds all humans responsible for their actions in every sphere of life is so basic to Christianity it cannot be denied without denying Christianity itself.

So a king who became Christian in a very real sense was demoted— from one who held a semi-divine absolute authority to one who exercised authority but who was accountable to an even higher authority. Just as his subjects were required to obey his laws, the king was required to obey divine law. But at the same time the Christian king was being demoted he was also being promoted. He now reigned on behalf of a power greater than his own, at least in theory. This idea of a divine right kingship would have a vast and formative impact on western political development.

Of course not all kings who claimed to be Christians acted in ways that were consistent with their professed beliefs. But those who failed to do so often found themselves being criticized, often severely, by the religious authorities in their territories. These were the Church's bishops and pastors, and the monastic movement's monks and holy men, part of the leadership elite but persons who had independent authority, and who were responsible for teaching and maintaining the Christian faith.

Kings could attempt to silence these critics, and often did so successfully, especially by co-opting them into financially and socially rewarding positions in a Christianized civil religion. But always there was the possibility, and often enough the reality, that one of these critics would choose martyrdom rather than submit to the king. Martyrdom was highly regarded in the Christian tradition and had always been. The deaths of the earlier martyrs were remembered each year and their graves became pilgrimage destinations.

As a result kings who were Christian, even if only in name, were faced with a difficult set of choices when confronted by a critic who was willing to be a martyr. If the king executed his opponent he was rid of a troublesome critic, but at the same time he had created a new martyr. There was always a good chance the people would regard this new martyr as a saint and make his or her grave a pilgrimage point. When this happened what had been a single individual's criticism became a powerful and permanent popular movement which could not be suppressed without endangering the king's right to be considered a Christian. The case of Thomas à Becket in England is the best known example of this phenomenon, but it is far from the only one.

Being a Christian king was not an easy task. But once having joined the Christian Church it was almost impossible for a king to leave it. And there were great benefits to being a Christian king as well.

In the final centuries of the first 1,000 years of Christian history the Christian Church came to regard itself as a trans-national political institution to which one owed an allegiance higher than ones allegiance to his or her nation or tribe, or even ones family. This identity which extended beyond and above the nation had many practical benefits. First, it linked the king and his nation to all other Christian nations, opening the way for profitable exchanges of many kinds—economic, educational, technological, and political.

It also freed the king, to some extent at least, from the need to be constantly prepared to defend his territory from attack by neighboring kings, since it was understood that Christian kings, at least in theory, did not attack one another. And finally it linked the king and his government to the Church and its widely respected local networks of dioceses and parishes, and to their extensive charitable activities—and to the increasingly important monastic communities that were emerging throughout Europe.

Term nation not real until 16-17th centuries

The Power of Christianity

Charlemagne's political revolution produced not just a new government, but even more important a new understanding of power. While the northern tribes and the imperial armies had been fighting increasingly bloody and inconclusive battles along their border for centuries, the Christian monks had been engaged in a very different struggle along both sides of the divide. Rather than seeking to dominate—a power which Christians in the early centuries never had, or ever sought to have—the early monks sought to convince and convert.

By Charlemagne's time there had been 400 years of continuous evangelism by Christian missionaries, most of them monks, and it had convinced enough people in all nations and social classes to adopt the new values of Christianity that it was possible to promote a new way of life. This new way of life which the monks lived was profoundly nonviolent. And the new institutions they were creating furnished living proof that it is possible to achieve high levels of social cohesion and political order without coercion.

Soldiers and military officers were included in the Church, but it was always agreed that the Church's leaders—its bishops, pastors and monks—were not to engage in warfare. Military combat was tolerated as an inevitable and unfortunate vestige of the old way, but it was clear in both the Church's Scriptures and in its doctrines that warfare had no permanent role in the new world which the Christian community was creating. The Christians' great heroes were not military leaders but the martyrs, ordinary people like themselves who had chosen to die voluntarily rather than submit to government coercion.

What slowly convinced Christians that it was possible to live without coercive violence was their experience of a new kind of spiritual power—a power which could convince people to voluntarily choose to live in orderly, socially constructive ways, and which gave them the capacity to do so. Christians did not need to be punished for not keeping the laws, or for not paying their taxes. They voluntarily chose to do so. They did not need to be defended against, for they voluntarily chose to live in mutually enriching cooperative relationships with their neighbors.

Christians believed the essence of divinity had been disclosed in the life, death and resurrection of Jesus. During his life Jesus had been a healer, one who devoted himself to the ordinary people, one who taught his followers how to be healers, how to voluntarily devote themselves to the welfare of others. In his death Jesus had voluntarily chosen to die unjustly rather than take up weapons in self-defense, or to allow his followers to do so.

As he was dying the most humiliating and painful death the Romans could devise Jesus had been able to pray that his executioners would be forgiven. And in his resurrection, the unique event which concluded Jesus' life on earth, Christians saw evidence that his life was grounded in divine reality itself. As a result they had come to believe that love was a force more powerful than death. Persons who had voluntarily adopted these beliefs not only rejected violence, but even more important they believed it was unnecessary.

Furthermore, the very fact that these new beliefs had been adopted without coercion changed the status of the individuals involved in a profound way. In the new societies forming around Christian beliefs the old pyramidal model was being replaced by the vision of a vast network with God at its center. No longer was it necessary to seek the support of someone higher in the hierarchy in order to act. Now every Christian could communicate directly with God, and was directly empowered by God.

This revolutionary new belief greatly increased human potential but it could only be realized gradually. Indeed this process is still underway. But its implications were so immense and so far reaching that even in its initial stages it had a profound impact, and the monastic communities were at the forefront of that impact. There were now two kinds of people. There were those who lived in the old way, constantly fearing violence and necessarily (they thought) involved in it. And there were those who lived in the new way, willing to accept death voluntarily rather than participating in the death and violence that raged all around them.

If the assumptions of the old way had been correct those who followed the new way would very quickly have been eliminated since they could be killed without resistance. That would have ended the Christian dream of a nonviolent society, but that is not what happened. Persecution and violence did not end the new way. To the contrary the way in which intentional Christians accepted death and lived with the constant threat of death made their way only more attractive to those who observed them.

The immense courage and peace with which the Christians faced death was in stark contrast to the fear and deviousness which characterized life in the old way, and people found themselves being irresistibly attracted to it, regardless of its cost. Humans cannot live if they do not have something to live for, and it was clear to nearly everyone in the centuries when western civilization was forming that the Christians had found something which was so valuable that for them any sacrifice on its behalf was worthwhile.

It was this power that came from within the human person which made Christianity impossible to ignore when the new civilization was forming. This new power in turn produced new institutions which although they lacked military power could not be ignored even by those who commanded large armies. These institutions were known collectively as "the Church," but in fact were immensely varied. They ranged from individual hermits who spent their lives in prayer and who instructed a few followers in wilderness places, to the Bishop of Rome who presided over the entire Church in what was still the major city in Europe.

In between these two poles were the parish churches that existed in most local communities, large or small, and the bishops in every city, representing the voluntary unity that bound the vast majority of Christian believers into a single institutional structure, one even greater than the old Roman Empire itself.

Anyone who wanted to rule, especially after the emperors themselves became Christians in the 300s, had to take the Christian Church and the amazingly active movement it embodied into account. If a ruler tried to eliminate Christianity from his kingdom what was there to take its place? The old religions had all been rendered suspect by the growth in rationality, and although there were still many people who clung to the magical practices of the past, there were no longer persons qualified for leadership who believed the old gods were real.

In recent centuries it has been believed by some western intellectuals that it is possible for humans to live without any religious beliefs, but that belief was not held by anyone in the ancient or medieval worlds. It would certainly not have been held by anyone in the northern tribes who were forming a new civilization. And since it was agreed that society-wide religious practices are essential, and since Christianity was the only religion with any real hope of being accepted society-wide, the only real choices were either to adopt Christianity as the civil religion, or else to have no religion at all.

CLUNY

The most visible product of Charlemagne's political, cultural and religious revolution would be a new kind of monastic institution. It was initiated by Charlemagne's grandson early in the 900s in a small French town called Cluny, and would become the dominant institution in Europe over the next three centuries. It consisted of a centralized system of Benedictine monasteries spread across the empire Charlemagne had established.

By the time this phenomenally successful institution building process had run its course there were hundreds of monasteries throughout Western Europe, all governed by a single abbot at Cluny. It has been estimated that by the year 1200 there were 10,000 Benedictine monasteries in Europe, and although not all were Cluniac monasteries, they were all deeply influenced by the institutional patterns established there. The Abbey of Cluny itself became the wealthiest and most powerful institution in Europe. Its massive church was the largest and the most richly decorated in the western world, and its abbots had a power that equaled and often exceeded the popes.

How did this happen? How was it possible for an institution which had no military or political power, and which depended economically on voluntary contributions, to attain such power? The answer appears to be that it represented Charlemagne's vision more successfully than anything else at the time, and that people found that ideal so attractive they enthusiastically supported an institution which embodied it. Cluny was living proof that Charlemagne's effort to combine Roman civilization with the Northern European indigenous cultures was possible. And it also provided living proof that the monastic way of life, based on combining spiritual, intellectual and social development, produced rich dividends.

The Cluniac federation was in fact a continuation of the Benedictine vision and at the same time a substantial departure from the vision of the original Egyptian monks. One can hardly imagine a greater contrast than, on the one hand, the young Pachomius along with the monk who was his teacher struggling to keep themselves awake at night in the 200s by carrying baskets of sand from one place in the Egyptian desert to another, and on the other, the architectural splendor and institutional power which had emerged at Cluny a thousand years later.

The early desert monks had deliberately separated themselves from society in order to be personally converted at a deep level; the Cluniac monks had integrated themselves into society in order to form a new civilization. But even though the Cluniac monks' social and political position had moved from outsider to insider, from counter-cultural to culture-creator, from prophet to teacher, there was also great continuity. Even as they became increasingly affluent the monks at Cluny continued to devote much of their day to prayer and to reading religious texts.

By the 1100s, 200 years after its formation, the Cluniac movement would begin to go into decline. Its power had become an end in itself, rather than a means to an end, and the result was inevitable. Political developments would also increasingly leave Cluny behind, until by the 1800s the French people would destroy its magnificent church and build a road through the place where it had once stood. A few archeological ruins are all that remain of this once great monastic empire.

In the centuries which followed Cluny's fall the monastic movement took an almost diametrically opposite path to the one that had been pursued there. But despite this the achievement at Cluny would never be forgotten, even though some of its more extreme features are now something of an embarrassment. Some of the most basic institutions of western civilization had their origins at Cluny, and even the new monastic movements that would emerge in protest to Cluny relied in many ways on the civilization-creating efforts that had taken place there.

THE LEGACY OF CHARLEMAGNIAN MONASTICISM

The reign of Charlemagne initiated a new epoch in the history of Christianity, and in the history of the world. He became the model for all future Christian kings, and his use of military force to compel Christian belief has left a mark on subsequent history that is quite substantial. His dream of a coalition of Christian nations in northwest Europe would guide European politics for the next 1,000 years, and would continue to provide the model for the present European Union whose headquarters building is named after him.

But none of his innovations had greater impact than the synthesis between the monastic movement and civil government which he initiated. It is this synthesis that provided the core around which a new civilization would form.

The Monastery as Model

The monasteries of medieval Europe were a model of what life could be when conducted according to the values inherent in the Christian gospel. One did not have to ask what a Christian society would look like, or whether it was possible. The monasteries provided convincing answers to both questions.

Around the monasteries there raged endless political and social chaos, and as a result endless warfare, both petty and large scale. Within the monastery peace reigned. Here men and women lived in voluntary cooperation, organized by law and rational government rather than by domination. Here people obeyed not by compulsion but by choice.

Outside the monastery sexuality was compulsive, an unmanageable instinctual force which produced rape and incest and a whole range of other actions which brought shame on all involved, and which made family life difficult if not impossible. Inside the monastery walls were individuals who demonstrated that humans need not be slaves to their passions.

Around the monasteries scarcity and hunger were everywhere, in sharp contrast to the ruling class's ostentatious luxury. Inside the monasteries there was an ordered and productive economy, which produced enough for everyone to have life's necessities. Nothing was wasted on luxury or warfare.

Outside the monastery there were radical differences in rank. A small minority held power and privilege, while the great majority was powerless and penniless. Inside the monastery there were also differences in rank, but these were functional rather than inherited, and existed within a context of fundamental equality. Most significant of all, monastic superiors were chosen by the freely given votes of those they ruled—a revolutionary idea unheard of elsewhere in the medieval world.

As a result people did not need to wonder what would happen if their society attempted to form a Christian culture. All across Europe these small but attractive islands of Christian community showed what would happen. They were like lighthouses springing up across Europe, pointing the way to a new world, and when people looked at the life taking place in these new places and compared it to what was taking place elsewhere they gradually but firmly came to the conclusion that the new way they observed in the monasteries was superior in every regard to the old ways.

Charlemagne had grasped this fact at a very deep level, and with great energy, skill and charisma had transformed it into a political vision, one that would remain in place—evolving but still fundamentally the same—until Napoleon and the French Revolution brought it to an end almost exactly a thousand years later.

In Charlemagne's new political culture the monastery had been given a privileged place as the architect of European civilization, in much the same way that the university has become the place where western civilization has been formed and defined and passed on in more recent centuries.

Good story
needs mne detail

THREE

From Bernard of Clairvaux
to Martin Luther

There was soon a sustained and powerful reaction to the changes the Cluniac monks had made in the Benedictine tradition. During the early centuries of the new millennium numerous more austere monastic communities would emerge across Europe, each an attempt to return to the original monastic traditions of asceticism and withdrawal.

Of these new monastic movements the three most significant, both in numbers and in influence, were the Cistercians, the Franciscans and the Dominicans. The Cistercians were founded in the 1100s, and the Franciscans and the Dominicans in the early 1200s. All were the result of a powerful evangelical movement that swept across Western Europe between the years 1000 and 1200.

This new monastic movement created a new kind of monastic institution, the religious order. Whereas the previous monastic movement had produced clearly bounded self-governing monastic communities, the religious orders that formed after 1100 produced international organizations in which the local communities were subordinate parts.

The new orders formed around a mission, not a place. The Franciscans and Dominicans consisted of men who had taken monastic vows but who traveled constantly, and who supported themselves by asking for voluntary contributions. They were thus known as 'mendicants'.

Equally important, the new orders placed great stress on the spiritual and mental development of the members of the institutional Church, in contrast to the first millennium monastic communities which had almost exclusively emphasized their own members' spiritual development.

This new development caused much conflict and controversy in both Church and society because it challenged existing institutional structures. But the new orders' vitality could not be ignored, and they received strong support from the papacy, which insured their success. They would play a major role in European religious and civil life until the Reformation of the early 1500s.

But in the end the new religious orders could not contain the ferment brewing throughout the Christian world. Although they took the laity seriously they still regarded lay Christians as inferior to monastic Christians, and lay Christians would eventually be unwilling to accept an inferior status in the Church.

Furthermore the new orders' commitment to the traditional monastic vows as the solution to all the great problems of sexuality, economics and political justice came to be doubted with increased intensity. These are the great issues that lay Christians struggle with constantly, and as Christian civilization continued to develop it became increasingly apparent, especially to the laity, that the traditional monastic ideals were not a sufficient guide for the new era the monastic movement had made possible. The end result of this dissatisfaction would be the Protestant Reformation.

BERNARD OF CLAIRVAUX

Early in the second millennium a new monastic movement emerged in France that would dominate religious life in Western Europe for the next two centuries. It would also create the spirituality upon which almost all intentional Christianity would be based throughout the entire second millennium. This new monastic order was called the Cistercians. It arose partly in reaction to the excesses of Cluny, but even more it resulted from a deep-seated and widespread desire for a more vital Christian faith, a desire which first millennium Christianity's immense success had produced.

The new movement began in 1112 when a young man from a French noble family knocked on the door of the new monastery in the nearby town of Cîteaux. He announced that he wanted to join the new community, but what was most astonishing was that he brought with him 30 other new members, including all his brothers and his uncle. Thus did Bernard of Clairvaux, a person of extraordinary talent and passion, enter the pages of Church history.

Bernard's abilities were quickly recognized and put to work. After only three years at Cîteaux he was sent to found a new monastery at Clairvaux, and the next year he was ordained an abbot at age 25. That was the only office he ever held, but his personal influence was so great that throughout his lifetime he was the preeminent leader of western Christianity, overshadowing even the popes.

Under Bernard's leadership the Cistercians spread with almost unbelievable speed across France and Germany and into the adjacent nations. He was personally responsible for founding 65 new monastic communities, and when he died at age 63 in 1153 there were some 300 Cistercian monasteries in Europe. By the year 1200 there were more than 500.

Opposition to Cluny

The Cistercian movement's rapid rise was due in large part to a popular reaction to the opulence and arrogance which had overtaken the Cluniac monastic movement.

While still in his twenties Bernard began condemning what he considered Cluny's great deviations from the monastic tradition. "Whereas bishops must use material beauty to arouse the devotion of their followers, who are not 'spiritual,'" he wrote, "the monks have left that world." To be a monk, he declared, is to "have reckoned all beautiful, sweet-smelling, fine-sounding, smooth-feeling, good-tasting things—in short, all bodily delights—as so much dung."

It was simple greed which motivated the monks at Cluny he said. "I don't know why, but the wealthier a place, the readier people are to contribute to it." As a result "there is more admiration for beauty than veneration for sanctity" in the Cluniac churches. They are decorated with crowns and candelabra "illuminated as much by their precious stones as by their lamps."

As a result "the church is resplendent in her walls and wanting in her poor," he declared. "She dresses her stones in gold and lets her sons go naked. The eyes of the rich are fed at the expense of the indigent. The curious find something to amuse them and the needy find nothing to sustain them."

Even the mosaics on the Cluniac churches' floors offended him. "What sort of reverence is shown to the saints when we place their pictures on the floor and then walk on them?" he asked. "Often someone spits in an angel's mouth." But he was equally offended by the secular art in the Cluniac churches. "What good are such things to poor men, to monks, to spiritual men?" he asked. "What is the point of those unclean apes, fierce lions, monstrous centaurs, half-men, striped tigers, fighting soldiers and hunters blowing their horns?"

"So many and so marvelous are the various shapes surrounding us," he said, "that it is more pleasant to read the marble than the books, and to spend the whole day marveling over these things rather than meditating on the law of God. Good Lord! If we aren't embarrassed by the silliness of it all, shouldn't we at least be disgusted by the expense?"

Bernard's Spirituality

Although there is no question that disgust with Cluny's excesses fueled the Cistercians' rapid growth, there is also no question that a rising desire for deeper personal spirituality played an equally significant role, and possibly an even greater one.

The Cistercians under Bernard's leadership introduced a new spirituality into Christian society, one that stressed the individual Christian's personal relationship with the divine. This new spirituality would profoundly shape Christian life for the next 900 years. ·

This new spirituality was a religion of the heart, and it contrasted sharply with the religion of the rule which had characterized European spirituality since Charlemagne. Over the 300 to 400 years before Bernard, Christian spirituality had become increasingly intellectual and doctrinal, whereas Bernard's spirituality was fundamentally emotional.

This is powerfully evident in the sermons on the *Song of Songs* which Bernard preached in the final years of his life, publishing them as the final summary of his spirituality. Bernard chose the *Song of Songs* as the Biblical base for his spiritual doctrine because he regarded its open affirmation of erotic love as the best metaphor for the Christian's relationship with Jesus.

His series of sermons begins with a long commentary on the opening verse of the *Song*, "Let him kiss me with kisses of his mouth!" This, Bernard says, is the beginning of a song which "only the touch of the Holy Spirit" can teach, a song that can be "learned by experience alone," a song that is "the very music of the heart."

Bernard said that he was ashamed of "the lukewarmness and lethargy of the present times" and he urged the other monks to join him in replacing that lukewarm faith with a new one based on a personal relationship with Christ, whose "living and effective word is a kiss—not a meeting of lips, which can sometimes be deceptive about the state of the heart," but instead a "wonderful and inseparable mingling of the light from above with the mind on which it is shed."

It signifies the bringing together of souls," and unites "the human with the divine," making peace "between earth and heaven." Bernard insisted that his new doctrine of Christian conversion was based on "the book of experience," not on theology. "I think no one can know what it is except he who has received it," he said. He did not try to prove his new doctrine from rational arguments. He simply stated it as a fact, borne out by his own experience and that of many other Christians.

Bernard and Politics

Although Bernard is now known almost exclusively for his spirituality, he was known during his lifetime equally for his involvement in politics. Midway in his career the Roman Church had split, electing two competing popes, and Bernard spent several years in Italy, mediating an end to this controversy—which because of the constitutional tradition Charlemagne had bequeathed to the medieval world crossed the boundary between Church and state. He was successful in doing so, which greatly added to his international prestige.

Throughout his life Bernard struggled with the tension between his commitment to spirituality and his involvement in political affairs, never really finding a satisfactory solution. On the one hand he considered things of the spirit so important they always deserved first priority—especially for a monk. But at the same time he realized that love, which he always proclaimed as the ultimate value for every Christian believer, demanded taking responsibility in the social realm.

Fr. Leclercq summarizes Bernard's position thus: "We exist in a society from which we receive and to which we must contribute, and this entails many practical consequences of which Bernard often spoke to his monks." He says that Bernard insisted on "social grace," and adds, "Everything that Bernard said about fraternal love in the rest of his work, and everything he did throughout his life in the service of his neighbor, was simply the practical application of the social character of love."

One of the political issues on which Bernard was called to offer an opinion was dealing with dissident Christians, who were appearing in constantly greater numbers throughout Europe at the time. He counseled that they should be dealt with by making rational responses to their mistaken beliefs, but if necessary they had to be executed he said,. The dissidents were seducers of the common people, presenting false but dangerously attractive doctrines which were causing women to leave their husbands, and husbands to leave their wives, in order to join communities of outcasts who made their living as weavers.

Bernard and the Crusades

The First Crusade had a profound impact on European society. Not only had it established a European colony in Palestine and provided secure access to the Holy Land for European pilgrims, its success had given the new civilization a powerful sense of its political potential. Bernard was a young boy while the First Crusade was taking place, and had grown to adulthood in its immediate aftermath.

A few decades later Pope Eugene called a Second Crusade and when the pope asked Bernard to promote it he readily agreed. Bernard spent 18 month in 1146 and 1147 traveling through Western Europe, successfully promoting the new Crusade. According to contemporary reports people were so moved by Bernard's sermons they volunteered in such great numbers to "take the cross"—that is to wear the garment of a crusader—that supplies ran out, and other clothing had to be found to make more. According to some sources Bernard's own habit was used in this way.

But the Second Crusade turned out to be as great a disaster as the first had been a success. In the First Crusade the Muslims had been divided, making it possible to defeat them, but by the end of the Second

Crusade the Muslims were united against the western invaders, and the Europeans were divided among themselves.

What was even worse this failed Crusade had poisoned relationships with the Christians of the East, with consequences that continue to the present. Rather than protect Middle Eastern Christians the Second Crusade had destroyed the image of western military power, and emboldened the Muslim states to undertake further attacks on the European colonies in the Middle East. Both the papacy and the west had been severely wounded.

Bernard received much blame for this disaster, since he had played such a prominent role in promoting the Second Crusade. When its full extent became known Bernard wrote a letter to Pope Eugene saying, "We have fallen upon grave times, which seemed about to bring to an end not only to my studies but my very life." Bernard recognized that God had "spared neither his people nor his name," and that those "who bear the label Christian have been laid low in the desert, and have either been slain by the sword or consumed by famine."

But despite this Bernard defended his role in the Crusade, placing the blame on the personal spirituality of the crusading soldiers. They were "a stiff-necked race" he told the pope, like the early Hebrews who had followed Moses out of Egypt, "forever contending against the Lord and Moses his servant." If the early Hebrews "had perished because of their iniquity, is it any wonder that those who did likewise suffered a similar fate?"

Earlier Bernard had written to a crusader in Jerusalem, telling him that when a Christian engages in combat everything "depends on the dispositions of his heart." If he fights for an unworthy cause he is a murderer. But when a Christian soldier "inflicts death it is to Christ's profit." He adds, "The Christian glories in the death of the pagan, because Christ is glorified." Bernard qualified this by saying that pagans are not to be "slaughtered when there is any other way to prevent them from harassing and persecuting the faithful," but in the end it is "better to destroy them" than allow them to treat Christians unjustly.

In saying this Bernard was simply passing on the tradition he and the entire medieval Church had inherited from Augustine, but by doing so in circumstances Augustine could never have imagined, and by lending his immense prestige to this tradition, Bernard left to the Christian churches a legacy that would not be challenged until after World War II, some 800 years later.

Bernard's Legacy

Before Bernard's time the Christian tradition had emphasized the other-ness of God. In this view God's power and perfection were so incom-patible with human weakness and imperfection that any human who experienced God directly would die as a result. For this reason the proper relationship of humans to the divine was described as being "God-fear-ing." But in Bernard's new spirituality this doctrine was replaced by a profound intimacy—almost the exact opposite.

In subsequent centuries this new spirituality would take root throughout Christian Europe, becoming the foundation on which virtu-ally all future religious developments would be based.

Both Francis and Dominic adopted this new spirituality as the basis for their movements, and the northern European evangelical movements which sprang up during the medieval period were also based on it. Even more important the Protestant reformers, including Luther and Calvin, were deeply imbued with Bernard's spirituality, and through them it has become the de facto spiritual doctrine of Protestantism.

This new doctrine would unleash massive amounts of human en-ergy and creativity. Surely if humans were able to "kiss Christ on the lips," as Bernard taught them they could, then they were capable of anything. But by emphasizing spiritual development so strongly Bernard also had the unintended consequence of promoting a kind of dualism in which Christians would so completely distinguish their spirituality from their lives in the world that entire communities of Christians would come to believe there was no connection between the two. This came to be true especially in regard to political actions.

FRANCIS OF ASSISI

Almost a hundred years after Bernard knocked on the monastery door near his home in France, another young man in central Italy went into a deserted chapel near his hometown to pray. The church was decaying, but an image of the crucified Christ still hung over the altar, and as the young man prayed he heard a voice saying, "Francis, don't you see that my house has collapsed? Go and repair it for me."

The young man answered immediately, "Yes Lord, I will, most willingly." This "Yes" would open a new chapter in medieval Christianity, and in so doing provide the spiritual foundations for many of western civilization's future developments.

Francis' World

This young man had grown up in wealth and privilege. His father was a successful businessman, one of the richest in the area, and Francis had grown up as what today would be called 'a rich kid'. One friend described him as a "spendthrift". His parents complained that he behaved as if he possessed "a fortune more like a prince's than theirs" but nevertheless they indulged him because "they were rich" and "very fond of him" and did not want to take any chance of "antagonizing him."

Every pleasure was available to this spoiled young man, and he availed himself of them all. The other young men of the town considered him their 'Lord of the Revels.' His most recent biographer says that Francis at 21 "still lived at home but if he heard during a meal that a party was going on in the town he would leave his food on the table and rush off to it."

There were about 5,000 people living in Assisi when Francis grew up there, and another 10,000 in the surrounding countryside. It was a typical medieval city, built on a hilltop and surrounded by stone walls, not previously noted for anything unusual. Today Assisi retains its medieval flavor, and is an oasis of peace and spiritual presence, a living monument to its famous saint, maintained by the people who live there.

But when Francis was growing up Assisi was anything but peaceful. The emperor had died when Francis was 16, creating a political vacuum that produced a fierce civil war in Assisi. The town's aristocratic families were pitted against the rising middle class—of which Francis' father was a leading member—and a fierce struggle for control ensued. The middle class emerged victorious, destroying the aristocrats' mansions and forcing them into exile. Rubble from the old mansions filled Assisi's streets during Francis' teenage years.

The young Francis became a soldier and energetically joined this great struggle, but one day the military company he had joined was massacred, and some 20 to 30 of his friends and comrades were killed. He himself was captured and became a prisoner of war, spending several months in prison until his father ransomed him. This experience would be a turning point in this life.

Francis had also been deeply influenced by the knightly tradition which was spreading across medieval Europe at the time. This new movement combined a new appreciation for the feminine and a commitment to romantic love with an equally strong determination to subject male sexuality to rational control. And it included a strong determination to combine Christian faith with an active life in the world.

All this was embodied in an artistic tradition that offered powerful new ideals, like the story of King Arthur and the Knights of the Round Table, and which produced popular songs and romantic poems in the vernacular languages. Francis had absorbed this artistic and cultural tradition from his mother, who came from the area in southern France where it had originated. She had named her son after her native France, and throughout his life he would sing the songs of this region, and draw on its inspiration in other ways. Francis often referred to himself and the members of his order as "troubadours" or "knights of the round table".

C. S. Lewis, the great literary scholar and Christian apologist, has said of the troubadour movement that "the most momentous and revolutionary elements in it have [formed] the background of European literature for 800 years." He adds, "Real changes in human sentiment are very rare—there are perhaps three or four on record—but I believe they occur, and that this is one of them."

But for Francis and most people living at the time, it was the Christian Church that was central to their lives. For a thousand years it had been the central force in their civilization, and under Bernard's leadership a great movement of religious revival had swept across Western Europe in the previous century leaving behind hundreds of magnificent new Gothic churches, and a newly empowered papacy in Rome.

However at the local level these great changes had often failed to make an impact. Pope Innocent III, who would play a crucial role in Francis' career, described local church life in these words:

> "Many priests have lived luxuriously. They have passed the time in drunken revels, neglecting religious rites. When they have been at Mass, they have chatted about commercial affairs. They have left

churches and tabernacles in an improper state, sold posts and sacraments, promoted ignorant and unworthy people to the clerical state, though they had others better suited for it.

"Many bishops have appropriated the income of a parish for themselves, leaving the parish indigent. They have gone to the enormous abuse of forcing parishioners to make special payments so as to have still more income. They have made a scandalous commerce of relics. They have allowed the illegitimate children of a canon to succeed the father in the benefice."

All was not well.

Francis' Twenty Years

One of the most notable aspects of Francis' story is the relatively short period of time in which it took place. His career began when he was 24, and it ended 20 years later when he died, worn out by his heroic austerities and broken by the failure of many of his ideals.

His career as a religious leader began in Rome where he had gone as a pilgrim. Here he was inspired to trade clothes with a beggar and to stand begging at the doors of St. Peter's. He returned home with a deep commitment to serving the poorest of the poor, and in Assisi these were the lepers. The young bon vivant had previously been so disgusted by their repulsive sores he could not even bear to look at them, but now when one day he saw a leper he dismounted from his horse, gave the man some money and then kissed his hand.

Within a few months Francis' life became a mirror image of his previous one. Instead of wearing the latest fashions he now wore the rags of a beggar. Instead of feasting he now ate whatever people gave him, often little more than garbage. Instead of seeking pleasure he sought humiliation. Rather than returning to his parents' comfortable home at night he slept in the open.

His father was so angry he cursed his son when they met on the street. His brother ridiculed him. Many of his neighbors thought he had gone mad. His mother's emotions can only be imagined. He ignored all this and each day went to the little chapel where he had first heard Christ's voice asking him to rebuild the Church, working with his own hands to restore it. When it was finished he took on another decaying building.

Then one day Francis heard this passage from St. Matthew's gospel read at Mass:

> As you go proclaim the message, *"The kingdom of heaven is upon you."* Heal the sick, raise the dead, cleanse lepers, cast out devils. You received without cost; give without charge. Provide no gold, silver, or copper to fill your purse, no pack for the road, no second coat, no shoes, no stick; the worker earns his keep. When you come to any town or village, look for some worthy person in it, and make your home there until you leave. Wish the house peace as you enter it, so that, if it is worthy, your peace may descend on it; if it is not worthy, your peace can come back to you. If anyone will not receive you or listen to what you say, then as you leave that house or that town shake the dust of it off your feet. (Mt 10:7–13)

Francis took that charge personally and literally. It would define the rest of his life—and the great religious movement that would form around him.

He began preaching, not in the churches but in the streets and public places, as Jesus had. His pulpit was piles of hay in barnyards, benches in the city square, the steps of public buildings. And when he spoke it was in the common language, the one ordinary people used, not the Latin used in the churches.

People flocked to hear him. The accounts of his powerful oratory are many, and moving. His biographer says, "If we do not know exactly what Francis said, witnesses graphically describe how he said it. His idiosyncratic delivery made full use of all his skills as a troubadour. His expression was friendly and cheerful; his voice clear and attractive. Eloquent and often witty, he became crisp and fiery when he denounced to their faces men commonly known to be guilty of greed, exploitation and cruelty."

To those who regarded Jesus' teachings as unrealistic and unattainable Francis offered the example of his own life. A contemporary reports that "A great many people of all classes decided to follow him and copy his way of life. They wanted to give up their worldly affairs to live under his discipline."

Francis was also a poet. His *Canticle of Brother Sun* is the first poem in the Italian language to have survived. It is believed that Francis' example inspired Dante to create *The Divine Comedy* in Italian rather than Latin. Dante would devote eighty lines of his great poem to Francis.

Above all Francis was a mystic. Throughout his life he experienced the direct presence of the divine in his life in the form of a voice which he believed to be Christ's own voice, instructing him and inspiring him. These experiences began with the voice he heard in the ruined church when he was a young man, and ended with his final retreat in the mountains where he received the stigmata. The followers of Francis would always tend to have greater faith in the emotions than in the intellect.

From Francis to Franciscan

A community began to form around Francis almost immediately after his conversion. At first its members were people who knew him, but within a decade they had grown into the thousands. They included women and men from every segment of society—nobles and peasants, old and young, rich and poor, the learned and the illiterate—all those who wanted to commit themselves to living as Francis did, by following Jesus literally in daily life.

When his first two followers joined Francis they had no idea how to structure their new community so they went to a nearby church where they knelt before the book of the Gospels which was on the altar. They prayed together for guidance and then opened the book at random. What they read was this:

> "If you wish to be perfect, go sell what you have and give it to the poor, and you will have treasure in heaven." (Mt 19:21)

They opened the Gospels a second time. This time they read:

> "Take nothing for your journey." (Lk 9:3)

When they opened it a third time they read:

> "If any man will come after me, let him deny himself." (Mt 16:24)

At the end of his life Francis said, "After the Lord had given me brothers no one showed me what I was to do, but the Most High himself revealed that I should live according to the pattern of the holy gospel."

Within a year Francis had twelve companions. He sent them on a recruiting mission, telling them that God had called them "to go throughout the world encouraging all men and women by our example and words." Even though they might appear "ignorant and not worth listening to" their words would have effect. Even kings and princes would be converted. When his colleagues returned Francis told them about a vision he had while they were gone. He had seen the roads "filled with Frenchmen, Spaniards, Germans, Englishmen and many others, speaking various languages and hurrying toward us."

That vision would accurately depict the growth of the Franciscan movement. Eight years after its founding the Franciscan community had a thousand members. Three years later more than 5,000 brothers would convene in the fields outside Assisi. Within 50 years there would be Franciscan churches throughout Europe.

Francis and the Pope

Pope Innocent III's support was crucial in the Franciscans' rapid growth. He was one of the most gifted of the medieval popes, and had come to the papacy about 10 years before Francis' movement began. He was pope for 18 years.

When Francis and his first followers traveled to Rome in 1209 to ask the pope for formal approval for their new movement he was presented with a real risk. Similar lay groups had formed recently, and all had turned out badly—at least from the Roman perspective. Why would this new movement be any different?

But Francis took an equally great risk in asking for papal approval. If the pope had refused Francis would have had to disband his movement and give up his vocation—or else form an independent and schismatic movement as so many of his predecessors had. And how would that fulfill the call to rebuild the Church which Francis believed he had received from Christ himself?

When they arrived in Rome Francis and his companions were questioned for several days by one of the older and most respected cardinals. At the conclusion this elder told the other cardinals, "I have found a really excellent man who wants to live according to the gospel, preserving precisely its evangelical spirit. I am convinced our Lord wishes to renew the faith of the holy church all over the world through him."

The next day the young Franciscans met with the pope and several cardinals. Francis addressed the pope and his advisers using his usual eloquence and honesty, telling them that the brothers were asking only permission to live in literal obedience to the commands of the Gospel.

The cardinals and the pope were wearing regal robes, and the young Franciscans were wearing ragged tunics.

When Francis finished the pope said, "My sons, your planned way of life seems too hard and rough. We are convinced of your dedication, but are afraid your rule may be too exacting for those who join you later."

But as the cardinals debated further, the pope recalled a dream he had a few nights earlier in which he had seen the papal cathedral tottering on its foundations. Only a single small man's efforts had kept it standing. The pope realized the small man in his dream was the one now standing before him. He did not announce his verdict immediately, but within a few days he granted Francis' request.

The way was now open. Throughout his lifetime Francis received unwavering support from the papacy, and he repaid that with unwavering support for the institutional Church.

The Third Order

Francis' new religious communities did more than take monasticism out of the monastic enclosures and into the streets. They also created a way for lay Christians to participate in the life of their communities, and that was to be one of the most significant innovations which the Franciscan movement bequeathed to the Church.

These new semi-monastic communities for lay people were called 'third orders'—the first order being the original one for celibate men, and the second the celibate order for women founded by St. Clare. Francis' central vision was to show it is possible to live in the ordinary world while following the teachings of Christ, and the Third Order Franciscans played a major role in making that vision a reality in the 300 years before the Reformation.

The example of the Franciscan Third Order would inspire other smaller groups to form throughout Europe, all of them driven by the same desire for a non-enclosed intentional Christianity open to lay people. A great many of these new groups were also lay-initiated and lay-led, and most had no direct links to the Church's existing institutional structures.

Many of the evangelical movements of the Reformation period and following had their roots in these pre-Reformation evangelical movements, which in turn had their roots in the Franciscan Third Orders.

Francis' Legacy

By any measure the Franciscan movement was one of the most successful in Christian history. There are few Christians in any of the western traditions who do not recognize Francis as a saint, and he has had virtually no enemies. He has often been ignored but he has seldom been criticized. The very fact that some 4 million people visit his tomb in Assisi each year is perhaps the best evidence of his continuing impact.

The fact that one of the world's great cities is named after St. Francis—not to mention some twenty smaller cities throughout the world, as well as numerous rivers, bays, creeks, mountain chains and islands—is enduring evidence of the impact which Franciscan missionaries have had in spreading Christianity throughout the world. The number of schools, hospitals and parishes named for St. Francis is in the thousands, and the impact of Franciscan missionaries continues into the present.

The Christmas traditions of western civilization, so treasured by religious and non-religious alike, are in large part a legacy of St. Francis. It was he who initiated the custom of the Christmas crèche, which invites everyone to experience the incarnation in the most human way possible, and in a way that is open to everyone, regardless of their beliefs or culture.

Surely among the most significant parts of Francis' legacy is the way it has provided an alternative to the just war doctrine. Francis never developed a carefully considered moral doctrine on warfare, but his example has always been a powerful reminder that to follow Christ without compromise requires the same nonviolence that Francis modeled.

It is surely significant that Pope John XXIII traveled to Assisi as a pilgrim to pray at Francis' tomb the day before he opened the Second Vatican Council. It was at this council that the bishops of the Catholic Church in effect rejected the just war doctrine and replaced it with an as yet unspecified new way of viewing warfare. And it is surely equally significant that in 1986 and again in 2002 when Pope John Paul II invited leaders from all religious faiths to come together to pray for peace the place he chose was Assisi.

These are substantial and far-reaching impacts, which together place Francis at the forefront of Christian leadership. But in the end St. Francis' impact cannot really be measured. That is because it has taken place in the hidden recesses of the human heart—a place so far above and beyond and below consciousness that we routinely forget it exists. It is in the deep core of our being, where rational argument is often inadequate, where Francis speaks to us—the place where we decide how to decide before we decide what to decide.

THE MENDICANT ERA

For 200 years after Francis' death new forms of monasticism sprang up everywhere in Europe. Rather than going into the desert as the original monks had done, these new monks went into the cities. And whereas the original monks had focused on their own conversion these new monks focused on the conversion of others. They were called mendicants because they supported themselves by asking for voluntary contributions.

The opportunity for this new monastic movement came from the success the previous monks had in converting Europe to the vision of a Christian civilization. But these new monks saw that this great vision was far from having been achieved, and that continuing to pursue it would require converting ordinary people at a much deeper level. They set out to do so with the same energy, the same sense of divine calling, and the same discipline that had made the earlier monks successful.

This new era in monastic history had been initiated by Francis, but it succeeded because of a seldom appreciated partnership with another great leader, St. Dominic. The two were almost exact contemporaries, and although very different people with very different gifts they shared a common vision. Together they opened a new chapter in Christian history—unleashing forces that would shape European religious life for the next three centuries, and which would eventually lay the foundations for both the Protestant and Catholic Reformations, and for the post-Reformation evangelical movements.

An Urban Movement

For members of the new mendicant movement the desert was in the new cities springing up all across Europe—and the way to counter the devils in this desert was to preach. One early mendicant preacher explained that he and his colleagues preached in the cities "because there are more people, and the need is greater, for in the city there are more sins."

But the mendicant preachers also located in the cities because at that point in European development commerce and trade were replacing agriculture and landowning, and that great economic transformation was producing a new urban culture. Most of the new monastics—who called themselves *friars*—had themselves been formed in this new urban world, and were thus able to preach the Gospel in ways that addressed their hearers' practical concerns. By contrast the older religious tradition had grown up in an almost exclusively rural environment, and was embedded in cultural and social customs that were no longer relevant.

The new urban population responded to the mendicant mission with an enthusiasm that remains evident to this day in the buildings they erected. By the year 1300 mendicant communities had been established in virtually every European city, and the mendicants' followers had constructed large preaching churches in most of them, corresponding in many ways to contemporary American mega-churches. These preaching churches were often the largest buildings in town, and were frequently paid for by the leading merchant families.

"The need for a well informed and devoted clergy, made all the more pressing by the emergence of an articulate and critical laity, was met by the mendicant orders," says the historian of this movement, Prof. C. H. Lawrence. "They offered a solution to the problems besetting the Church by providing a second force—a new body of pastors parallel to that of the secular clergy and highly trained for the task. They did not change or renew the ecclesiastical structure; they simply bypassed it."

Dominic and the Dominicans

The rapid spread of the mendicant movement in late medieval Europe was due in large part to the synergy between the two quite different branches of the movement, one intellectual and the other rooted in popular culture and its emotional life. Both movements were evangelical, both were devoted to preaching and to forming a new Christian laity, and both focused on the cities of Europe, but their founders—St. Dominic and St. Francis—were quite different people, and the institutions they created were equally different. Fortunately they complemented each other in an unusually productive way.

The founder of the Dominicans had been an Augustinian canon, a pre-mendicant clerical order, and from the outset his order was clerical.

Whereas Francis had been inspired by an essentially lay vision, Dominic's envisioned a community of ordained men who had the education required to be effective preachers, and his early followers came primarily from the new European universities.

Because only educated persons could be members the Dominicans grew more slowly than the Franciscans, but even so by the 1350s some 635 Dominican houses had been established throughout Europe. About twice as many Franciscan houses had been established by then, but the Dominican houses tended to be significantly larger.

In addition to their preaching and evangelization the Dominicans made two other major contributions to western civilization. The first was the new kind of international organization they created. It was based on direct representation to a degree that had never before been attempted. From the local level to the international Dominican leaders were elected by those they led, and were held responsible for the conduct of their office by those they served. The obvious success of this new kind of organization had much to do with eventually making it virtually universal in the western world.

The other major Dominican contribution was the academic system they created, one which has come to be adopted everywhere in the west. It reflected an entirely new view of human learning and mental development, one based not simply on absorbing the knowledge that already existed, but in adapting learning and knowledge to the needs of the time. This was a decisive break with the prevailing intellectual tradition, which regarded the classical Greek and Roman past so highly that no one could imagine anything of value being discovered or written in the present.

Almost immediately the Dominicans began founding houses of higher education in the major university cities of the time. They were soon followed by the Franciscans, and later by the other mendicant orders. The mendicant students attended classes at the university, but lived in their orders' houses.

But the mendicants believed that only Scripture was a suitable topic for monks who were preparing for missionary preaching, and therefore did not allow their members to study the traditional classical subjects. This produced serious conflicts with the secular university faculties, who would not allow the mendicant students to proceed to graduate study, even in theology, without first graduating in the arts.

The friars responded by setting up their own schools, and these schools began attracting students with their fresh approach to learning, including many of the ablest students. This in turn posed a serious threat to the older secular faculties, resulting in some violent confrontations in Paris and Oxford in the 1250s.

There were great advantages to being a mendicant in the 1200s, 1300s and 1400s. Whereas other students would teach for a few years and then move on, it was possible for university teaching to become a lifetime career for members of the mendicant orders. Unlike their secular colleagues the mendicants did not have to repay debts accumulated as students, which could only be done by finding a place in the ecclesiastical or governmental bureaucracies.

As a result members of the mendicant orders were able to pursue scholarship with a freedom their secular colleagues did not have, and as a result it was very often the friars who wrote the most influential books and developed the most important new ideas during these centuries.

In large part it is due to the mendicants, and especially the Dominicans, that we have come to believe that the disinterested pursuit of truth is essential both to true Christian faith and to human progress in general.

The Mendicant Legacy

The mendicant preachers introduced into European society an entirely new way for lay persons to be Christians. Their message was that committed Christians could be 'in the world yet not of it', and that the way to build the Kingdom of God was to live a life of simplicity and to forsake the pursuit of personal privilege, imitating Christ by engaging in evangelization and service to the poor. It was a message that proved to be as attractive to the newly emerging middle class as it was dangerous to the old aristocratic social and political structures.

The very act of preaching was itself a major innovation. Before the mendicants appeared on the scene the church-going laity rarely heard a sermon. But now there were interesting and intellectually stimulating sermons being preached in the mendicant churches, and people flocked to hear them—especially the growing number of merchants who were necessarily literate and informed, and the growing number of lawyers and physicians and other professionals which the increased economic activity in the cities both required and made possible.

And the mendicant preachers not only preached in a new way, they also preached a new message. To those lay Christians who chafed under the status of being passive spectators to religious ceremonies they did not understand, and who were hungry for a more personal role in a religion that had become almost totally clerical, the mendicants offered new opportunities.

In the mendicant churches they were told that lay people could live as devoutly as monks, not by trying to imitate the monastic life but by the way they lived in the world. It was a message based on a new theology of the secular life developed by the mendicant intellectuals, and it was based on a fundamental theological reappraisal of the relationship between grace and nature.

The person most responsible for this theological revolution was the Dominican Thomas Aquinas. He stated the new point of view in the simple phrase, "Grace does not remove nature, but perfects it."

That viewpoint is now so firmly established we can hardly imagine that it was once revolutionary, but in the medieval centuries it was. What it meant was that Christians who were engaged in secular occupations—especially the merchants who had been viewed very negatively by earlier theologians—no longer needed to feel guilty for their work, or to view themselves as second-class Christians.

This new view of the relation between nature and grace also meant that sexuality could be viewed in a much more positive light. This in turn began the long slow process of freeing women from the terrible misogyny which many earlier Christian leaders had acquired, both from their pre-Christian cultures and from their personal struggles to live celibate lives with the resulting experience of relating to women only as sources of temptation.

Although the mendicants are little known to most modern Christians we all owe a great deal to their three centuries of ministry.

- They are the ones who put preaching back at the center of Christian life.

- They pioneered the educational innovations which laid the foundations for the modern university.

- They introduced the idea of fundraising on which all non-profit institutions are now based, an idea which at the time was completely new and which radically challenged the power of the existing elites.

- With their insistence that Christian faith and secular activity are completely compatible they produced the intellectual atmosphere in which western scientific thought would eventually develop.

- They put the Bible at the center of Christian life, not only through their preaching but by publishing the first Biblical concordances, and by pioneering the study of the original languages in which Scripture was written.

- Their influence extends far beyond Western Europe, for they became the European Church's first missionaries, providing the model for what would make Christianity a global religion in later centuries.

- Less happily, they became the backbone of the Inquisition, serving as the inquisitors whose sentences of heresy led to the execution of thousands, a blot on their record that has yet to be acknowledged or dealt with.

THREE MEDIEVAL LIVES

Despite their great preaching the mendicant orders were unable to satisfy the hunger for a more truly Christian way of life which hearing the Gospel faithfully proclaimed will always produce. Their preachers offered a powerful new vision, but they could not offer their hearers a new way to live out this vision, and so the great hunger their message fed on only became more intense, until finally it exploded in the Protestant Reformation.

In retrospect it is clear that a great political and social crisis was building up in European Christianity and that the friars had no way to address it. Indeed they were for the most part unable even to see the crisis, insisting again and again that only the spiritual mattered. But for lay people living in a world where the material and the political are essential to survival this answer was becoming increasingly unsatisfactory.

It is difficult for us to understand the crisis that gripped Europe in the fifteenth century. The lives of our ancestors who lived then were so different from our own that we must make a conscious effort to understand them, but unless we are willing to do so we will never fully understand our own era, for it has been shaped to a very substantial degree by the events of that period.

One way to enter into this period is by looking at the lives of three European lay Christians who lived during the 500 years between 950 and the mid-1400s. Their names are not world famous—Peter Orseolo of Venice, Angela of Foligno in Italy, and Walter Hilton of England—but they each left a mark on history, and they are persons we can perhaps more easily identify with than the great saints.

The Governor of Venice

Peter Orseolo became the governor of Venice in the 970s. Born into one of Venice's noble families at a time when it was the wealthiest and most powerful city-state in Western Europe, he had already at age 20 commanded a naval fleet charged with hunting down a pirate fleet preying on Venice's lucrative Mediterranean trade.

In his mid-forties Orseolo joined in a political coup which overthrew the existing governor by trapping the governor in his palace and then setting it afire. The next day Orseolo was elected to take his place, making him one of the most powerful governmental officials of his time.

But the fire that brought Orseolo to power had also badly damaged the city, destroying not only the governor's palace but damaging the adjacent cathedral as well and destroying some 300 nearby homes. According to contemporary accounts the new governor (called by the Venetians their *doge*) paid to repair the damage from his own funds.

He also resolved the grave political crisis which the coup had caused, restoring peace to the city. He was, says a contemporary, "a man of saintly character" who possessed "higher qualities of statesmanship than were to be found in his predecessors."

One day a year or two after becoming the doge Orseolo heard the passage from the Gospel of Luke being read at Mass in which Jesus tells his followers, "Whoever does not carry his own cross and come after me cannot be my disciple." (14:27).

The new doge was struck deeply by these words and he decided to leave his position of power and become a monk. He left Venice one night with a Benedictine abbot, and they crossed the border into southern France and went to the abbot's monastery where the doge became a Benedictine monk.

For many months no one knew where the doge was or what had happened to him. Needless to say his action created a sensation. It was talked about in Venice, and elsewhere in Europe, for decades after.

According to contemporary accounts the former nobleman and governor became a model monk, seeking out the most menial tasks and undergoing severe penances. He had already been living in a celibate relationship with his wife since the birth of his son 30 years earlier. He eventually built a hermitage for himself near the monastery, and that is where he died, nine years after entering monastic life. One of his biographers believed that he became a monk to atone for his role in his predecessor's murder.

Orseolo's son eventually replaced him, becoming one of the greatest of the Venetian doges. His father wrote to him from the monastery, instructing him in how to be a Christian ruler.

After his death Orseolo's contemporaries declared him a saint, and a thousand years later his memory is still venerated in Venice and in some European monastic communities. Many miracles were reported at his tomb following his death.

An Italian Housewife

Almost exactly 300 years after Doge Orseolo's dramatic conversion a married woman living in a central Italian town named Foligno underwent a similar conversion. Her name was Angela and she lived in the small town just a few miles from Assisi, where she had been born about 25 years after St. Francis' death. Her parents were well-to-do and possibly noble, and she had grown up in a house near the Franciscan church.

At age twenty she married and had several sons. Reputed to have been "rich, proud and beautiful," she lived a life of luxury and passion during her twenties and thirties. She was, she said, preoccupied with her appearance, dressing expensively and wearing fine perfumes, and she frequently indulged in gossip, fits of anger, and in maligning others. She also reports that she engaged routinely in seductive behavior and illicit caresses, "offending God by each of the senses of the body, and all of oneself" as she put it.

At some point in mid-life her life took a dramatic turn. She became overcome with guilt and experienced a profound spiritual crisis. It was caused by some sexual transgression, one so deeply shameful that she believed she was in danger of "being damned to hell." There is a local tradition that she was having an affair. Whatever the cause she "wept bitterly" she says, but her shame was so deep she could not bring herself to confess it.

In despair she began praying to St. Francis, asking him to help her find a confessor "who knew sins well" and to whom she could go for help. She says that in answer Francis appeared to her in a dream saying, "Sister, if you would have asked me sooner, I would have complied with your request sooner. Nonetheless your request is granted." The next morning Angela heard a Franciscan friar preaching, a man to whom she was related, and she went to him and confessed. He helped her resolve her paralyzing guilt, and would eventually become her spiritual director and biographer.

For the next five and a half years Angela struggled to begin a new life, but despite her best efforts she made "only small steps". Finally in her early 40s she made a complete and radical break with her past. She began praying that her children, her husband, and her mother would all die so that she could devote herself entirely to Christ. Her prayers were answered and her entire family died in a short period of time and she began a new life based on the Franciscan ideal.

This event is reported by Angela herself in her published autobiography. It appears not to have horrified her contemporaries in the way it does us. Indeed it appears that some of her contemporaries, who regarded Angela as a saint, saw her willingness to suffer the deaths of all those most closely related to her as a sign of her commitment to follow Christ without compromise.

Unencumbered by family responsibilities Angela now stood before a crucifix and stripped herself naked, pledging perpetual abstinence so that she could become Christ's lover. She gave away her fashionable clothing, and sold her country villa and gave the proceeds to the poor. Needless to say her relatives, especially her husband's family, feared she was possessed by a diabolical fanaticism. Angela herself, and her Franciscan spiritual advisers, were unsure this was not the case.

But after a pilgrimage to Rome Angela returned to Foligno and sold everything she still possessed and gave it to the poor. At this point the local Franciscans invited her to join their community as a Third Order member, and she took the required vows.

Shortly after she became a Third Order Franciscan Angela went on pilgrimage to Assisi, and en route had a powerful vision of the Trinity that would mark the beginning of her career as one of the first female Christian mystics. When she and her companions reached the Franciscan basilica near Assisi she went into a profound mystical ecstasy, throwing herself on the ground in the basilica doorway, shouting inarticulately. Her spiritual director was so embarrassed he angrily ordered her never to return to the basilica.

After that experience Angela regularly reported her visions to her spiritual director, and he recorded them. The end result was a book that would be widely read in medieval Europe, and which 700 years later was translated into modern English.

A lay Franciscan community formed around Angela in Foligno, which continued until her death 18 years later, and likely much longer. After her death she was acclaimed a saint by the public, and her status as "Blessed" was confirmed by a pope 400 years later. Although she has never been officially canonized by the Roman Church she continues to be considered a saint by many.

An English Lawyer

About a hundred years after Angela's conversion, a less dramatic but no less radical conversion took place in England. This one involved a young lawyer, Walter Hilton, who was a recent Cambridge graduate. His education opened some lucrative professional opportunities to him, but for reasons we do not know he chose instead to devote his life to spiritual development.

In earlier times his decision would have almost automatically resulted in his becoming a monk, but for this young man that choice was not automatic. He would eventually become an Augustinian (the same order Martin Luther would join a hundred years later) but he regarded his choice as optional, not a necessity.

He would spend his life proclaiming the message that the kind of radical conversion which had previously been thought possible only for those who lived in monastic communities was now possible for all

Christians—and that even more significantly it was the calling of all Christians.

Hilton's major work, *The Scale of Perfection,* has been described as "probably the most complete, lucid, and balanced treatise on the interior life that the late Middle Ages produced." It was written in English, a revolutionary act at the time, and it circulated in handwritten copies throughout the 1400s. After the invention of printing in the late 1400s it became one of the first English books to be published in print. For many years Hilton's reputation was so great he was believed to have been the author of the *Imitation of Christ.*

One of Hilton's books was written specifically to convince lay Christians they should not try to imitate monastic spiritual practice. Instead, he wrote, they should adapt monastic disciplines to their own situation in the world, balancing their inner development with service to their fellow humans. They should follow this course, he said, even when it meant being less purely spiritual than members of the monastic communities.

He complemented this message by reminding those who lived in monastic communities that it was possible for Christians living in the world to be more truly spiritual than they were.

In a letter to a fellow lawyer and government official who had undergone the same evangelical conversion he had, Hilton discouraged his friend from joining a monastic order. The letter was eventually published and became part of the spiritual literature of the time. Hilton told the readers of this small book that attempting to live like a monk or a friar when one's calling is to live in the world, caring for his family and other dependents, is a mistaken view of Christian faith.

There are "perfect souls" outside the cloister as well as in it, Hilton wrote, and a truly generous person living in society could very possibly acquire as much Christian love and the "other spiritual gifts" as a person living in a monastery. Hilton supported this by quoting Pope Gregory the Great who had counseled pastors to live a "mixed life", one that combined action in the world with private prayer and contemplation.

Hilton's teaching is summed up in this sentence, his very free English translation of another medieval spiritual writer's thoughts:

> Many seek after Christ by withdrawing and fleeing from all men,
> in the belief that he cannot be found except in that way. But it is
> not so. If you would be a spouse of Jesus Christ and would find

him whom your soul loves, I shall tell you where . . . you can find him—in your sick brother who is lame or blind or afflicted with any other disease. Go to the hospital and find Christ there.

The Secularization of Conversion

The journey marked out by these three lives rather vividly illustrates a major event in Christian history—the increasingly secular understanding of Christian conversion that would come to be adopted everywhere in the Christian world. The change in viewpoint which occurred between Doge Peter Orseolo's lifetime in tenth-century Venice and Walter Hilton's in fifteenth-century England—with Angela of Foligno's midway between them—is an epic transformation which the entire Christian community experienced in different ways during those 500 years.

When Peter Orseolo heard Jesus' call to take up his cross and follow Christ, whatever the cost, it meant only one thing to him—that he should become a monk. When Angela of Foligno heard that call 300 years later she had a second alternative—she could become a Third Order Franciscan. And when Walter Hilton heard it in the 1400s he could imagine yet a third alternative—living a life of uncompromised Christian discipleship independently of a religious order.

But none of them could imagine that it was possible to live a truly intentional Christian life and also be married and have children. That is why Angela believed all her family members had to die before she could be a true follower of Christ. The institutional framework of monasticism was open to endless adaptation, except for the tradition of celibacy.

What this did was to create two classes of Christians—those who were celibate and could therefore live completely Christian lives, and those who were not celibate and therefore could only live partially Christian lives. Underneath this was a seldom acknowledged theology which held that sexuality itself was inherently evil. Although to have openly advocated this position would have resulted in charges of heresy, it nevertheless reigned unchallenged in the shadows, producing ever increasing anger and frustration in married Christians.

Hilton was clearly moving beyond this position, but he was still living in the shadow of Bernard of Clairvaux whose influence remained immense well into the modern era. Bernard had convinced western civilization that the spiritual was real, a contribution of almost epic significance, but in so doing he had unintentionally opened the door to the obviously mistaken belief that only the spiritual matters—that physical and social concerns are of only secondary importance, and occur in a realm separate from the one in which our spiritual development takes place.

Not only did Orseolo, Angela and Hilton share the belief that they could not be fully Christian and engage in the sexual life, they also shared the belief that in order to be fully Christian they had had to withdraw from political and economic affairs. This again reflects the medieval belief that there were two classes of Christians—those who are spiritual, and those who are secular.

This is a view that has been explicitly rejected in the twentieth century by Christians of virtually all traditions, but we have yet to institutionalize this view. Given that reality we should not be surprised to find that our distant ancestors, with so much less experience to guide them, should have had such great difficulties in overcoming the legacy their past had bequeathed to them.

MARTIN LUTHER AND THE REFORMATION

The European civilization that had formed around the model provided by the monasteries was firmly established throughout Europe by the end of the medieval era in 1500. No one wanted to tear it down, or give it up; it represented the almost unanimous aspiration of a very large group of people. But as the 1400s unfolded it became increasingly clear that the aspirations at the heart of European civilization were no longer being realized in their major institutions.

Everywhere people looked they saw bishops who preached Christ but practiced Machiavelli. If they looked to Rome for hope what they found was constant warfare between the pope and the secular rulers— and often open warfare between competing popes. When they looked to the monasteries they found wealthy land-owning institutions filled with men who claimed St. Benedict's legacy but who lived semi-aristocratic, self-indulgent and often non-celibate lives in direct contradiction to Benedict's Rule.

Their kings claimed legitimacy because they were Christian kings, but these Christian kings very often governed as tyrants, denying even elementary justice to their people. Everyone agreed that Jesus taught his followers to love their neighbors, but what the working classes and farmers experienced were lives controlled by wealthy landowners who made a great show of personal piety but who treated their fellow Christians as virtual slaves.

If these glaring defects were not enough to cause people to lose confidence in the existing social structures, there had been the abysmal failure of the Crusades—followed now by an invasion from Turkey that threatened all Europe. And hanging over everything was the terrible epidemic that had swept across Europe a hundred years earlier, leaving people dead by the hundreds of thousands, and reducing some towns and cities to less than half their original numbers.

Something had to change. The steadily growing disconnects between the ideals being proclaimed in the churches and what was actually taking place in the societies of which they were a part was becoming increasingly intolerable, creating unsustainable pressures in every area of life. These pressures were often invisible to people living at the time, but visible or not they continued to build up decade after decade and century after century, making a major religious and political explosion increasingly inevitable.

This inevitable event took place in Germany, where the situation was most intolerable and where there had been an animosity to the European ruling establishment ever since Charlemagne had used military power to force his new civilization on the Germanic people.

The eventual outcome would be the Protestant Reformation, and one of the major results of that Reformation would be the near annihilation of the monastic movement. And the explosion would be ignited by a German mendicant.

The Civilizational Crisis

Exactly what was at the heart of this great civilizational crisis was not clear to anyone at the time, and it is still not clear to many historians. What is clear with the benefit of 500 years of hindsight is that this crisis forced a profound reform on European society—one that involved every area of human life, and which culminated in the triumph of democracy in the twentieth century.

But for our medieval ancestors there was no way they could have known this epochal process was taking place, and so they simply reacted to their situation as best they could, making the incremental changes possible in their circumstances, seeking to survive.

What gave meaning and coherence to this otherwise random process was the persistence of Charlemagne's ideal—the vision of Europe becoming a new kind of civilization, a Christian civilization. Although there was widespread disagreement in the medieval era about what constituted a Christian civilization—and even less agreement about how to achieve it—there was virtual unanimity that creating it was the goal. Thus every great issue in this period, whether political, social, economic or otherwise, ultimately became a religious issue.

But what was the answer? By 1500 there had been more than 300 years of attempts to remedy the all too obvious defects in medieval society. New religious orders had been founded, many of them by saints, but they soon became replicas of the old orders they had replaced. Protest movements had demanded justice, but after they had run their course things reverted to the old pattern of two social orders, one for the wealthy and another for the poor.

Lawyers and scholars had tried to initiate an international rule of law, but despite great support warfare and petty violence continued to reign everywhere. Church councils had tried to bring unity and reform to the Church, enacting much far-reaching and worthwhile legislation, but in the end the institutional Church became even more corrupt.

Gifted and highly trained theologians had debated the great issues, but in the end ordinary Christians found their situation unchanged or even worse. For the most part the Church's intellectuals were engaged in debating other intellectuals while the people in the pews starved for lack of spiritual and intellectual nourishment.

The result was a kind of deep-level desperation that historians today find it difficult to understand. But we do not need to understand it to recognize that it existed, and that it had profound consequences. And if we were to regard it as a collision between the ideals European society had inherited from its medieval past on the one hand, and on the other hand its inability to attain those ideals, we will probably not miss the point.

We would like to think that if cooler heads had prevailed the great changes that took place in western civilization in the 1500s and 1600s could have been made without the bloodshed and anarchy that in fact did occur. But that is to ignore the fact that this crisis had been left to fester for so long that it appeared to a very large portion of the northern European population that it could only be resolved by a complete and radical break with the religious and political institutions then in place.

With the benefit of hindsight we can imagine a reformation of the medieval Church that would have avoided schism, and the deviations from the great tradition which schism always produces. But given how deeply embedded in the cultures of the time the defects that needed to be changed were, and the determined efforts by those who benefited from these defective social structures to make sure they remained, we can surely understand why the Protestant reformers were unable to see these nonviolent options at the time.

The answer, we now see, was to act. But action on a civilizational level requires great leadership, and for centuries Europe had failed to produce any great leaders. Martin Luther would change that.

Luther as a Mendicant

Before Luther was a Protestant reformer he was a mendicant friar. He became a friar, he said later, because as a young man he was once caught in a violent thunderstorm. Believing his life was in danger he cried out to St. Anne (the woman who medieval Christians believed was Jesus' grandmother) promising her that if his life was spared he would become a monk. He later wrote that "not freely or desirously did I become a monk, but walled around with the terror and agony of sudden death, I vowed a constrained and necessary vow."

Needless to say with this as its foundation the young friar found his vocation to be a terrible burden. Armed only with his will he made heroic attempts to live up to the profession he had adopted—in opposition to his father, who had wanted him to become a lawyer, the profession for which he had been trained as a university student.

The mendicant movement was almost 400 years old when Luther joined the Augustinian friars in 1505. In those four centuries it had evolved from a revolutionary force in European society into an established part of it, becoming an essentially conservative voice of conventional orthodoxy rather than an innovative or prophetic movement. To a large extent the friars' original mission of evangelistic preaching had been replaced by academic study.

Luther entered into this academic world with great talent and resolve and quickly distinguished himself. His superior, who led the Augustinian order in Germany, became his personal mentor. This resulted in a trip to Rome which left the young Luther shocked at the lack of rigor he witnessed in the Roman Church. By the time he was 30 Luther was a professor of biblical theology, and that would be his occupation for the remainder of his life.

But the young Luther's great professional success only intensified his personal distress, for he found himself teaching things he was aware he was not living. He would later write,

> For however irreproachably I lived as a monk, I felt myself in the presence of God to be a sinner . . . I did not love, indeed I hated this just God, if not with open blasphemy, at least with huge murmuring, for I was indignant against him, saying, "As if it were really not enough for God that miserable sinners should be eternally lost through original sin, and oppressed with all kind of calamities through the law of the ten commandments, but God must add sorrow on sorrow, and even by the gospel bring his wrath to bear.

Luther resolved this personal crisis by in effect adopting the spirituality of Bernard of Clairvaux, with its emphasis on personal religious experience.

Luther became a reformer as a direct result of his academic work and his leadership in that world. His famous 95 Theses, nailed to the church door at Wittenberg in 1517, were an invitation to academic debate, but they would initiate a chain of events that eventually revolutionized both European Christianity and western civilization. This document was broadcast throughout Europe, thanks to the newly invented printing press, and the eventual result would be the Protestant Reformation.

This much of Luther's history is well known, but what is rarely studied or discussed is the role Luther's early formation in the mendicant movement played in his subsequent career. Both Catholics and Protestants tend to be embarrassed by his mendicant years—Catholics because they regard him as a traitor, and Protestants because of their antagonism against monasticism in general. But surely Luther's nearly 20 years as a friar had some impact on his career as a reformer, and if we are willing to move beyond the intense emotions bequeathed to us by the reformation he ignited they appear to be rather obvious.

Could he have produced his great German translation of the Scriptures—surely one of his major and most lasting contributions—without the extensive education in the Biblical languages and sources he had received as a mendicant? Could he have reached the masses of the German people as he did without the training in preaching he received as a mendicant, and the authority his membership in a mendicant order gave him?

Could he have arrived at the profound theological insights that were to prove so formative in the subsequent development of Christianity—even to those who disagreed with him—without the theological training he had received as a mendicant, and without the freedom to reflect on both the Scriptures and the Church's previous traditions which his membership in a mendicant order had provided?

In a word, why should we not consider Luther, and indeed the entire Protestant movement, as a result in some substantial way of the medieval mendicant movement?

Surely what happened in the 1500s is connected in some way to Francis' and Dominic's revolutionary preaching in the 1200s, and to the evangelistic movement they initiated throughout Europe—in the same way that we can now see the mendicant movement was based on the new spirituality introduced by Bernard of Clairvaux in the 1100s.

Luther's Legacy

Luther moved from being an obscure teacher of theology in a small town in Germany to becoming the most significant leader of sixteenth-century Europe in only a few years. How do we account for this almost amazing burst of popularity and for its lasting influence? Surely in large part it was due to the fact that at long last Christian believers in Europe were being offered courageous and clear leadership in moving toward what they had so long sought—a new way to be Christian that involved the laity as full participants.

The fact that the tectonic-scale change which Luther initiated took place so rapidly and over such a wide area indicates he had unlocked forces which had been building up over a long period, only awaiting new leadership to be released. Here was someone who took a stand outside the established hierarchical structures, claiming the authority to act in opposition to them but at the same time able to use all the resources of intellect and spirit which until then had only been available to those who were part of the established structures.

The fact that people in such great numbers flocked to support him—buying his portrait to hang on their walls, printing and reading his pamphlets, affording him political protection in numerous ways—is powerful evidence that they shared his personal goal, which was to act freely as an individual guided primarily by his own conscience.

The Italian scientist Galileo had modeled this same personal autonomy, along with many others who were involved in the Italian renaissance. But these earlier secular reformers had only sought to make room within the existing paradigm for their new ways of thinking. They wanted change, but not fundamental change. Luther by contrast introduced an entirely new paradigm into western society, and it would become the dominant paradigm for the next 500 years.

In the old paradigm everything had revolved around an omnipotent God whose wishes were revealed to an equally omnipotent hierarchy, whose responsibility in turn was to enforce the divine will on everyone below them in the social pyramid. In the new paradigm each individual had direct access to God, and thus was able to decide for himself or herself what God's will was, not only for that person as an individual but for society as a whole.

The well known image of Luther standing before the imperial governing body of his time and announcing, "Here I stand. I can do no other," captured the mood of Europe at the time, and it has remained iconic ever since, especially among Protestants. It almost perfectly embodies the clash between Europe's medieval past and its post-medieval future—what would eventually be called the modern era.

In the modern era Protestants have viewed Martin Luther as their founder, and have regarded it as heretical to criticize him. Catholics by contrast have viewed Luther very differently, as an almost demonic figure responsible for destroying medieval Christianity and causing a terrible schism. But from a post-modern perspective, with its ecumenical outlook, we are able to see that neither viewpoint does Luther justice. He had never set out to establish a new Christian tradition, much less a schism. His only goal was to reform the Church, which he loved and which so badly needed reform.

He can be criticized for many things, but one thing is inescapably clear—he did produce a reform of the Church, and not just of the northern European churches which became Protestant. The Catholic Reformation was equally significant, and it is very difficult to imagine it having occurred had Luther's challenge to a corrupt status quo not been successful.

FOUR

The Monastic Legacy

Although the days when monasticism was a formative force in both Christianity and western civilization are now several centuries in the past, its impact remains, often in ways we are not aware of. On the whole the legacy of monasticism has been richly beneficial, but there have also been negative aspects to its legacy which need to be acknowledged.

MONASTICISM AFTER THE REFORMATION

After the Reformation the story of monasticism is chiefly the story of new religious orders which turned their focus from personal spirituality to institutional service to the Church and the world. The original monastic commitment to conversion and prayer was not abandoned, but after the Reformation monasticism became an almost exclusively Catholic activity, and the emphasis in it shifted to combining spiritual development with specific institutional activities.

In the Protestant world monasticism would in effect be eradicated. Despite their many other disagreements the Protestant reformers were in complete agreement on two things. One was rejection of any allegiance to Rome, and the second was an absolute rejection of monasticism. In every nation where the Protestant Reformation took root the monasteries were closed, their members turned out to fend for themselves, and their lands and buildings sold off to the highest bidder. Much of the capital that initiated the present western economy came from these confiscations.

In Catholic nations the old monastic institutions continued to exist, but their influence and power were greatly diminished. There were new post-Reformation religious orders founded to defend the Catholic Church against the new Protestant challenge, but increasingly the monastic impulse was absorbed into the institutional Church. The Society of Jesus, or Jesuits, was preeminent among these new orders.

Other new Catholic orders would be formed to carry out evangelism in the newly discovered parts of the world, especially Asia, Africa and Central and South America. This was not an entirely new development by any means. Gregory the Great had initiated it in the early 600s, and it was a crucial component in the evangelization of Europe. Even in the medieval period, when monks had largely remained in their monasteries, they had played a key role in evangelizing the areas immediately around them.

But missionary activity became a major focus of Catholic monasticism in the nineteenth and twentieth centuries, with numerous new religious orders formed specifically to engage in evangelism in previously non-Christian areas. The impact of these monk-missionaries has yet to be fully measured and appreciated, but it is difficult to imagine the present process of globalization having occurred without the contributions of the missionaries in creating many of the first trans-national links.

Many other Catholic religious orders were formed to staff the Church's numerous schools and universities, and still others were founded to carry out the Church's charitable activities, including hospitals and service to the poor. The best known member of a Catholic religious order in the twentieth century was Mother Teresa of Calcutta who devoted her life to serving the poorest of the poor in her adopted nation of India.

There were a few attempts to revive monasticism within the Protestant world, but none achieved great popularity. Perhaps the most successful were the Lutheran orders of deaconesses.

THE MONASTIC ACCOMPLISHMENT

When the Egyptian monks went into the desert in the 200s they did not know what they would find or what the consequences of their actions would be. They knew only that this is what they were being called to do. Surely they could not have imagined the vast impact which the movement they began would have on the development of human civilization.

Many of western civilization's most fundamental features come from our monastic past. Most are positive, but some are not. We must confront and understand both if we are to continue moving forward. The past does not control the future but the future is always built on the past, whatever it is. Everything else is a utopian dream.

Monasticism as Intentionality

Although seldom recognized, there has been a foundational assumption upon which all monastic life has been based from its beginnings to the present. It is the belief that human persons can choose their actions. This belief is also the basic assumption upon which all intentional behavior is based, and the belief that intentional behavior is possible is fundamental to western civilization.

Monasticism is in fact the earliest form of institutionalized intentionality in our history. The members of monastic orders are by definition persons who live a highly intentional life style, and the monastic communities have always assumed that those who wish to do so can follow Christ without compromise, that they have the capacity to live their lives in a way that conforms to certain specific expectations.

Today that expectation is pervasive in western society. People everywhere cooperate in staffing very large institutions which are governed by rules, and which assume that people have the capacity to follow those rules. Large business corporations employing hundreds of thousands of people scattered throughout the world would be impossible without this assumption. The same is true for large government agencies. The military could not function without it.

This assumption is now so firmly embedded in our cultures that we cannot imagine a time when it was not the case. But such a time has existed, and it still does exist for a large portion of the world's people. It is possible our ancestors might have acquired their capacity for intentional activity from some other source. We will never know. What we do know is that they learned it from the monks who were in effect their teachers for more than a thousand years.

Fundamental to our way of life as this part of the monastic legacy is, it does however have a dark side. Almost inevitably people will want to have the benefits of intentionality without bothering with the spiritual development that makes it possible. When this happens intentionality becomes a grim burden, not the freeing of human capacity it is intended to be.

Humans cannot simply decide to become intentional. Like any other human ability it must be acquired, and doing so requires long and sustained effort. Above all it requires courage to live intentionally, since doing so makes one responsible for what happens. It is always much easier to assume the role of a passive victim who has no real control over events. This courage can only come from a sustained belief that the universe itself has been created in such a way that it enables and rewards intentional behavior.

If it was possible for Jesus of Nazareth—who lived as a human at a certain time and a certain place, both known to us—to have been both fully human and fully divine, then surely it is possible for other humans to be at least partially divine. And if it is possible for us to be divine in some way and to some degree—if it is possible for us to claim to be "children of God"—then surely it is possible for us to behave intentionally.

That realization is the great gift of the monastic movement to western civilization.

Monasticism and the Ordering of Time

An equally basic development which we now take for granted is the ordering of time. Everything for us now happens according to certain pre-determined schedules. We go to work at a certain hour. We eat at certain times. Our children go to school at certain times. Certain days are work days, and others are weekend days. We meet both for business and socially at previously arranged times. Without the clock our way of life would be unimaginable.

Furthermore we study history. This book is an example. We recognize that time is real, that what has happened in the past has produced what is happening in the present, and will play a major role in what will happen in the future. As a civilization we have acquired a strong sense that human life takes place in linear time—a time that has a beginning and will have an end, a time in which events matter.

But when the first monks came on the scene time was regarded in a very different way. Rather than being linear time was assumed to be an accidental and unimportant byproduct of unordered and essentially meaningless cycles of constantly repeated events—not at all what we would think of as time. Last year was no different than the year before it, and next year would be no different than this year. Time had no destination, no purpose.

The monks changed this view. Their time started at creation, and would come to an end when Christ returned to earth. God in person had chosen to participate in history, at a particular time and place, and with that overwhelmingly important event all time everywhere had acquired new significance. The result was that the universe itself became charged with a numinous energy. No longer was existence a dreary succession of nearly identical days, punctuated only by changes in the seasons, and marked only by occasional feasts, remembered more for their unrestrained passions than for their meaning in history.

By contrast each day in the monastery was viewed as an opportunity for prayer, for reading Scripture and the writings of those who had spent their lives praying and reading Scripture. This work was holy; it had eternal meaning. It was part of a great movement which had begun with Noah and Abraham, and with Moses and the people of ancient Israel who had been formed by the Exodus—a movement which continued with the prophets, and after the prophets with Jesus and the apostles, then with the martyrs and saints—and now with all who believe, and with all who will believe in the future.

Each day brought this new people nearer to a place where humans had never been before, a place where justice would reign. It was for this reason that every day mattered. It was to be occupied, to be used, not simply endured. At the end of each day one could be closer to God, and that had eternal significance. If one was not closer to God a precious thing had been wasted.

And so each day gradually came to be named, and incorporated into a vast liturgical system, a cycle proceeding toward heaven itself. Either the monastic community was celebrating some great event in the history of Christian belief or it was awaiting such an event. And at the end of each cycle the community was nearer to its goal, to its homeland, than it had been when the cycle began.

Each hour was also named. Either the monks were at prayer or they were looking forward to the next time of prayer, which at the most could be only a few hours away. There was no time to kill here, no empty dead time with nothing to do. Every action mattered and every moment mattered.

Is it any surprise that the clock—as basic to western civilization as the wheel—should have been created in the monasteries of medieval Europe?

Monasticism and Work

The monastic contribution to our attitudes toward work has been equally as significant as the monastic contribution to our appreciation of time.

When one joined a monastic community in the formative years of the Benedictine movement it was not to withdraw from the world of manual labor but to enter into that world in an entirely new way. By creating a culture that combined spirituality and economic activity, and successfully maintaining it over sustained periods, the Benedictine communities contributed to western civilization a new attitude toward work, one in which the work which humans did was regarded as equally significant to prayer.

In these communities prayer was no longer regarded as a fearful and ultimately self-centered plea for mercy from an angry and inscrutable god or gods. It was now a free and mutual exchange with a divine being whose primary characteristic was love. In the same way work was no longer a dreary and unpleasant obligation imposed on us by malevolent fate. It was now an opportunity to serve the world, to create as God had created—a gift given us by an ever-present God who wishes only good things for the humans who have been created by God.

The impact this has had on the formation of western civilization is enormous. Rather than regarding work as a lowly thing to be avoided at all costs, something fit only for slaves and servants and those able to do nothing else, manual labor of all kinds has come to be regarded as a noble thing in the western world, something that contributes to the good of society and which should be appreciated and rewarded appropriately.

This in turn has enriched all the societies which have come to adopt this new attitude by bringing many more people into the productive economy, eventually enriching everyone in that society. The emergence throughout the western world of labor unions, and of laws which recognize the importance of labor of all kinds, is the ultimate consequence of this revolution. The self-evident prosperity and vitality of western civilization is based on it, and the monks laid the foundations for it.

Monasticism and Rationality

From the very beginning the European monasteries were places where learning and rationality were promoted and prized. The Rule of Benedict is very explicit that growth in holiness includes both prayer and intellectual development, and throughout its long history the monastic movement has been at the forefront of intellectual life.

Before the monastic era learning was largely the privilege of the wealthy and aristocratic, but in the monasteries everyone was expected to learn, to the extent of their capacities. Everyone in a monastery was assumed to be capable of becoming holy, at least to some degree, and everyone was assumed to be capable of becoming learned to some degree.

Furthermore a new intellectual tradition emerged in the monastic community. It was based on viewing reality in historical terms rather than in mythical terms. This new attitude had originally formed around the practice of viewing the stories in Scripture as history rather than myth, in contrast to the traditional religions whose stories were regarded as conveying timeless truth rather than as accurate descriptions of past events.

By regarding themselves and their movement from an historical perspective the monks would slowly but surely create an intellectual world in which evidence mattered above all. Timeless truth was regarded as existing, but timeless truth was always expected to be verified in the events of history. That unique combination would have immense consequences for the development of western civilization, by allowing us to combine vast general concepts and laws with the evidence of ordinary experience.

The mendicant movement opened up a new world to the Christian laity by enabling St. Thomas Aquinas to produce the great philosophical synthesis which embodied this combination. No longer did one have to choose between being a Christian believer or an intellectual, and no longer would one have to choose between the spiritual and the material. They were now part of a single whole, both available to be understood by human intelligence, and both available to be applied in ways that benefited everyone.

Although the tension between Christian belief and Greek rationality would continue to the present, the ultimate outcome was now decided. Despite occasional reactionary efforts to reverse its course, rationality would thrive within western civilization as it had never before thrived. And that would give enormous power to the laity.

Monasticism and Democracy

The legacy of monasticism also includes its contribution to the major political event of recent centuries, the emergence of democracy.

With the benefit of a thousand years of historical perspective we can now see that the central issue during the entire 1,500 years from the collapse of the Roman Empire to the collapse of Communism in 1989 has been the struggle between two very different ways of organizing human society. It was the monastic movement which pioneered the one that eventually prevailed.

The old way of the pyramid and the empire had prevailed for so long that no one could imagine an alternative. It had maintained social order by giving unlimited authority to male military commanders who occupied the apex of clearly defined social pyramids. These military rulers derived their power from two sources—the common desire for social order, combined with their ability to inflict unlimited amounts of morally sanctioned violence on anyone they deemed necessary in order to maintain order.

Ultimately these great pyramids rested on the people at the base— women, children, peasants and slaves. Although such persons constituted the vast majority in their societies, everyone else ranked above them and no one ranked below them. And for pyramidal societies to function effectively it was essential for everyone at the base to do what they were told, expecting little or nothing in return but survival itself.

A person's position in this rigidly organized society was determined by birth. If one's father was a king, he would be a king, or at the least a member of the aristocracy. If one's mother was a slave, he or she would be a slave, regardless of the father's status. If one's father was a soldier, he would be a soldier, or if a daughter, most likely the wife of a soldier. If one's father was a peasant, he would be a peasant and till the land his father and grandfather had tilled.

If one were a woman her life would be determined by her father and her other male relatives, and lived by the clearly established rules of her society. A husband would be found for her, selected on the basis of the benefits that marriage would bring to the extended family with little or no regard for her well-being or wishes. If one were a child, she or he had virtually no rights at all. Until one reached adulthood, which came early in this world, the child was simply a liability.

The monasteries were a decisive break from this old and long-established pattern. By the very act of joining a monastery one rejected the fundamental assumption upon which it was based—that one's place in society was determined by birth.

But that act of freedom was only the beginning. A way of life based on prayer and study of the Scriptures simply could not be reconciled with the basic assumptions on which the ancient social pyramid was based. Everywhere in Scripture one encounters the belief that any human person can communicate directly with God, and every time people pray they act on that assumption—actualizing it, making it real, declaring that they believe it to be true.

This belief in the fundamental dignity of all humans is the foundation upon which all successful democracies have been based. Our belief in human rights is now so widely held that its origins in religious faith are largely forgotten, but forgotten or not the record of history is unambiguous—the first western institutions based on social equality and elected leadership were the European monasteries.

Monasticism and the Laity

Monasticism's impact on lay Christians is an important but seldom discussed topic, but even though it is clear we have much to learn there is little question that the impact is considerable. How could it be otherwise when monasticism was one of the most powerful institutions in Europe during the formative centuries of western civilization?

The medieval monks maximized human potential in a way that made lay Christians want to imitate them, and that was a clear benefit. But with that benefit there came a serious problem: how were people to share in the monastic way of life if they were married and had responsibility for children? For that matter how were they to share in the monastic way of life even if they were single but for one reason or another could not live in a monastery?

Various answers to this dilemma evolved in the medieval centuries. People, especially the wealthy and politically powerful, supported and even established monasteries in order to have their children educated there, and in order to receive counsel and spiritual support from the monks. The emerging middle class—small farmers, merchants and artisans—for their part often settled near a monastery in order to share in its life, both spiritual and economic.

But despite this the very success of the monastic movement had introduced a sharp divide into the medieval Christian community. Either one was 'religious' or one was 'secular'. Either one lived in a monastery, or one lived in 'the world'.

In the monastery there was order and moral perfection (in theory, never fully in actual practice), and sexuality was thoroughly sublimated (again in theory, not always in practice). By contrast, in the secular world social and moral chaos prevailed. Violence and treachery of every kind were endemic, and undisciplined sexuality dominated the lives of many people. Clearly the monastic way was preferable, even given its failures.

But just as clearly not everyone could live the monastic life. Someone had to conceive and bear children. Someone had to create and maintain stable families for children to grow up in. Someone had to provide them with food and shelter. Someone had to establish the political order on which every family depends for its wellbeing and survival. Someone had to deal with the ugly and often intractable disputes which threaten the order of every social and political community.

The end result of this dilemma was to inject a deep dualism into Western Christianity, one that has had profound and tragic consequences to the present time. In order to maintain the split between 'religious' and 'secular' the Church has been forced to develop a double set of ethical standards—one for its members who are religious and another for its secular members.

This difference is especially apparent in warfare, where the religious are forbidden to participate, while secular Christians are virtually required to do so. This duality also extends to the realm of sexuality, where intercourse is strictly forbidden to the religious but virtually required—or at least regarded as the normal condition of life—for those who are married.

There are many other areas of life where the differences are equally as stark. Greed and avarice—indeed personal property itself—are institutionally prohibited for religious Christians, whereas the pursuit of wealth has become the de facto primary measures of success for Christians living in the secular world.

What this has produced is a prevailing belief that full Christian morality is meant only for the heroic few, and that everyone else must live by an essentially Darwinian morality, in which virtually any action is considered legitimate so long as it results in the short term survival of that person and his or her social group.

The Franciscan Legacy

Because the impact of St. Francis and the movement he inspired have been so great it is especially important that we confront the way his extraordinarily popular example, and the extensive influence of the Franciscan orders, have impacted subsequent lay Christian development.

We must begin with the tendency toward a spirit-matter dualism which is inherent in the entire monastic legacy, and which is an especially troubling part of St. Francis' legacy.

Francis identified with the poor so completely that he became poor. This has inspired millions of Christians in the centuries since to make care for the poor a part of their lives as Christians, and that is obviously a major gain. But at the same time we have learned that we cannot give what we do not have, and that our becoming poor is not really helpful to those who are already poor.

In retrospect it appears that Francis' response to his father's aggressive materialism was an equally excessive anti-materialism. No one after him has been able to live out Francis' ideal of living in society without owning anything, not even the religious order which he founded. It is simply impossible, and the attempt to do so verges on an un-Christian dualism which holds that the material domain is inherently evil. The result has been that many Christians have justified their materialism by pointing to the impossibility of its opposite.

Francis' approach to peace has proven to be equally problematic, despite its being rooted in the Gospel and in a deep commitment to the sacredness of all life. He was essentially a pacifist, who believed that good will could solve all political conflicts, even those embedded in hundreds of years of history—such as the conflict between Western European Christians and the Muslims of the Middle East which dominated foreign affairs in his lifetime as it does in ours. His efforts to end this conflict by converting the leader of the Muslim forces to Christianity is notable equally for its courage and for its naiveté, and has bequeathed to our civilization the widely held view that being in favor of peace requires one to ignore the realities of injustice, inherited conflict and cultural factors.

Francis' attitude toward institutional matters was of the same type. He appears to have believed that everything could be governed by personal relationships, a belief that proved to be seriously mistaken when the order he founded expanded across national and cultural boundaries.

His negative view of institutions forced him to leave the organization of his movement to others, and the result was that after Francis' death his movement split into numerous warring factions. Within a hundred years after Francis' death members of his order were burning each other at the stake, and it has remained seriously divided to this day—surely a counter-witness to its central message, and a dangerous inducement to individualism for those who have adopted Francis as their model.

Francis' adoption of celibacy as a requirement for uncompromising Christian intentionality must also be questioned. It is now obvious that a major evangelical crisis was developing in medieval Christianity, and that the tradition of clerical celibacy was a major cause of this crisis. But rather than helping resolve this crisis Francis and his associates, without intending to do so, in effect extended the life of the clerical subculture for several centuries, and in so doing unintentionally contributed to the belief that sexuality is inherently evil.

Had the early Franciscans found a way to carry out their mission without adopting the discipline of forced celibacy it is conceivable that the Protestant Reformation would not have been necessary.

Francis' great poem in celebration of creation, written at the end of his life, indicates he had come to realize, at least intuitively, that for Christianity to progress it must develop a more robust integration of the spiritual and the material. It is entirely conceivable that if he had lived longer his legacy might be very different.

The mendicant orders which Francis and Dominic founded offered conversion and Christian intentionality to everyone, but this conversion was almost exclusively spiritual. It was a personal conversion involving the inner life, not a cultural or political change. But that is impossible. Humans cannot change their spiritual beliefs and leave their political and cultural behavior unchanged.

Monasticism had thrived because it had formed stable communities, but there were very few communities for intentional lay Christians— places where they could combine prayer and work, *ora et labora*. The result was an increasingly self-absorbed monasticism, and an increasingly frustrated laity—both of which could quite possibly have been avoided had the Franciscan movement taken a more balanced approach to human existence.

That of course is speculative. What is not speculative is that Francis was a pioneer of the first order, confronting problems which had never before been confronted. If he had made no mistakes he would have been the equivalent of Christ, which he was very conscious he was not. Francis was one of the greatest Christians of all time, but for that very reason we must be careful to recognize his errors so that we do not repeat them.

MONASTICISM AND THE FUTURE

Even the negative legacy of monasticism can be a gift to us if we will let it be. To recognize that a major element of dualism is embedded in the monastic legacy can help us recognize that for Christians neither spirituality nor materialism is the goal—that what matters is integrating them, in imitation of the incarnation itself.

Surely the task of the future is to combine our spirituality and our existence in time and space into a single harmonious whole, making what we feel and think and desire consistent with what we actually do. If we wish to continue on the path Christians have followed for the past two thousand years we will need to make increasingly intentional efforts to conform our work to our beliefs, to actually live day by day in new ways, establishing relationships with our family members and with the citizens of other cities and nations which are consistent with our spiritual commitments.

We all experience a constant inclination to make life simpler and easier by either privileging the inner spiritual world or the outer material world, but when we do either life only becomes more difficult. We have been created as an integrated whole which combines the spiritual and the material in ways we do not yet fully understand, and only when we embrace that combination do our lives become successful.

St. Benedict understood that, at a profound level, and he initiated a tradition in which prayer and work are integrated into a single way of life. That combination is what has made our civilization so successful. To go on we must continue to make that connection in new ways.

That is why we await, in the words of the philosopher Alasdair MacIntyre, a "new Benedict". Just as the first Benedict gave the world a new vision of virtue and a new way to institutionalize following Christ—a way that combined the inner and the outer, the spiritual and the practical, the ordinary and the eternal—we are being called 1,500 years later to a new way of following Christ which combines the feminine and the masculine, the scientific and the mystical, the personal and the political, the family and the prophetic.

Jesus has already accomplished this, in a profoundly life-giving way, and he continues to invite us to "Follow me."

Oversells the monastic but excellent insight into legacy of dualism.

PART TWO

Evangelical Intentionality

Just as the monastic movement increasingly came to dominate first millennium Christianity, the lay evangelical movements would increasingly come to dominate second millennium Christianity. These two forms of Christian intentionality are fundamentally similar, especially in their motivation, but the ways they have developed over the centuries have been quite different, and as a result their stories are quite different.

The story of monastic intentionality is one of great institutional success, extending across the world and across seventeen hundred years of Christian history, and it is one that is well known. By contrast the story of evangelical intentionality is less well known, and although it extends across an even longer span of time, and an equally large area, it has until recent centuries been dominated by persecution at the hands of other Christians, and by often serious deviations from the great traditions of Christian orthodoxy.

But despite these tragic chapters the evangelical story is equally inspiring—and at this point in time it is unusually important. Even though the history of evangelical intentionality is little known even by those Christians who consider themselves evangelicals, and despite its having been largely ignored by past historians, evangelical intentionality holds a place in Christian history as central as monastic intentionality.

In the twentieth century the evangelical movements have experienced the greatest growth in the Christian community, which provides an additional reason to focus greater attention on them than has been the case in the past. It now appears virtually certain that the development of Christianity in the new millennium will be strongly influenced by these rapidly growing evangelical groups. They are now spread across the world, and routinely exhibit a kind of vitality which the older and more traditional forms of Christianity often lack.

Although most Christians are unaware of their evangelical heritage, it is very much there—as this overview of the major evangelical movements which have emerged over the past two millennia makes quite clear.

Defining Evangelical

The word evangelical is currently used in three different ways. The first is the one we have inherited from the medieval era. Members of the monastic orders were referred to then as persons who followed "the evangelical counsels"—meaning the literal commands of Christ as they appear in the Gospels. This primary meaning came from the word 'evangel' which is equivalent to our word 'gospel'. In that sense evangelical meant those who took the direction for their life directly from the gospel, and that meaning is still used in the Catholic world.

In the post-Reformation era the word evangelical came to be used in two other ways, both related to the medieval usage but somewhat different. The earliest of these is the Germanic usage which is essentially synonymous with Lutheranism. The Lutheran Church in the United States is called the Evangelical Lutheran Church, and in Germany the same terminology holds.

A third meaning of the word 'evangelical' has emerged in the Anglo-American world. In this case it refers to a movement which emerged in the nineteenth and twentieth centuries in both English and North American Protestantism and which emphasizes individual religious conversion, the authority of Scripture, and a congregational ecclesiology and polity.

To choose a word which has been used in three different ways is less than ideal but the only alternative is to coin a new term, which is even less satisfactory. But because there are multiple uses of this term it is important to clarify which one is being used. In this book the word evangelical is used in a generic sense to refer to all the movements throughout Christian history which have emphasized individual religious conversion, immersion in Scripture, the role of the Spirit in Christian life, and voluntary lay-controlled institutions.

FIVE

From Jerusalem to the Millennium

Although the major impact of the evangelical movements would come in the second millennium of Christian life, there were precursor movements in the first millennium which would point the way toward both the potential and the problems these later movements would encounter.

THE JERUSALEM COMMUNITY

The first community of intentional Christians is also the first Christian community of any kind. It is the one which formed in Jerusalem immediately after the first Easter and Pentecost. All the Christian communities that have formed since are descended from this original Christian community.

There is a detailed account of this community's early years in the *Acts of the Apostles*, the first book of Church history, a book which appears to have been written by a member of the original Jerusalem community. The history of the founding of this community—in many ways the founding of Christianity—is recorded in the first seven chapters of the *Acts*, and although this account does not tell us everything we would now like to know it tells us a great deal.

The People

The Jerusalem community consisted of people who believed Jesus had physically been raised from the dead. Some of them had encountered him in his risen body on that first Easter Sunday, others had only heard reports from others, but in either case they shared the belief that this unprecedented event had actually occurred, and it was this belief that brought them together and kept them together. They had known Jesus before the Resurrection, but when he was executed by the Romans they had lost hope, and without this miracle they would not have continued, and could not have continued.

Prior to Pentecost this community was small. It consisted of the twelve apostles chosen by Jesus, a few anonymous women, Jesus' mother Mary and her closest relatives, and the others who had followed Jesus during his lifetime. Originally it numbered at best a few hundred persons. (Acts 1:13-15)

Although new and untested—and strongly opposed by the religious authorities—the community took its responsibility to propagate Jesus' story very seriously. Their first action as a community was to choose someone to take Judas' place in the Twelve. Peter, who served as their leader, said "It is necessary that one of the men who accompanied us the whole time the Lord Jesus came and went among us, beginning from the baptism of John until the day on which he was taken up from us, become with us a witness to his resurrection" (1:22). The other members concurred and agreed on a way to choose Judas' successor from among their number.

This group, which would form the nucleus of the Christian tradition, was remarkable equally for its diversity and for its utter lack of any social or political power. Many were Galileans living in a city where people from their region were regarded as uncultivated country people. And indeed they were largely uneducated, and for the most part poor. Their leaders were former fishermen. There were no priests, no aristocrats, no wealthy individuals among the original community.

Furthermore the community included both women and men, something which at the time was not only unprecedented but was associated with sexual license and other forms of immorality. There appear to have been no qualifications for membership in this community, other than the belief that the stories which the apostles told were true. Their very existence was revolutionary.

The opposition to Jesus that had brought about his execution was immediately extended to his followers, and for the first several weeks this little group lived in constant fear they too would be arrested and executed.

But then an event took place that was as inexplicable as the Resurrection itself, and which would have as great an impact on subsequent history.

This took place on a Jewish holiday called Pentecost, when suddenly and inexplicably they were filled with an energy they had never before experienced, nor had ever witnessed in others. When this happened they lost their fear, unlocked the doors behind which they had been hiding, and began proclaiming their message openly and aggressively.

What was even more amazing was their ability to communicate in languages other than their own. People by the thousands joined the community that day, and in subsequent days thousands more joined them. This event made the new community even more disparate, and even more revolutionary. Now there were people by the thousands, including priests, proclaiming that Jesus was the Messiah long predicted by the Jewish prophets. The global spread of Christianity had begun.

Needless to say the governing establishment could not tolerate this and ordered the new movement's leaders be arrested and jailed. But once again a miraculous event took place and the leaders simply walked out of prison, only adding to their fame.

The community's original members had all been observant Jews, but increasingly non-Jewish persons joined them. To comprehend the significance of this we must understand the hostility that existed at the time between Jews and non-Jews. If we were to compare it to the hostility that currently exists between Jews and Muslims in the Middle East it would be similar. But this first Christian community experienced their unprecedented diversity not as a problem but as proof they were truly following Jesus.

The Community

What this still small but rapidly growing community believed and preached was radical enough, but the way they lived was equally so. Each day they met in the temple for worship, and then went to one of their homes for a fellowship meal, where they shared their amazement at what was happening. Their neighbors and family members looked on, equally amazed, and many decided to join the new community.

These first Christians were participating in a miracle—something which actually happens but which people had previously believed could not happen—and even at the time the members of this tiny community realized it.

The same unexplainable healings which had occurred throughout Jesus' ministry were now occurring under the apostles' hands. A 40-year old man who had been born deformed and who had spent his entire life begging at the temple gate suddenly acquired the ability to walk, and his almost incredible story spread through the city. Peter used the occasion to proclaim once again that Jesus was the Messiah (the Hebrew word for Christ)—and that the Resurrection had proved this.

The temple authorities responded by once again arresting Peter and putting him in jail overnight. The next morning when Peter and his fellow apostles were brought before the Jerusalem religious establishment they were asked how it was possible for ordinary uneducated men like them to have done such a thing? What was their source of power? By what authority did they act? Peter boldly replied that it was very simple—it was the power of Jesus the Messiah, "who you crucified, and who God raised from the dead." Peter had added, "There is no salvation through anyone else."

The authorities of course could not accept this, but when they saw the formerly deformed man standing among the members of the community the best they could do was to order the apostles to quit proclaiming their new story, an order which the apostles immediately rejected. "Whether it is right for us to obey you rather than God, you be the judge," they told the authorities. "It is impossible for us not to speak about what we have seen and heard."

The judges wanted to punish these men for their boldness, but could not because they feared the people, who were grateful the deformed man had been healed. When the apostles returned to the community and recounted the story of their trial the members began praying ecstatically, experiencing such spiritual intensity they felt the earth shake under their feet.

Many people who had seen the deformed man made whole and who had heard Peter's explanation for it responded by joining the new community, which continued to grow rapidly, soon including more than 5,000 members. When the apostles were rearrested and once again put in jail an angel opened the doors and let them out, they said.

The members of this unique community not only preached to others and healed anyone who came to them, they also took care of each other in a radically new way. "No one claimed that any of his possessions was his own," the author of the *Acts* says. "There was no needy person among them, for those who owned property or houses would sell them" and give the money to the apostles, who in turn distributed the community's resources "to each according to need."

This early example of what we would today call voluntary socialism was even more radical then than now. In the first century one could imagine a wealthy person distributing his surplus to his children, or even to other family members, but no one could imagine treating a person with whom there were no blood ties, or who could not somehow repay the gift, in this same way.

It does not appear that economic community was a requirement for membership in the first Christian community. There are abundant examples later of persons becoming Christian without any mention of this requirement. But it was an option, and it was an option that many first generation Christians chose.

The *Acts* includes the story of a married couple who said they had chosen this option, but who secretly kept some money for themselves. Peter caught them in their lie, and when confronted with it both the man and the woman immediately fell dead. The point of the story appears to be not that a Christian should not own property, but that one should not pretend to have made a commitment she or he does not intend to carry out.

What is clear is that caring for the poorer members of the community was so central to the Jerusalem community's way of life that very soon they had to appoint a new group of leaders to carry out the community's charitable actions. They were called deacons, from the Greek word for service. They had an equal standing with the apostles, whose job was proclamation. The deacons' job was to translate the proclamation into a way of life.

The Legacy of the Jerusalem Community

In the life of this first Christian community we find the essential traits that would characterize the numerous evangelical groups that would emerge in subsequent centuries. These communities would also be founded by ordinary and often uneducated persons who had experienced a spiritual transformation that made them bold and able to take extraordinary actions. At the center of the <u>lives of these communities</u> would always be the sense of Jesus' resurrected reality, both in their lives and in history, which the first generation Christians had experienced.

They would also claim the Holy Spirit's enabling power, a power that they will insist is greater than any earthly power. They would also have the confidence to say, as Peter had said to the religious authorities of his time, "We must obey God rather than men."

And they will have a confidence that enables them to literally risk their lives on the ultimate truth of their beliefs. They will be notable for their evangelism, especially among their peers in the less privileged segments of society. And they will take care of each other, as the members of this first Christian community did. And they will not only serve each other, they will serve all those who are suffering or are in need.

The example of the Jerusalem community has inspired Christians throughout history, and still does. Their way of life is so inherently attractive that it is difficult to read their story without saying, "I would like to belong to a community like that. Why can't I? Why can't we all live like that? That's the truly Christian way to live."

Why do we find this story so attractive? Why have so many Christians through the centuries tried to imitate it in some way? The answer appears to lay in reality itself. We have been created to love, and to live in community with other loving persons, and we have a profound and undeniable urge to do so.

But if this is the case why have so many of the communities which have set out to follow the example of the Jerusalem community failed? The answer to this question appears to be that we have increasingly—often without being aware we were doing so—separated the apostolic from the evangelical.

The Jerusalem community—a lay evangelical community if ever there was one—formed around the twelve apostles themselves, who were very much a part of that community. It was this combination of apostolic authority and lay intentionality that made it possible for this tiny, powerless community to found what has come to be the world's largest religious community.

Unfortunately over the centuries maintaining the apostolic tradition and creating intentional communities of lay Christians have come to be separated. Christians have in effect been forced to choose one or the other, and the result has often been tragic.

THE MONTANISTS AND DONATISTS

In the first three hundred years of Christianity the constant threat of persecution would require all Christians to be highly intentional. There was no other reason to be a Christian at a time when becoming one meant putting your life at risk.

But even under these conditions two substantial lay evangelical movements emerged—and several smaller ones. Both of the larger evangelical movements emerged because some Christians at the time had serious disagreements with the way the Christian community was developing. In both cases these disagreements involved matters on which the Christian community remains divided more than eighteen hundred years later, and which Church leaders have been unable to successfully address.

The role of the Holy Spirit in Christian spirituality is the first. The second is the Church's responsibility in dealing with issues of structural social injustice, issues which by their very nature can only be resolved through political action. In the twentieth century the first of these issues produced the Pentecostal and Charismatic movements, and the second produced the Liberation Theology movement. The movements which these same issues gave rise to in the 100s and 200s are similar in many ways.

The Montanists

The first major evangelical movement that would emerge in the post-Apostolic period—the period following the death of the apostles and those who had known the apostles—was a group now known as the Montanists. It originated in Phrygia, an area in what is now southwest Turkey which had originally been evangelized by St. Paul. The Montanist movement originated in the 150s, some fifty to eighty years after the apostles' deaths, and it would spread rapidly for the next hundred years, both in Turkey and elsewhere.

The movement's founders were three lay people, one male and two female. The two women had abandoned their husbands and joined a small group gathered around a man named Montanus and had begun prophesying in ecstasy, at times and in ways which more conventional believers thought were inappropriate.

These "new prophets", as they called themselves, believed they received messages directly from God. These messages, they said, were intended for the poor and marginalized and were intended to prepare Christians to die as martyrs. The new prophets proclaimed the end of the world, and said the New Jerusalem promised in the Revelation of St. John would appear in a small town near where they lived.

Needless to say this produced much opposition among other Christians, who believed all this was a departure from the tradition they had received from the apostles. But many other Christians at the time regarded it as a return to the charismatic component in the apostolic tradition—clearly reported in both the *Acts of the Apostles* and in Paul's letters.

The significant impact which this movement had on the entire Church at the time is apparent in the significant number of Church leaders who commented on it. Unfortunately almost all the surviving contemporary reports are negative ones, focusing on the movement's defects and giving us very little information as to why this movement grew so rapidly and why it survived for so long, despite determined efforts to stamp it out.

Our only friendly reports come from the writings of Tertullian, the great North African Christian apologist. He joined the Montanist movement in the early 200s, after having been a Christian convert for some years, and defended the new movement with great fervor.

Many subsequent Christian historians have viewed his association with the Montanists as a defection from Christian orthodoxy, but Tertullian's most recent historians have pointed out that despite his being a Montanist Tertullian was highly regarded by St. Cyprian, a later leader of the North African Church and one whose orthodoxy is unquestioned.

Tertullian's writings indicate that the Montanist movement was sometimes schismatic, but not always. He himself appears to have joined the Montanist movement—or The New Prophecy as it members called it—because he shared its commitment to lay discipleship, something he as a lay Christian felt strongly about. He appears to have viewed the movement as 'a little church within the Church' not an alternative to it.

His writings indicate a movement which supported rigorous ethical standards, and a non-hierarchical organizational structure in which all believers were regarded as priests. It was based on a sharp distinction between a pneumatic 'Church of the Spirit' and a visible institutional Church.

Tertullian appears to have regarded military service as forbidden to Christians, and it is probable that other Montanists shared his point of view. What the Montanists stood for was a clear distinction between the way Christians lived and the way non-Christians lived, and Tertullian believed Christians in his time were losing the fervor of the original Christians and were accommodating to the prevailing culture in order to avoid persecution.

Although the Montanist movement survived and grew for more than a century, in the end it died out. In the early 400s one of the popes outlawed Montanism as a heresy, leading to its decline in the Roman Empire, and 150 years later the Byzantine emperor repressed it with considerable violence. The Montanist movement however was only driven underground, not entirely destroyed. In 601 Pope Gregory the Great was still discussing the validity of Montanist baptism with the Spanish bishops, and 300 years later the Patriarch of Constantinople once again urged the emperor to take action against the "Phyrigian heretics".

But suppressing the Montanist movement did not resolve the issue that had brought it into being, which was the role of the Spirit in the life of the Church, and especially in the ordinary life of the laity. By failing to address this issue the early Church simply passed it on to later generations, where it still remains largely unresolved.

There is good reason to fear the destructive actions which people who believe they are directly inspired by the Holy Spirit all too often engage in. The history of Christianity is filled with horrific examples, ranging from the numerous prophets who have inaccurately predicted the end of the world to tragic instances of religious fanaticism. But the Church's history provides equally tragic examples of what happens when the energy which comes to individuals from the Holy Spirit is not present. In that case the Church quickly degenerates into a stale traditionalism, with equally deadly consequences.

The Donatists

The controversy over Christian behavior in the face of persecution, which had originally brought Tertullian into the Montanist movement, would in the next century produce another major protest movement in North Africa.

In the final persecution of Christians by a Roman emperor, which took place under Diocletian in 303-05, the bishop of Carthage had avoided martyrdom by handing over some books to the imperial authorities. The books had not been the Christian Scriptures demanded by the authorities—they were books by Christian heretics instead—but for the strict party this made no difference. They believed their bishop should have refused to hand over anything to the persecutors and thus have died as a martyr, as so many of his predecessors and colleagues had, and like many lay members of the Church had.

This very serious controversy, which raged throughout the Christian Church at the time, produced a major split when it came time for the North African Christians to elect a new archbishop of Carthage. On one side were the urban bishops and on the other were a large group of bishops from the countryside. The city party was the largest faction and elected one of their members as the new archbishop. The smaller country party was led by a bishop named Donatus, who would give his name to the opposition movement that would emerge from this conflict.

What lay behind this conflict was not simply a disagreement over persecution, but even more a long-standing conflict between the Roman colonists who had lived in North Africa for centuries and who held all the major positions of power and privilege, and the native peoples called Berbers who had long considered themselves a conquered people.

The Donatists refused to accept the bishop their largely Roman colleagues had elected, and instead elected one of their own. The resulting dispute threatened the political stability of North Africa and so came to the Emperor Constantine's court. For three times in succession he asked the Bishop of Rome to convene councils of bishops from other nations to adjudicate this dispute. In all three cases the bishops in other nations listened to the evidence and ruled against the Donatists.

While all this was going on Donatus was energetically organizing what would become in effect a separate church of the indigenous Berber population. He ordained bishops and created a separate hierarchy, who presided over a separate set of congregations with their own buildings.

When the Donatists' third appeal had failed the emperor ordered this new religious body to be suppressed and their churches confiscated. However the imperial authorities rescinded it when it became apparent that enforcing the suppression order was causing dangerous unrest among the indigenous population.

The hostility between the two communities of North African Christians was now permanent and armed guerilla groups continued to wreak havoc on life in the region for the next century. Imperial authorities made several attempts to end the conflict but none were successful. The Christian religion instead of being a unifying force in society had become a battleground between two warring political and ethnic groups, and there was nothing in the Christian tradition at that time which equipped its leaders to deal with this tragic situation.

Theologically the debate continued to center around the original controversy over persecution, but it now appears this theological dispute had been the occasion for forming the Donatist movement rather than its cause. It is becoming increasingly clear that what accounts for the tenacity of this movement over more than a hundred years was the long-standing conflict between the indigenous Berber community and the Latin-speaking Roman colonists—the kind of social and political conflict that is inevitable wherever colonialism takes place.

When Augustine returned to North Africa in about 390 he inherited this conflict, and when he was made a bishop he undertook great efforts to resolve it. Donatist guerillas were threatening the members of his parishes and attacking his churches. The situation had evolved into a de facto civil war and a resolution had to be found.

Augustine approached the matter with rational argument, using his legal training and experience. He compiled a record of what had happened, then analyzed it as objectively as possible before proceeding to show the error of his opponents. But none of this mattered to his opponents. They had committed themselves to changing their political and social status, and once having committed themselves to military action had crossed a point of no return.

After struggling with this conflict for some 15 years Augustine came to the conclusion that the Donatist revolt could only be ended by governmental coercion. He came to this conclusion reluctantly, and after trying in every possible way to solve the problem theologically and rationally. But the problem was not theological or rational—it was political, and it demanded a political solution, and the only one Augustine could imagine involved appealing to Roman imperial authority.

Augustine justified this position theologically with a series of homilies on the *First Letter of John*, a portion of Scripture that emphasizes the centrality of love in Christian faith and which contains the phrase, "God is love." Augustine set out to prove that the use of government coercion could in certain circumstances be an act of love, and with that he laid the foundations for the later Christian doctrine of just warfare.

Needless to say the Donatists did not view their repression by violence as an act of love. Instead they pointed to the floggings they received, the confiscation of their property, and their being forced into exile as clear evidence that they were the true successors to the early Christian martyrs, and that the Catholic party had become the successors to the Roman imperial authorities who had persecuted the early Christians.

The Donatists survived, but were much weakened by persecution and by their own internal divisions. 200 years later they were still in existence, and would continue to exist until the Muslim conquest destroyed the entire North African Christian community.

What we know about the Donatists had until recently come almost entirely from St. Augustine's writings, which contain numerous references to them. As a result the Donatists' reputation has been almost largely negative. But recent historians have uncovered evidence from Donatist sources and this is causing a major reassessment. We had known only that this group had an exceptionally loyal following and that it thrived for more than a century. We had not known why its followers joined the Donatists, nor why they were so persistent in their commitment to it. It is likely that will change and if so it will be important information.

What has often been overlooked in Augustine's dealings with the Donatists is the great lengths he went to in dealing with them as fellow Christians. Even though they held positions that he and the other Church leaders regarded as mistaken and heretical, he nevertheless made persistent and serious efforts to restore these Christians to fellowship with other Christians. But why did he not succeed?

The ecclesiological debate that took place in fourth-century Africa continues unabated today between Catholic and evangelical theologians. But what has yet to be taken seriously is Donatism as a social justice movement, representing the legitimate grievances of the indigenous people in their struggle with the dominant Roman colonists.

The exceptionally high regard in which Augustine has been held by subsequent Christians has made it virtually impossible to even entertain the possibility that he might have supported the use of violence against a group which has a legitimate claim to respect by later Christians. One can disagree with Donatist theology—at least as it has been reported to us by their opponents—but at the same time agree with them that a serious discrepancy existed between the gospel which the Catholic bishops were proclaiming and their support of the Roman imperial government.

As the international Christian community came to be centered in Rome, and as Latin became its common language, there was a strong tendency to emphasize the benefits with the Christian community received from the empire. It provided the Church with political stability so that its missionaries could travel freely. After Constantine the empire provided Christians with freedom of religion. In many cases Christians had the active support of government officials, which gave them many advantages.

But this calculation failed to take into account the many disadvantages which Roman imperial rule brought to those on the bottom of the social, political and economic pyramid. The issue of social justice had not yet emerged on the horizon of Christian thought, and principles that are now quite clear to us, and which are affirmed in numerous confessional Church documents, were then unknown.

Once again this issue has been passed on to later Christians, largely unresolved. And once again throughout the centuries other evangelical movements would take it up—in a great variety of ways, some successful and some tragic.

OTHER EARLY EVANGELICAL MOVEMENTS

In the early centuries of the post-persecution Church, lay evangelical communities would continue to emerge throughout the Mediterranean world. None would survive, and most have been lost to history, but the records of those which survived the longest and which have left some mark on the historical record indicate the persistence of this ideal in the Christian community, even at this early stage in the Church's development.

Whereas Monatism and Donatism emerged in the period of persecution, these later movements formed in the centuries following persecution, when the Christian community had a freedom it had not enjoyed before.

Eustathius of Sebaste

At the same time the Donatist movement was developing in North Africa, another quite different lay evangelical movement was forming in the Greek-speaking area in the eastern Mediterranean. We know about this community because of a remarkable family that was among its members. This was a noble land-owning family, probably of senatorial rank, which lived in Pontus, an area now part of Turkey. This Christian family had maintained its noble standing, but had also been heroic in withstanding the fierce Diocletian persecution which had immediately preceded Constantine's reign.

It appears that three generations of this family had formed an intentional community on their estate, under the inspiration of a bishop named Eustathius of Sebaste. He was promoting monasticism of the kind being practiced at the time in Egypt, and this family apparently attempted to conform their life to that ideal. They did so with such success that since their deaths seven members of the family have been regarded as saints by Greek-speaking Christians. They include St. Basil the Great, a major figure in the history of eastern Christianity; his grandmother; both his parents; his two brothers; and his sister. Both Basil and his sister founded celibate monasteries, and Basil himself is regarded as the founder of Eastern monasticism.

Unfortunately we do not yet know a great deal about the community which produced such an astonishing result, except that it existed. Was it strictly a family affair, or were there other members? Did similar communities exist elsewhere in the Greek-speaking Church? What were its practices and beliefs? Were the members of this community regarded by contemporary Christians as a 'little church within the church' or were they considered an aristocratic family that lived an unusually ascetic life?

One significant fact which the existing record does report is that despite Basil's parents' extraordinary commitment to the Christian faith they did not have their children, at least not their sons, baptized as infants. But we do not know if that was unique to this particular community, or whether this was the pattern elsewhere in the Eastern Church at the time.

Nor do we know a great deal about this community's connection with Bishop Eustathius. Was he their founder or simply their spiritual director? Did he seek to establish other similar communities? We do know that Eustathius had the same difficulties with the developing theology of the time which many other evangelicals were having, and that for that reason Basil would eventually part ways with him.

Subsequent historians have criticized Eustathius for questioning elements of what would become the orthodox theological tradition, but once again the only information we have comes from his opponents. We do learn from them that the movement Eustathius founded was devoted to works of charity, including homes for the poor and hospitals.

It is entirely possible that Eustathius criticized the theological efforts of his time not so much for their content but because he viewed the great amount of energy then being devoted to theological disputation to be a distraction from the essential tasks of the Church, which were evangelism and serving those most in need. If so that would put him in the company of many subsequent evangelical leaders who have shared a relatively low regard for theology.

In any case it is surely significant that St. Basil the Great, unquestionably a major figure in the development of the institutional Church in the east, would have grown up in and been formed by an evangelical community.

The Pricillianists

At the same time Eustathius was forming evangelical communities in the east a somewhat similar evangelical movement was emerging in Spain. Here the leader was a recent convert named Priscillian of Avila. He is described by his biographer as "a devout cultivated layman of high, probably senatorial standing" who began by asking his fellow Christians to take their baptism more seriously and to "give more time to special spiritual study."

Priscillian's vision of Christian intentionality was similar to the monastic vision, but differed in incorporating not only celibate individuals but all Christians, both lay and ordained. His followers did not live in monasteries but they did take long retreats at isolated places in the countryside. Often the retreat leaders were laymen, including Priscillian himself.

Priscillian formed communities of people devoted to reforming the Church, not to founding intentional communities outside it. His movement first appears in the historical record in southern Spain but it soon spread north and west in the mountainous area called Galicia, named after the Celtic peoples who had settled there, and then across the Pyrenees Mountains into southern France, inhabited at the time by the same ethnic group.

The attraction of the new movement to people at the time was so great that it spread quite rapidly, in much the same way similar religious revivals would in later centuries. The Spanish bishops became alarmed by this sudden emergence of a new movement in their churches and in 380 called a council to discuss it. At the conclusion of their deliberations they issued a document condemning the Priscillian movement for these reasons:

- Women were attending Bible study groups in the houses of men they were not related to.
- Its members sometimes fasted on Sunday, and especially on Sundays in Advent and Lent
- They sometimes received the eucharistic elements at Mass without immediately consuming them.
- They withdrew into monastic cells and retreats in the mountains.
- They sometimes walked about barefooted.
- Some of their ordained members had given up their pastoral duties to become monks.
- Some young women were taking vows of virginity before reaching the age of 40, and were doing so without the approval of their bishops.
- The title of teacher was being used by laymen.

Today none of this sounds heretical, but at the time each of these actions were apparently regarded by the bishops as sufficiently dangerous that they had to be stopped to prevent grave danger to the Church and its members. We must remember that at the time most Christians were only recently emerging from traditional pagan practices and that things like going barefoot had cultural and religious meanings which they would not now have.

But even by the most generous standards the reaction of the Spanish bishops appears to have been excessive, and in any case they were not accepted by the members of the new movement. In the ensuing controversy Priscillian was forced to engage in a theological defense of his position, something he was not equipped by training or temperament to do. The result would be that once again an evangelical movement would be pushed into defending positions that were not essential to its core mission, but which its enemies would use to condemn it as heretical.

The Pricillianists responded by offering their own members for ordination, and eventually found other Spanish bishops willing to ordain them. Priscillian himself was ordained a bishop. But this only stiffened the conservative opposition, which was growing increasingly alarmed by Priscillian's popularity.

What motivated Priscillian was his belief that lay persons could experience a more vital religion than the one available to them in their ordinary church services. For some of his followers this expectation led them to return to the occult traditions that had dominated pre-Christian religion, but the coercive opposition of their bishops did little to change their minds.

In an effort to resolve this conflict Priscillian did what the Donatists had done some 60 years earlier—he appealed to the emperor. Unfortunately his appeal became entangled in the imperial politics of the late 400s and his appeal was denied. He was immediately executed on charges of sorcery.

Priscillian's followers in Spain reacted to his execution by making him a martyr. They regarded him as having been put to death by worldly bishops who were jealous of his popularity and who were threatened by his commitment to lay Christian discipleship and to the presence of the Holy Spirit in the Church: Women among his followers were especially fervent in perpetuating his memory because he had championed their equality in the Church, even ordaining women to the diaconate.

Other Church leaders of the time, including St. Ambrose in whose diocese Priscillian had been executed, condemned his execution, although they also condemned some of his particular beliefs. Martin of Tours was involved in Priscillian's trial and to the end of his life deeply regretted his participation in that entire process.

Priscillian's body and the bodies of those executed with him were brought back to Spain where they were immediately revered as the relics of holy men. He was buried in Galicia and his tomb became a pilgrimage point. His name and the names of some of his fellow martyrs were added to some official lists of the Church's martyrs.

For many years his memory would have an impact on Spanish politics and religion, and his popularity in the mountains of Galicia would help produce a separate culture there. There is even archeological evidence which would support the hypothesis that it was Priscillian's tomb that eventually evolved into the shrine at Compostela—a holy place which played a major role in medieval lay spirituality, and which remains one of the most popular Christian pilgrimage sites in the world. The origins of Compostela have never been otherwise accounted for.

The Paulicians

The most successful of the first millennium evangelical movements—measured by the time it survived, the number of persons involved, and its long-term impact—would originate in Armenia, the first nation to adopt Christianity as its national religion.

This movement would be called the Paulicians—perhaps because they patterned themselves after St. Paul and his associates, or perhaps because their opponents wanted to identify them with a previously rejected evangelical group called Paulicians who held the views of a third century bishop of Antioch whose Christological views had been declared heretical.

The founder of the Paulicians was a layman, a mule driver named Constantine, who in the year 653 had offered extended hospitality to an unnamed Assyrian Christian, a deacon who had just been released from prison. The visitor may well have been a Nestorian missionary, but that is not known. Constantine was converted through this encounter, and when his Assyrian guest left he gave Constantine a copy of the Gospels and the Pauline Letters to repay him for his hospitality.

Constantine devoured the books he had been given, and was deeply inspired by their message. As he traveled through the surrounding area as a mule driver—the equivalent of today's truck driver—he shared the New Testament story with his peers. His message took hold among the country people, and he soon devoted his life to preaching the message of the Gospel as he had learned it from reading the Gospels and St. Paul's letters to the first century churches.

Constantine eventually took the name Sylvanus, choosing it because one of St. Paul's associates had that name, and for the next 27 years he devoted his life to itinerant evangelism. Other leaders of his movement would also take the names of St. Paul's associates, and named their new communities after the ones Paul had founded.

Eventually an organized movement emerged, similar in many ways to the early Methodist evangelical movement that would emerge in England a thousand years later. The Paulicians called their buildings "houses of prayer," probably equivalent to the modern term "chapel."

When the Greek imperial authorities discovered that this new movement was threatening their political control over one of their subject territories they sent a government official named Simeon to capture and execute Constantine. Simeon did as he was ordered, but he was so impressed by Constantine's martyr death that he later joined the Paulicians—remarkably imitating the story of St. Paul himself. Simeon would become Constantine's successor as the Paulician leader, taking the name Titus. He further expanded the movement until he too met with a martyr's death six years later.

Once again we are left to gather our information about this movement from those who condemned it as heretical, and who regarded its religion and practices as utterly evil and without value. Despite this nineteenth- and twentieth-century historians have been able to arrive at a fairly detailed consensus view of the Paulicians. The most careful recent study has summarized the evidence for Paulician beliefs in this way:

- Jesus was human before his baptism, but was adopted as God's son at his baptism.

- The importance of Jesus' own baptism makes the baptism of all subsequent believers equally important. For that reason baptism should be reserved until the believer is at least 30 years old and has become a mature Christian. Children should not be baptized.

- Through baptism every believer becomes Christ-like, and has the same privileges and power as Christ, since the believer has received the Holy Spirit through baptism.

- Only believers who have received adult baptism are true heirs to the apostolic tradition, and therefore all orthodox practices, including the sacraments, veneration of images, and liturgical worship are rejected.

- The Church is created by its members' belief. This is summarized in the Paulician saying, "The church is not the one which is built by men, but we ourselves."

This early adult baptism community, despite repeated attempts to stamp it out, thrived in the rural areas of Armenia and adjacent areas. It would play a major role in that part of the world until well into the second millennium, and would eventually gain several hundred thousand members, remaining in existence in various forms into the nineteenth century.

The Paulician movement became deeply involved in the great iconoclastic controversy that convulsed the Eastern Church in the century after its founding. Paulicians in the villages tore the crosses from the Orthodox churches to show their antipathy to the way the institutional Church was developing.

This antipathy between the evangelical Paulicians and the established Church would eventually grow so great that it produced organized warfare. At first the Paulician armies were victorious, even establishing their own cities, but eventually the Paulicians were defeated and their religious movement was driven underground.

A large group of Paulicians were then deported to what is now Bulgaria where they eventually became involved in establishing a similar evangelical movement, the Bogomils. This movement would in turn aggressively evangelize in Western Europe, probably producing the important French movements called the Cathari and Albigensians. The memory of the Paulicians survived in the Christian world, and the Waldensians, an early Western European evangelical movement, would claim to be descended from the Paulicians, by way of the Cathari.

There is obviously a great deal more to be learned about this group, and it is important that we do so. It is clear that mistakes were made, but it is also clear that an exceptionally vital movement of lay evangelical intentionality once existed in Armenia. We need to know the reasons for the mistakes that were made so they can be avoided in the future, and we need to know the reasons for this movement's exceptional vitality so it can be imitated.

THE LEGACY OF FIRST MILLENNIUM EVANGELICAL INTENTIONALITY

The history of the first millennium has left us with a double legacy. On the one hand there is the permanently attractive example of the original Christian community in Jerusalem which has inspired Christians throughout the world in numerous ways in the centuries since. It draws us like a distant lamp, reminding us always of what is possible, and forcing us to compare the ways we are living to the way the first Christians were able to live in the afterglow of the Resurrection.

On the other hand the first millennium has also bequeathed to us the histories of the various lay-initiated groups which emerged after Jerusalem—groups which set out with great confidence and commitment, convinced it was possible to realize in their own time and place the kind of Christian communities they had learned about from reading the New Testament accounts of the early Church.

But what began in Jerusalem with such great hope and love would over the next centuries become a tragic story of constant conflict between the newly emerging evangelical communities and their fellow Christians in the institutional churches, especially their bishops.

The lay evangelical communities formed around charismatic leaders who realized that the Christian faith provided a potential for the laity that was not being realized by the institutional structures then in existence. These leaders were motivated—and strongly motivated—by their belief that new opportunities to live fully intentional Christian lives existed, and they were frustrated because they believed those opportunities were not being acted on by the existing Churches

The already established communities, led by the bishops, saw things rather differently. When they looked at the new evangelical movements they frequently saw people who were undisciplined and impetuous, and who were led by persons, often recent converts, whose intemperate behavior and frequently heretical doctrines endangered everything that had been built up over the centuries through the careful and patient efforts of less passionate Christians.

A clash was inevitable, but the legacy this clash has left behind is less in the clash itself than in the way it was resolved. By resorting to violence, both verbal and physical, both sides would give their support to the belief that this disagreement could only be resolved by one party defeating the other. The result would be a tradition in the institutional Churches which came to view doctrinal conformity as primary and lay discipleship as secondary, and a tradition in the evangelical community which came to regard the institutional Churches as permanent adversaries.

St. Augustine's involvement in this clash, more as a bishop than a theologian, would play a major role in forming the institutional Church's tradition. His fateful decision to use military coercion to resolve the conflict with the Donatists would establish the principle that maintaining civil order takes priority over all other ethical considerations, and the corollary principle that maintaining civil order requires the use of governmental coercion to enforce religious uniformity.

On these two principles both the Crusades and the Inquisition of the next millennium would be based.

Bishop Augustine surely had the right and the responsibility to safeguard his members and their churches from the often ferocious Donatist guerilla attacks which were then taking place. But equally as surely the Donatist leaders, who represented the indigenous population, had the right and the responsibility to insist that the systemic injustice which their members had long endured at the hands of the colonial establishment—to which Augustine and his members belonged—had to be addressed.

It is now clear that the Donatists were mistaken in teaching that Christians create the Church by their will-based ethical actions. But the Roman Christians were no less mistaken in using governmental authority to enforce religious orthodoxy. When the Roman Catholic bishops at the Second Vatican Council adopted *The Declaration on Religious Liberty* in 1965 they in effect convicted St. Augustine of a grave error for calling on state power to resolve a dispute which involved religious belief.

The first millennium disputes between the evangelical movements and the institutional Church would also leave an important doctrinal legacy, involving our understanding of both orthodoxy and heresy.

All the first millennium evangelical movements were rejected by the institutional Churches because of their deviations from the consensus theological position that slowly emerged in the Church's early centuries—what would come to be called orthodoxy. All those who rejected some part of this consensus tradition would henceforth be excluded from the institutional Churches as 'heretics'—a label that was as politically and socially significant as it was religiously.

There is now little doubt that all the early evangelical communities were indeed heretical, at least as they eventually developed. But it is also evident after 20 centuries of dealing with doctrinal deviation that the doctrinal deviations which have emerged in the evangelical movements over the centuries have often been the result of exclusion from the institutional Churches as much as the cause of that exclusion.

This exclusion of the evangelical communities from the institutional Church's structures would also play a role in the development of clericalism. The evident success of the monastic movement in the first millennium occurred at the same time as the exclusion of the lay evangelical movements, and the result was that Christian intentionality gradually came to be equated with celibacy. This development was greatly reinforced by the fact that many of the Church's leaders in the late first millennium and early second millennium came from the monastic movement, and were deeply committed to the discipline of celibacy.

As we have seen in the first part of this book, monasticism was on the whole able to avoid heresy and to develop strong accountability to the Church's other institutions. These results were of great benefit to both groups, and to the emerging new civilization, but there was a price to pay. That price was the belief that Christianity consists of inter-locking hierarchies of professional religious persons whose leadership and actions constitute the Church.

This belief inevitably produces a two-tier institution, populated by two sharply distinguished classes of members—one lay and sexual, the other religious and celibate. But this pattern so obviously contradicts the New Testament accounts of first century Christianity that it can never hope to be accepted by the laity, especially those most deeply committed to Christian belief. Had the evangelicals been kept within the Church's institutional confines it appears unlikely that this exclusive emphasis on doctrine and celibacy would have developed.

The long term result has been a deeply entrenched divide between belief and discipleship. Those who have emphasized the importance of orthodox doctrine have tended to place a lesser value on Christian discipleship—what has been called *orthopraxis*. Those who emphasize the importance of individual belief and action have tended to place a lesser value on the Church's doctrinal tradition. But in fact the orthodox tradition has always held that Christian faith requires appropriate action, and the evangelical tradition has always insisted that correct belief is essential, even when it has not been able to agree on what constitutes correct belief.

As we will see as we move to the pre-Reformation period of Church history in the next chapter, this division between doctrine and action will increasingly lead to an increasingly divided Christian community. The final result will be a Church so deeply in conflict with itself that a massive series of schisms will occur, causing severe damage to all parts of the Christian community—and eventually to the entire world.

SIX

From the Peace of God to the Reformation

The 500 years between the year 1000 and the Reformation were a decisive era for the lay evangelical movements. In these five centuries the institutional Church and the evangelical movements would engage in a deeply antagonistic struggle which has had a major impact on both the Christian Church and on the development of western civilization.

This division could have been avoided, but it was not and the result has been a Christian community increasingly divided against itself throughout the second millennium.

THE MEDIEVAL RELIGIOUS REVIVAL

Between the years 1050 and 1250 Europe was transformed from a pre-literate rural society still based on the traditional cultures which its peoples had inherited from the distant past, becoming in only a few centuries an essentially urban society based on the new values that now characterize western civilization:

- Rational as opposed to magical thinking;
- Political and religious institutions based on law and justice rather than military power;
- The belief that each individual possesses a God-given dignity and value independent of birth, age or social status, a status which cannot be taken from that person by any other human;
- The belief that truth exists independently of human opinion, and that truth should govern all human actions and social structures;

- The religious belief that Christ is the model for all human behavior, and that everyone is ultimately to be judged by Jesus' life as described in the Gospels—good if that person's actions in ordinary life conform to Jesus' actions in his ordinary life, and evil if they do not.

How these values emerged in western civilization is still a matter of dispute among historians, but the fact that a major religious movement took place throughout Europe in the centuries when this civilizational change was taking place can hardly have been coincidental.

We have already met with this movement in the first part of this book, especially in the sections devoted to Bernard of Clairvaux and Francis of Assisi. But the great popularity of these two religious leaders is only a portion of the evidence that a massive religious revival occurred throughout Western Europe in the first 300 years of the second Christian millennium.

There is equally significant evidence in three events which primarily involved the laity:

- The first is the unprecedented Peace of God movement which suddenly appeared in Europe in the opening years of the millennium without any apparent single cause.
- The second is the construction of dozens of enormous Gothic cathedrals throughout Europe in the 1100s, again an event without precedent.
- The third is the willingness of thousands of lay Christians to voluntarily leave their homes to fight in the Crusades, also an event without any prior precedent.

Regardless of whether we regard these events as progress in the Christianization of Europe, or as regrettable incidents in what earlier historians called the 'Dark Ages', there is no question that they took place and little reason to doubt their impact on people living at the time. We have now largely lost memory of this period in our history, but people who lived at the time could not have forgotten what they and their immediate ancestors had experienced.

The persons who heard Bernard of Clairvaux preach—the overwhelming majority of them lay persons—would never forget what they had heard, or the enthusiastic reception which the great evangelist's words had produced in the enormous crowds which gathered to hear him whenever he preached. Nor would they ever forget what this great saint had told them—that Christ desires an intimate relationship with every living person.

This revolutionary doctrine meant that Christianity was more than a religion—at least as that word was commonly understood—referring to a combination of defined cult and doctrine. Christ wants to kiss his followers "on the lips" Bernard had told them, and people drew the obvious conclusion—that Christianity was something that touched ordinary people at their deepest emotional and practical levels, as the old religions had not.

Nor would the lay people who had contributed vast sums of money and millions of hours of labor building great Gothic cathedrals in the 1100s ever forget that experience. It would remain engraved in their collective memory, a constant reminder of the vast human potential that is unleashed when people who are motivated by common beliefs devote themselves to a common goal.

Nor would their descendents ever forget this experience. How could they when these great buildings, which still inspire wonder 800 years later, towered over their towns and cities? They were a constant reminder that something extraordinary had happened, something which involved everyone from the lowliest to the highest. These buildings existed because everyone had played a part, and it was obvious to anyone that only lay Christians could construct such buildings.

The soldiers who returned from serving in the Crusades had also experienced the immense power which lay Christians have when bonded in a single purpose by common beliefs. As Crusade followed Crusade in subsequent centuries the vast majority of European Christians retained their commitments to the crusaders' mission, even when their military expeditions had failed. They had come to believe so deeply in Christianity that they were willing to make any sacrifice necessary for their faith to prevail throughout the world.

The Crusades have now been pushed to the edges of western historical memory, but they remain a major event in the formation of western civilization, whether remembered or not. They had involved the entire population of the Christian world for over 300 years, and their impact is still with us. What is important about them for our purposes is that they were essentially a lay movement. The decision "to take the cross" was a religious one, but it was a decision only open to lay Christians.

The thousands of men who volunteered for these great military campaigns returned to Europe utterly changed—much in the same way that American soldiers who returned from World Wars I and II were changed in some fundamental ways. Their experience in a foreign culture had severely challenged things they had previously taken for granted, and their experience in combat in a distant place had raised disturbing questions about established power relationships, especially between Church leaders and the laity.

Furthermore the Crusade armies had put people from all parts of Europe into extended contact for the first time, and their efforts had given European leaders a sense of their combined power—and the potential of the new civilization they were creating.

At a religious level the Crusades put the members of the new civilization in direct touch with their spiritual roots, an event that took the form of the numerous relics, most of them spurious, which they brought with them when they returned from the Holy Land. In addition their contacts with both the Islamic and Byzantine civilizations introduced Europeans to new intellectual currents which would have a profound impact in subsequent centuries.

Politically the Crusades created a large organization based on a common cause, rather than on the power of a single king, or allegiance to a single nation. They had also rewarded ability over birth, giving many non-aristocrats a new sense of their worth and talent. Once Europeans had experienced these new forms of power they would never forget them, and they would become major features of western civilization.

In addition to these three major events lay people in Europe increasingly began moving from magical thinking toward rational, fact-based thinking and when they did they inevitably began to think about their religion, and to question its traditions and practices. And when they did they came to see what is apparent to nearly everyone today, that many of these traditions and practices included significant amounts of the magical outlook which had characterized their pre-Christian traditional religions.

When increasing numbers of lay Christians combined all these experiences with the new spirituality which they had been taught by St. Bernard it was inevitable that at least some of them would conclude that the way to be truly Christian was to follow Christ in daily life, just as the people who had encountered Christ in his own time had done—those earlier laypersons whose stories from the Gospels were read in their churches each Sunday.

Exactly that did happen, beginning in the 1000s and 1100s and continuing to the present.

THE PEACE OF GOD AND THE PATARINES

The earliest lay movements in the second millennium were unique in successfully uniting the Church's laity and its clerical leadership around a common political purpose, successfully combining the spirituality which medieval Christians had inherited from the first millennium monastic movement with political action of an entirely new kind.

The Peace of God

Around the year 1000, an amazing and utterly new event took place in France. A mass movement, one that was both political and religious, suddenly emerged which swept up the entire population and left society fundamentally changed. This movement, called the Peace of God, had no known precedents in human history and would remain largely unique.

What happened was this: people by the thousands marched together from their homes to meeting places in the open countryside—the only spaces large enough to contain the immense crowds that assembled—and there inaugurated a new social order based on what we would today call the rule of law.

Throughout Europe central authority had broken down after the collapse of the Roman Empire, and the new empire established by Charlemagne had also lost its power to govern. The result was that local militias had constructed castles everywhere, using them as bases from which to plunder the surrounding territory and extort property and services from its residents. There was no superior power to call on for protection when the castles' soldiers stole your livestock or raped your daughter.

Charlemagne's great vision was still very much alive, but 200 years after he had been crowned Christian emperor in the West his vision hung by a thread. The institutions he had established throughout France—the diocesan bishops and the Benedictine monasteries—were both seriously endangered.

No one yet knows who initiated the great Peace of God movement which emerged to resolve this crisis. It may have been the Benedictine monks at the monastery where the first gathering was held, but whatever its origins what made it a success were the thousands of lay people who voluntarily participated.

Throughout the Peace of God's history there would never be a single individual who could claim to be its leader. From the beginning this movement appears to have had a life of its own—something that so clearly answered a profound need sensed by people at the time that it needed no leadership.

The first of the great Peace of God marches took place in the year 989 near a monastery in western France. The local bishop presided at the gathering, and the monks from the nearby monastery came in procession, bringing with them the relics of their founder, a Benedictine abbot from the 500s who was revered as a holy man throughout the area. Lay people by the hundreds, and probably the thousands, came from the surrounding area, often traveling long distances on foot.

This unprecedented gathering adopted a proclamation that prohibited armed men from breaking into churches and plundering them. It prohibited stealing a sheep, an ox, a donkey, a cow, a goat or a pig from any peasant or from any other vulnerable person. And it prohibited attacks on unarmed priests or deacons. (Clergy who were armed were not included in the prohibition.)

These prohibitions were enforced by the bishop's power to excommunicate, and that would be its major source of juridical power. But what was equally as important, if not more so, was the virtually unanimous popular support the movement had among the laity.

A contemporary historian reports that the religious leadership of the time would summon "great councils of the whole people" and that the priests and monks brought to these great gatherings "the bodies of many saints and innumerable caskets of holy relics." The goal of the gatherings was always to "reestablish peace and consolidate the holy faith." An observer of one of them reported that the local people, both the middle class and the poor, "came rejoicing and ready, one and all" as though they had been commanded "by a voice from heaven speaking to men on earth."

This observer also reports jubilant throngs gathering in 1033 to celebrate the one-thousandth anniversary of Christ's crucifixion and resurrection, raising their palms toward the sky and shouting in unison, "Peace! Peace! Peace!"

What was politically revolutionary about the Peace of God movement was the partnership between the common people and the monks—particularly the Benedictines in the new Cluny federation. In this great movement, which continued across France for more than 40 years, both the people and the monks participated as equals and the result was a profound transformation of European society.

This movement was also revolutionary in being completely non-violent. The entire movement depended solely on moral authority and the power of excommunication to achieve its ends, and it now appears that was a major reason for its long-term success. In refusing to use military coercion to counter military coercion the movement practiced what it sought to establish.

After about 1040, when the movement was some 50 years old, it gradually evolved into a similar but actually rather different movement called the Truce of God. In the new movement citizen militias were formed to enforce the rules adopted by the Peace of God councils, and the governing elites began to find ways to incorporate the movement's principles into the established structures.

A rule was adopted which held that to shed the blood of another Christian was to shed Christ's own blood, since every Christian is part of the Body of Christ, but at the same time the killing of non-Christians was legitimated, opening the way for the Crusades, the Inquisition, and the execution of Jews.

It has been customary among historians in the twentieth century to regard this movement as a failure, since its great goals were not immediately achieved. But fundamental social and political change is always the work of centuries, and often of millennia, and establishing the rule of law is a prime example. The important fact is not that the Peace of God movement failed to achieve its goals in its own time. The truly significant fact is that a thousand years ago our predecessors in the Christian faith had the ability and the motivation to initiate a centuries-long process that would eventually create a rule of law in western civilization, and increasingly throughout the world.

Like all the medieval lay movements the Peace of God has not received the attention it deserves. One notable exception is Prof. Richard Landes of Boston University, and we conclude with his summary of this event:

> In fact, the lack of coercive power, so often cited as the cause of the movement's failure, may have been precisely what made the Peace of God so influential. For without recourse to force, it had to depend on more fundamental cultural activity: building a wide and powerful social consensus, developing courts of mediation, educating a lay populace, high and low, to internalize peaceful values. In this sense, the Peace movement laid the groundwork for later developments:
>
> - It awakened the populace, both rural and urban, to the possibilities of self-organization . . .
> - It helped to "Christianize" the nobility, encouraging the development of chivalry
> - It gave enormous authority to the Church, which, having mediated the Peace, became a major player in the political and social organization of lay society
> - It opened up an often fervent, if occasionally tragic, dialogue between cleric and layman on the true meaning of Christianity.

Landes says, "The Peace of God changed the history of Europe," and he believes it did so by introducing into the newly forming civilization a new "moral vision" based on a "sense of nonviolent community." Above all, he concludes, "it introduced the populace as an autonomous actor on the stage of European history."

The Patarines

The Christian laity in northern Italy would also become deeply involved in the religious and political affairs of their societies in this same period. Although the situation was different than in France, the issues that produced this movement of lay activity were similar.

In the city of Milan an entrenched group of land-owning families had gained control over the institutional Church and were using the Church's resources to enrich themselves. A recent historian describes the situation thus: "The Archbishop bestowed the lands of his cathedral on the greatest families of the region, from whose sons were drawn the upper clergy of the diocese, including the canons of the cathedral, who in turn elected the archbishop himself—usually of course from their own number."

But what seemed to the ruling classes to be "a perfectly ordinary and elegantly self-sustaining system of elite support," came to be viewed by the increasing numbers of evangelical Christians being created by the great religious revival of the 1000s as a scandalous abuse of the Church.

The Roman popes at the time were also a product of the revival, and had set out to restore the independence of the Church. They had allied themselves with the emperor, who was a German, and he in turn had supported the election of several German popes.

This reform movement culminated in the career of Cardinal Hildebrand, who eventually became Pope Gregory VII and who gave his name to this great institutional reform. He and his fellow reformers would eventually take the radical step of commanding the laity to ignore those bishops and priests who had purchased their offices or who were married—and even more significantly to refuse to take communion and the other sacraments from them.

The resulting conflict involved all Europe. "Nothing else is talked about, even in the women's spinning-rooms and the artisans' workshops" said a contemporary. It had produced a "confusion of all human laws" he said, and the result was a "sudden unrest among the populace" which affected everyone. There were "treacheries of servants against their masters" which in turn produced the "masters' mistrust of their servants"—and it was all supported "by those who are called the leaders of Christendom."

It was in this situation that a hermit named Ariald began supporting the reform movement in the countryside near Milan—one of most important European cities at the time. Ariald soon moved into the city and in about 1057 began preaching in public places, attacking his fellow clergy with great verbal violence. He described them as "the blind leading the blind" and said their richly ornamented churches were really no better than stables, and the sacraments they offered were as worthless as a dog's dung.

People who heard Ariald's sermons responded by setting themselves up as a de facto church police force. They went so far as to forcibly remove priests from the altar, and even to prevent other lay persons from taking communion in Masses being celebrated by priests who had purchased their ordinations. Mobs entered the homes of some married priests, demanding that they dismiss their wives (and presumably their children) and sign pledges of celibacy. It was by all indications a reign of terror.

But many of the married priests were not evil men. They were simply following a tradition that had been established in Milan for centuries, dating back the time of St. Ambrose some 700 years earlier. This tradition gave the Church in Milan considerable autonomy and had long permitted its clergy to marry. The conflicts were thus not simply a struggle between the old aristocracy and the new religious reformers, but a battle between Milan and Rome as well. A contemporary historian reports that it divided the people of Milan across all classes, and even within families, for nearly 20 years.

The battle in Milan immediately produced an appeal to Rome. The response was to appoint an investigative commission in 1057. The commissioners ruled against the archbishop and many of the clergy, but allowed them to remain in office if they would agree to reform. But this did not settle the matter and the conflict continued for another nine years.

Finally the pope gave the Patarines formal authorization to serve as the Church's police force, and simultaneously excommunicated the archbishop of Milan. This radical act produced a severe reaction against the Patarines—and within a few months their leader, the former hermit Ariald, was murdered.

After Ariald's assassination a layman named Erlembald took his place and formed a military band which successfully controlled the city for eight years. This new lay leader would also be killed when he set off a brawl by deliberately trampling on some chrism oil that had been consecrated by a corrupt bishop. With this death the Patarine movement came to an end, after some 18 years of struggle. Erlembald came to be regarded as a martyr and was declared a saint some 20 years later by Pope Urban II.

The name Patarine would spread throughout northern Italy. There is a tradition that the name came from the word for rag pickers, but that is not certain. What is known is that the movement's opponents in the upper classes were unanimous in declaring that its members came from the lower classes. However evidence now indicates that the movement's leaders often themselves came from the upper classes, and that its core strength came from the new middle class—the merchants, lawyers, judges and other urban leaders who would increasingly dominate European life.

THE EASTERN DUALIST MOVEMENTS

At the same time the Peace of God movement was thriving in France, and the Patarines were supporting the reform of the Church in Milan, a third independent lay-led movement was emerging in Western Europe. This movement had its origins in the Greek-speaking East, where Christians had formed a tradition significantly different than the one being formed in the Latin-speaking West.

The Paulician movement, described in the previous chapter, had been forced from its homeland in Armenia in the 900s and had taken root in Bulgaria. There a preacher named Bogomil had reformed this older evangelical movement, now more than 200 years old, creating a vibrant set of new local communities.

The Bogomil communities began sending missionaries to Western Europe, where they first appear in the historical record shortly after the year 1000. These missionaries formed small communities throughout France and northern Italy, and over the next 250 years their efforts would produce a substantial movement which would leave a permanent mark on European Christianity.

In the historical record, both medieval and modern, this movement is referred to by a wide variety of names—Cathari, Manicheans, and Albigensians being the most common. The movement appears not to have been centrally organized, although there is evidence of ongoing ties to the mother churches in Bulgaria.

Over the centuries considerable diversity emerged within this movement, but despite this the vast majority of the communities that resulted appear to have adopted some variety of ontological dualism. Its severity ranged from a moderate spirit-matter dualism to a more radical dualism that proclaimed two equally powerful gods, one evil and one good.

These beliefs now seem rather bizarre to most Christians, but at the time they appear to have offered an attractive alternative for those Christians who were dissatisfied with the increasingly formal and clericalist church order evolving throughout Europe. People by the thousands eventually joined these new independent communities—mostly peasants and other ordinary persons, but also including a few priests and members of the nobility.

Once again our information about these groups comes from their enemies, but in this case that information is so voluminous, and extends over such a wide geographic area and such a long period of time, and comes from so many independent sources that some conclusions can be drawn with a strong degree of probability.

The following core beliefs and practices appear to have been shared by the movement as a whole. All are secondary to the radical spirit-matter distinction on which the movement was based.

- The concept of a visible Church was rejected, even to the point of believing in some instances that to construct a church building is sinful. The dominant belief was that the Church is an entirely spiritual thing which has no connection to the physical world or to human society.

- For the same reason the movement rejected the idea that Jesus was fully human, and that Mary had been his mother. The movement's Christology was thoroughly docetic.

- The movement also rejected the idea of sacraments, believing that only the interior spiritual disposition of the individual believer mattered, and that the material can never convey grace.

- Infant baptism was categorically rejected. There are reports that members of the movement would turn aside and spit on the ground when they saw a child who had been baptized, since the child could have played no intentional part in his or her baptism.

- Baptism in this movement was an adult ceremony involving the laying on of hands and the reception of the Holy Spirit. It was through this ceremony that the believer became a full member of the movement.

- The movement tended to be strongly anti-sexual, with many members attempting to live celibate lives even when they were married. They did not eat meat because all biological life is the product of sexual mating.

- They prohibited the swearing of oaths.

- They were non-violent. There is no known instance of their resisting their suppression by violence, or of their being accused of violence. Some of them appear to have welcomed martyrdom.

- They held to a perfectionistic moral code, which some later observers have called puritan. One man who was being led through the streets of Toulouse to be burnt at the stake because he had been accused of being a member of the movement successfully proved that he was not by shouting to his neighbors, "I have a wife and I sleep with her. I have sons; I eat meat; I lie and swear and I am a faithful Christian."

Theologians and bishops at the time immediately saw this new movement as a return to the third-century religion of Mani the Persian, which the young Augustine had adopted then later denounced. They regarded the movement's teachings as a grave danger to their newly converted flocks and they believed it was their responsibility to prevent its spread by any means necessary. To them it was the exact equivalent to an infectious epidemic that could destroy the entire community if its infected members were not isolated and banned.

Political leaders at the time shared this view and frequently took matters into their own hands, burning these unorthodox believers alive, often over the protests of the bishops. To have allowed dissidents the right to act independently of existing authority structures would have been a revolutionary political event. No one then had that right, and it was widely assumed that granting it would produce social chaos on a catastrophic scale.

But despite widespread and determined opposition the dualist movements continued to spread throughout Western Europe for some 300 years. Of all the pre-Reformation evangelical movements the dualist movements would gain the most adherents, they would last the longest, and they would have the greatest impact on events in their time. The numerous mentions of this movement in contemporary records and the repeated efforts to repress it all indicate rather clearly that its appearance was a major event in Europe in the 1100s and 1200s.

The dualist movement would especially flourish in southern France, where by the 1200s it had established its own hierarchy, and where for a time it became the dominant religion in certain areas. This French community was called the Albigensians, and it would be ruthlessly destroyed by a French king in a series of military actions that are still remembered for their violence and treachery.

This violent suppression, combined with its own internal dissensions, brought the dualist movement to an effective end by the year 1300, but it survived as an underground force, leaving a permanent and substantial impact on the subsequent independent evangelical movements which emerged in Europe in later centuries.

The Legacy of the Dualists

Probably the dualist movement's most important legacy has been to equate lay evangelical Christianity with heresy in the minds of most other Christians. The fact that this movement was in fact heretical, even by the most generous standards, meant that for most people living at the time all evangelical Christianity would come to be almost automatically viewed as heretical. The final result was a situation in which evangelicals were regarded as guilty of heresy until proven innocent.

Beginning from this basic assumption most Church leaders drew the conclusion that the best way to protect their people from doctrinal heresy was to prevent evangelical movements from forming—or if they did form, to supervise them very closely. The result was that avoiding heresy would virtually always take precedence over providing a place in the Church's structures for its lay members, evangelical or otherwise.

This in turn would push the evangelicals to the Church's periphery—and very often beyond it into schism, where their isolation would produce even greater doctrinal deviation. In this situation it was almost inevitable that these disrespected and persecuted evangelical Christians would come to believe that their treatment proved that the institutional Church had departed so far from the apostolic tradition that it could no longer be considered the Church. From this base they drew the conclusion that the Church's traditional doctrines and theology were to be rejected precisely because they were being taught by a corrupt institution.

This poisonous atmosphere, with equally committed Christians accusing each other of the most terrible crimes in the vilest possible terms, made it virtually impossible for even the most orthodox lay evangelical movement to succeed.

Most tragic of all, the dualist movement's violent suppression would establish the principles on which the Inquisition would be based, and would set the precedent for the shameful crimes that would be committed by that institution in the name of Christian orthodoxy over the next few centuries—crimes which have so blackened the Church's reputation that Pope John Paul II at the end of the second millennium felt it necessary to publicly ask forgiveness for them.

Furthermore the Church's decision to deal with the dualist movement by force rather than reason and dialogue left the movement's central challenge to orthodox Christian belief largely unanswered. The result was that dualistic belief was merely pushed underground, where it has remained to the present, emerging from time to time in movements based on an exaggerated spirit-body distinction, and adopting the impossibly perfectionistic moral codes which always accompany this belief.

The dualist movement of the medieval centuries is today an embarrassment to nearly everyone. To Roman Catholics its violent repression, especially the massacre of the Albigensians, is a major blot on the Roman Church's reputation. It is a part of our history that virtually all Roman Catholics would now prefer not to remember.

For their part current evangelicals find the movement's dualistic beliefs repugnant, in effect agreeing they were heretical. Although the medieval dualists obviously shared some beliefs and practices with twentieth-century evangelicals—and some Baptist historians have claimed them as precursors to the modern Baptist movement—no evangelical group today would be prepared to defend their beliefs as a whole.

Secular historians for their part tend to admire the dualists for having been the first dissidents to oppose the medieval authority structure, but find their religious enthusiasm deeply embarrassing. Like modern intellectuals the medieval dualists insisted on the right to think and act as they wished, but unlike modern intellectuals they regarded the spiritual as primary, not the material.

It is tempting to pass over this difficult chapter in western civilization's history in silence, but doing so leaves many subsequent events difficult if not impossible to explain. Furthermore to ignore this movement is to deprive ourselves of a valuable experience, one that is of permanent importance to the Christian community.

Dualism is permanently attractive to humans, especially at an early stage in their spiritual development, and has remained so to the present. There are Christians today who would recoil in horror at the thought of two gods, but who have made the devil so powerful in their thinking that this evil force in effect functions as an equal to God. Dualism is a simple solution to the great unsolved problem of reconciling a good God with the existence of evil in a world which this good God created. It also excuses a good deal of personal evil by allowing us to say, "The devil made me do it," or an equivalent.

If St. Augustine in his younger years was taken by dualism's attractions why should we find it surprising that others, lacking his great intellect and without anyone to teach them an alternative, have found it attractive in later centuries? But taking this theological shortcut, as Augustine came to understand, in the end only adds to the evil in the world. By raising the power of evil to such heights the people and communities involved are plunged into despair, living in constant fear that they too will be overtaken by the forces of evil. It results in lives dedicated to spiritual warfare, a warfare that will always eventually result in physical warfare of some kind.

Above all the medieval dualist movements are perhaps the clearest evidence of the high price the Church pays when it allows itself to be divided between a clerical leadership and a powerless laity. In the end the greatest heresy of all is the belief that the evangelical and the institutional can be separated, and when this belief is adopted it causes great damage to all Christians.

The institutional Churches' leaders come to believe the Church can be healthy without nurturing its lay members, and without learning from them. On their part the laity, especially its evangelical members, come to believe they can be healthy Christians without holding themselves accountable to the institutional Church and to the traditions it preserves.

Neither is true.

THE WALDENSIANS AND OTHER LAY MOVEMENTS

There is no more tragic story in the history of the pre-Reformation evangelical movements than the Waldensians. Here we find a lay movement of unquestioned doctrinal orthodoxy, founded in large part to counter the dualistic doctrines of the Cathari, a virtual model of what we can now see the religious revival of the 1100s required. But it too would be rejected by the institutional Church, and eventually violently suppressed by the Inquisition.

What makes this tragic story even more tragic are the dozens of other smaller evangelical movements which emerged in the 1100s and 1200s, many of which would also be condemned as heretical by the Church's hierarchy, and thus ignored and finally destroyed by the Inquisition. Both the Catholic Church and the civilization that was forming around its beliefs and structures would pay a very high price for this mistake.

The Waldensians

In the city of Lyons, the old Roman city in southeastern France, a wealthy merchant named Valdesius experienced a profound religious conversion in the year 1173, an event typical of the religious revival taking place everywhere in the western Christian world at the time.

Valdesius had experienced deep guilt for the way his wealth had been acquired and he finally went to a priest, asking how he could henceforth live a fully Christian life. The priest answered him with the story from the Gospels recounting how a wealthy man had come to Jesus in the first century with this same question. "Go and sell what you have and give it to the poor, then come follow me," Jesus had told that man.

The man in the Gospels had refused Jesus' advice because he did not want to give up his privileged position in society, but Valdesius made the opposite choice. Exactly as the young Anthony had done a thousand years earlier, this successful merchant from Lyons took Jesus' words literally, but his life thereafter would be very different that Anthony's.

Valdesius divided his property with his wife, then proceeded to give everything remaining to the poor, at one point literally throwing his money on the street. As St. Francis would do some 50 years later Valdesius began living as the poor did, begging his food from people who had been his associates. His wife, seeing him living in this way, went to their bishop and begged him to order her husband to rely on her for his food, which the bishop did.

But before distributing his money to the poor, Valdesius had used some of it to pay two priests to translate the Scriptures from St. Jerome's Latin into the language which was spoken in southern France at the time. This would result in the first known translation of the Scriptures into a European language and would initiate the efforts by evangelical Christians to produce vernacular translations of the Scriptures, an effort which has continued to the present, eventually producing thousands of translations.

Valdesius then began preaching from Scripture, much of which he had memorized. He emphasized personal conversion and solidarity with the poor. There was nothing new in any of this—except for the translation of the Scriptures, and that was not controversial at the time. What Valdesius preached was much the same as Bernard of Clairvaux had preached throughout France earlier in the 1100s, and Valdasius' rejection of the opulence of the institutional churches and the corruption of the hierarchy was shared throughout European Christianity, including several popes.

Furthermore Valdesius and his followers supported one of the institutional Church's major goals—combating the dualist doctrines of the Cathari which had taken root in southern France. The members of this new movement were not rebels against the Church but members of the Church who wished to strengthen it and make it more authentically Christian.

Within three or four years after Valdesius' conversion a small community of like-minded believers had formed, joining him by living in poverty and preaching to their peers—not in the Churches but in the places where the public lived and naturally gathered, and preaching to them in their own language rather than the Latin of the churches, which they did not understand.

Their preaching proved to be popular, and as a result began raising concern among the institutional Church's ordained leaders who had come to equate lay preaching with the dualist movements. As a result Valdesius and his followers traveled to Rome where an ecumenical council was taking place, asking for papal approval of their efforts. They presented a copy of their Biblical translation to the pope and requested papal authority to preach from it. They received a limited oral approval from the pope, but it was subject to approval by local authorities.

While they were in Rome the Poor of Lyons—as they were called at the time—were subjected to a theological examination by an English theologian named Walter Map. This unfortunate man, whose autobiography depicts a cynical participant in the political and religious events of his time, and a person whose lack of charity is matched only by an arrogant sense of superiority to everyone whose intellectual abilities and education were less than his own, asked his visitors a trick question which would have been understood only by a few members of the theological elite at the time—and which is understood only by a few historical specialists today.

When the evangelicals from Lyon answered the question as any ordinary Christian would have they were openly ridiculed by Map and his colleagues and branded as heretics. This small but telling incident is sadly typical of what would happen frequently in subsequent decades, when religious professionals would treat the lay evangelicals as a threat to their privileged positions and use every means at their disposal to discredit them as heretics.

In an effort to establish their orthodoxy the Poor of Lyons produced a profession of faith that clearly established their doctrinal orthodoxy and their rejection of all the Cathari deviations. But even that would not be enough. The local leadership in Lyon asked Valdesius' followers to demonstrate their orthodoxy by not preaching, and when the new movement responded by quoting the apostles, "We must obey God rather than man," a split was unavoidable.

Eleven years after Valdesius' conversion he and his movement were declared heretical by a papal council, along with a similar Italian lay evangelical movement, the Humiliati.

Being branded heretics did not of course end the new movement, only forcing it underground. It would continue to be propagated throughout Europe by itinerant missionaries who established communities as far away as Austria and Eastern Europe. Cast out of the Church's protective embrace, this growing and tenacious movement would in many instances deviate from its Catholic roots, some of its members going so far as associating with the also persecuted Cathari, who their movement had originally been founded to oppose.

The remnants of this movement, which is now known as the Waldensians, was persecuted with increasing violence by the Inquisition in the 1300s and 1400s but would survive underground until it finally achieved the right to exist after the Reformation. It exists in the present as a small Protestant denomination in Italy.

At this point in time we cannot avoid asking what might have happened if the institutional Church's leadership had chosen to nurture and guide this new evangelical movement rather than viewing it as a threat. Given the information we now have, and the 800 years of Christian experience we now have to guide us, the failure of the institutional Church's leaders to make a place in the Church's institutional structures for this evangelical movement at this crucial period in the Church's history appears to be a lost opportunity of immense consequence.

Other Early Lay Movements

The historical record also reveals a sizable number of other evangelical communities emerging in the 1100s and 1200s alongside the Waldensians, revealing how powerful the lay evangelical impulse was at this period in Christian development. Furthermore it is virtually certain that the evangelical movements known to us from this period are only a portion of those which existed. Many are unknown because no historian has researched their story, and many more can never be known because no evidence of their existence has survived.

But even a brief overview of the movements known to us at this point in time indicates how significant the evangelical impulse was in pre-Reformation Christianity:

The Humiliati emerged in northern Italy in the late 1100s, at about the same time as the Waldensians. This lay movement had a great deal in common with the French movement, and was condemned along with it in the late 1100s.

The Humiliati were lay Christians, both married and single, primarily from the middle and upper classes, who lived in communal voluntary poverty and wore a unique costume of undyed wool. They were known for their penitential practices, and for their rejection of military service. They supported themselves by laboring as cloth weavers. The women cared for the sick, especially lepers, and the men devoted themselves to promoting social justice—providing work for those who had none, helping workers form trade unions, and otherwise assisting the working class and the poor.

Pope Innocent III, who had also approved the new Franciscan movement in the early 1200s, would rescue this movement from the condemnation of heresy by forming it into a quasi-religious order at about the same time. He gave it an organizational form similar to the Franciscans, and in that form it would survive for several decades, until its lay members withdrew in 1272. The clerical branches of the new order survived until the late 1500s, but had long since abandoned their original ideals.

Lay Confraternities emerged throughout northern Italy in the 1200s. These were lay-initiated and lay-led groups which may have been inspired by the Humiliati, but were not part of its organization. Several of these communities formed a federation in 1221, drawing up an agreement to dress plainly, to observe set periods of fasting, especially from meat, and to either recite the monastic office each day, or if they were illiterate to pray the Our Father. The members met monthly for a Mass, at which each member contributed a set amount which was given to the poor.

What is perhaps most striking about this community was its non-violence. Like the Humiliati its members were prohibited from serving in the military. This had important political ramifications in the chaotic situation of the time, and may have been responsible for attracting numerous government leaders and professional men to the movement. On one occasion a local community appealed to the pope for his support because the city authorities were demanding that their members serve in the local militia.

The Caputiati were a group of laymen formed by a French carpenter at the same time the Waldensian movement formed. Its purpose was the same as the Peace of God—to bring civil order to a community being terrorized by roving bands of soldiers protected by the local castle owners. The movement's name came from the white hoods the members wore, on which they placed a medal of the Virgin and child and a phrase from the Mass, "Lamb of God who takes away the sins of the world, grant us peace." The members prohibited themselves from cursing and swearing, from gambling and drunkenness, and from dressing ostentatiously.

With the support of both the local clergy and the French king the movement spread quickly and succeeded in ending extortion by the local castle owners. The Caputiati exercised their newly gained political power by massacring a large number of the soldiers who had been terrorizing their area, and in retaliation the local castle owners brutally repressed them soon after.

The Order of the Holy Spirit, an evangelical group which established some of the earliest hospitals in Europe, was also formed at the same time as the Waldensians. The founder was a layman named Guy de Montpellier, who formed a hospital in his home town in France and created a semi-monastic religious community to staff it. The movement grew rapidly under Innocent III, and included both celibate members and lay people of all ranks. The celibate members devoted their lives to the care of the sick and the lay members both donated money and volunteered several days of personal service each year.

This movement spread rapidly during the 1200s, and by the end of the century had established hospitals throughout Europe. It brought medical care to higher levels throughout Europe and to wider numbers than had ever received it, including the poor. It also pioneered in medical education by establishing schools of anatomy, surgery and pharmacology. By the 1400s its support by the papacy had become a liability rather than an asset and its early vitality was lost.

The Third Orders established by the Franciscans early in the 1200s would also attract many lay Christians who were seeking a more active form of Christian life. The first such persons were a married couple, people of some wealth who gave all their possessions to the poor after being converted by St. Francis in Assisi in about 1213. They spent the remaining 47 years of their lives seeking out and caring for poor people who were sick, and begging food for those who had none.

A few years later a young queen of Hungary who had recently been widowed joined the Third Order, spending her dowry to build a hospital in St. Francis' name, in which she cared for the poor, sick and outcast.

Dante was reported to have been a member of the Third Order—certainly his great poem indicates a deep devotion to Francis—and many others at the time were either members or deeply influenced by the Third Order Franciscan movement. Unfortunately no historian has yet told the story of the Third Order.

THE NORTHERN EUROPEAN MOVEMENTS

In the three centuries prior to the Reformation a new kind of lay Christian intentionality would emerge in northern Europe. Whereas the earlier western evangelical movements had emerged in Italy and France, these new movements would form in the quite different cultural and political conditions which prevailed in the area now called the Netherlands and Belgium.

This area was unique in being both part of medieval Europe and at the same time culturally distinct from it. What made it distinct was that its roots were almost entirely in the pre-Roman northern tribal groups, from which it residents had inherited a strong aversion to centralized control and an equally strong dedication to individual rights. The people in this area, unlike their neighbors to the south, did not have the memory of the Roman Empire in their background and thus were free to grant a much greater degree of religious and political freedom to individuals than were the people of southern Europe, where social order had for millennia been equated with hierarchy.

In addition to this the northern Europeans had by now been more or less thoroughly converted to Christianity and thus saw themselves as equals in the Christian community. The disarray of the Roman Church in the centuries immediately prior to the Reformation added greatly to their sense that non-Roman ways of being Christian were not only possible but preferable.

Out of this unique situation would emerge two evangelical movements which had no precedent when they first appeared, and which have remained largely unique to the present.

The Beguines

Up to this point the great majority of the highly intentional Christians who have appeared in our story have been male. That is not because only men chose to be intentional Christians. Quite to the contrary, there is solid evidence from the very beginnings in Jerusalem that women were equal partners with men in forming the intentional evangelical communities, and that women very often shared in their leadership.

This fact set these new communities on a path that was profoundly counter-cultural, since the societies in which they lived assumed male dominance and female submission. The Christian community has slowly but persistently challenged these very old and very deeply ingrained customs—sometimes more successfully than at other times—but it has taken 2,000 years to reach the present awareness that women have the same rights and responsibilities as men. Christianizing society is a long, slow process and no aspect of that process has been more difficult than creating new gender relationships.

This background makes the fact that a movement of women which remains unique to the present emerged in northern Europe in the centuries prior to the Reformation. In what is now Belgium and the Netherlands, women began to create evangelical communities that resembled monastic communities in being clearly bounded but that were unlike monasteries in not requiring vows. And unlike any previous Christian community they were governed by women.

Already in the early 1200s a cardinal of the Catholic Church wrote that "many holy maidens had gathered in different places" in that area. "Although their families were wealthy," he reported, "they preferred to endure hardship and poverty, leaving behind their family and home" in order to avoid the temptations of riches and "worldly pomp." They supported themselves with manual labor and "despised the riches of the world for the love of the heavenly bridegroom," choosing to live in poverty and humility.

These women came to be called Beguines, for reasons that are not clear at this point, and that is the name that has remained. Their movement spread rapidly, and by the time of the Reformation there would be nearly 300 of these "cities of women" in more than a 100 towns and cities in Belgium and the Netherlands and adjacent areas. Some were quite small, others fairly large. Already by 1243 it was reported that there were some 2000 Beguines in the Cologne area alone.

The buildings they eventually constructed were like small walled villages, always with a church at the center, built on the edge of a city. Each woman had her own residence, and some brought children with them. The historian of this movement describes these unique places as "islands of contemplation and seclusion, whose inhabitants often worked in town, and to which many outsiders had access during the daytime." A few of their buildings still exist.

What is perhaps most remarkable about the Beguine movement was the way its members combined the ideals of voluntary poverty with a deep commitment to spiritual development. There appears to have been no strict rule which governed life in these intentional communities, but despite this they preserved a way of life that combined service to the poor with manual labor and a sustained life of prayer and ongoing conversion. Their contemporaries regarded them as a middle way between monasticism and the secular lay life.

The Devotio Moderno

In the late 1300s a young man from an upper middle class family in the Netherlands returned to his hometown after spending 15 years studying at the University of Paris. The young man, Geert Grote, had many lucrative professional opportunities open to him but instead chose to become a sort of urban monk without an order.

He gave the large house he had inherited to a group of religious women, probably Beguines, and spent the next 5 years in spiritual development. At the end of that time he became an evangelical preacher, securing permission to do so from his bishop. His preaching was effective, but within only four years he would be gone, killed by the plague which was then ravaging Europe. But despite his early death he left behind a movement similar in many ways to the Beguine movement, but one which included men as well as women, some of them married.

People at the time called this new movement the Devotio Moderno, a Latin phrase that is probably best translated the New Devout. This movement would have a major impact on the northern European laity during the 150 years immediately preceding the Reformation. It is best remembered today for the devotional classic which it is thought to have produced, Thomas à Kempis' *The Imitation of Christ*, and for the impact it had on Erasmus.

A recent historian has identified seven general characteristics of this unique movement:

- They formed communities of both lay and ordained persons who lived in economic community and supported themselves by their own work, and who referred to themselves as "brothers and sisters of the common life." They were deeply critical of the endowed wealth which the Benedictine monasteries had accumulated, and equally critical of the constant fund-raising of the mendicant monks.

- They worshipped in their local parish churches and made it clear they had no intention of forming either a new religious order or of creating new congregations of lay believers. Like the Beguines they refused to take religious vows and insisted on the right of voluntary association, but unlike the Beguines they lived in ordinary urban houses and attended the local parishes.

- They were completely orthodox in doctrine and practice. Given the growing numbers of dissident movements emerging at the time this was essential to their success. They in effect set out to prove that it was possible to be both evangelical and orthodox. Their devotion to the settled traditions of the Church was so great

that they were sometimes persecuted for not joining local dissident groups.

- They combined spirituality and morality to an exceptional degree.
Indeed their concern with moral behavior was so great that they
were criticized, both at the time and by subsequent historians, for
being puritanical. What was important for them was that their ordinary behavior be consistent with their spiritual commitments.

- They were profoundly devoted to Scripture. They read it personally each day, and played a major role in translating it into the vernacular and in publishing it. They were committed to publishing
Dutch translations of other religious texts which had previously
been available only in Latin. These included the works of many
medieval spiritual writers, including Bernard of Clairvaux.

- They met for private in what today would be called small groups
devoted to Bible study and faith sharing. These were open both
to members and to other interested persons. By this means they
were able to proclaim their message without falling under the medieval Church's prohibition of lay preaching.

- They engaged in what they called "fraternal correction," holding each other accountable for their high spiritual and ethical
standards with a kind of brutal honesty that few today would be
willing to accept. They regarded this not as an alternative to the
medieval practice of sacramental confession but an addition to it.

Out of this movement three separate groupings emerged in the 1300s
and 1400s. The first was the Sisters of the Common Life, which would
have more than a hundred local houses by the time of the Reformation. A
second was the Brothers of the Common Life, which was smaller but still
significant. The third was a semi-monastic order that was numerically
the largest and institutionally the most successful, becoming a major
publishing house in the pre-printing era and founding an important set
of schools.

Why was the movement so successful? The answer appears to be
essentially the same as for the earlier lay evangelical movements we have
noted. The conclusion which Prof. van Engen arrived at after long study is
that "these houses offered a devout way of life, rooted in the model of the
first apostles, without requiring them to leave town or church and with-

out imposing any of the difficulties and obligations that came with taking vows and joining an order." He adds, "When the Reformation came the brothers and sisters mostly did not join, in part at least because…they did not need to." Luther himself was an admirer of the movement.

WYCLIF, THE LOLLARDS AND THE HUSSITES

Until almost the year 1400 the medieval evangelical movements had not reached England, at least not to any significant degree. But beginning in the late 1300s an evangelical movement emerged in England that would increasingly come to dominate evangelical Christianity over the next 600 years. That movement was initiated by a leader whose impact on evangelical Christianity is as significant as Luther's would be in forming Protestant Christianity a hundred years later.

This leader was John Wyclif, a professor of theology at Oxford University in the 1360s and 1370s. His writings and his preaching and teaching would provide a rallying point for the widespread but unfocused discontent of his time, and eventually give rise to an underground movement of lay evangelical Christians in England who would be called the Lollards. This movement would survive for 150 years after Wyclif's death and would provide the foundations for the post-Reformation English evangelical movement of the 1700s which we now call Puritanism.

Wyclif also deeply influenced events in the Czech nation through some of his Czech students. They took his new theology back to their homeland where it played an essential role in the development of the Hussite movement—a movement that provided essential foundations for the Lutheran Reformation that would take place in neighboring Germany in the next century.

Wyclif

When John Wyclif was ordained by the bishop of Lincoln at about age 30 there appears to have been no reason to suspect he would become a major dissident leader. He seems to have been viewed by his superiors as one of Oxford's most gifted young theologians, and to have been destined for a comfortable place in the English clerical establishment. By the time he was 40 he had received an important assignment from the king's court, and by his late 40s he was included in the entourage of a leading member of the English royal family.

But as his public standing grew so did scrutiny of his theological writings, and these revealed some rather radical positions, positions that challenged the foundations of the very establishment from which he and his clerical patrons drew their power. These views can be described as fundamentally opposed to what we would today call clericalism—the view that the clergy essentially constitute the Church and that the laity's role is therefore to be passive recipients of the sacraments over which the clergy have exclusive control.

In late medieval England this view of the Church had reached such lengths that the clerical leadership was able to charge relatively high fees for performing the sacraments and as a result had become quite wealthy. This in turn had drawn persons to Church leadership whose primary goal was enjoying the wealth and social status which these positions provided. They often had to purchase their positions, and even when they did not had to prove to others in the leadership elite that they could be counted on to preserve the status quo. Wyclif was a part of this system and profited from it in his early career.

This situation had predictably produced two kinds of discontent. On the one hand the middle and lower classes felt their bishops and priests were extorting money from them in order to live privileged lives. On the other hand the secular establishment was growing increasingly envious of the Church's wealth and had begun to look for ways to appropriate some of the Church's resources and income streams for their own benefit. Wyclif's writings appealed at first to both groups. He argued in learned scholastic Latin that only those who were true Christians were entitled to receive income from the Church's properties, a position that supported the goals of both the middle and the upper classes.

Why did Wyclif turn against the clerical establishment he was part of? We do not know the answer to that question. He wrote and published a great deal but there is virtually nothing autobiographical in any of his writings. We can only infer his motives from his actions, and the most obvious explanation for his actions is that he had experienced an evangelical conversion similar to the ones so many of his contemporaries were experiencing, and would continue to experience over the next centuries, at all levels of English society.

Wyclif's theology went to the heart of the clerical establishment's power, which was a belief in the semi-magical power of the sacraments. It was this belief upon which the clerical establishment's political and economic power ultimately rested. By rejecting this basic belief he was able to argue that the institutional Church's great wealth was derived unjustly and therefore amounted to theft. This of course produced enormous hostility within the Church's leadership, and soon Wyclif was facing papal charges of heresy.

He had sufficient popular and political support to withstand these charges, but increasingly it became clear he had started a movement that was larger and more powerful than he had expected or intended. He retained the support of his colleagues at Oxford—apparently as much from their desire to preserve academic freedom as from their agreement with his opinions—and he continued to use the legitimacy which his position at Oxford provided to preach and publish to large audiences.

He also encouraged some of his younger students to translate the Bible from Latin into English, a move that would have immense impact on the future development of the English-speaking evangelical movement.

As Wyclif's thought took hold in the 1370s it increasingly became obvious that although both the middle and upper classes had a common enemy in the clerical establishment, they had very different long-term goals. The upper classes wanted to take the power and wealth currently held by the Church's leaders for themselves, whereas the lower and middle classes wanted the Church to become an independent source of power that would support their demands for greater social justice.

At the end of his life Wyclif appears to have been disappointed and even somewhat confused. He clearly knew that something was seriously wrong in both Church and society, and he knew that whatever it was involved the leadership of both. But what exactly was wrong seems to have been less clear to him, and as a result he often lashed out rather incoherently, even at times contradicting himself.

The one thing that was clear to him was that English society, which had formed around the Christian faith, must return to its foundations—and that doing so required a return to Scripture, especially the Gospels. For that reason he was known to his followers as *Doctor Evangelicus*—the great teacher of the Gospels.

Wyclif retired from public life after some of his middle and lower class followers formed a mob in 1381 and murdered the Archbishop of

Canterbury. Wyclif died of a stroke a three years later, apparently a broken man. His impact would not be felt in his lifetime, and would not become fully apparent until after the English Puritan movement emerged in the 1600s, but it would eventually come to be recognized by nearly everyone.

His most recent historian has summed up Wyclif's impact in these words: "Luther declared in 1520, 'We are all Hussites.' He might more accurately have declared, 'We are all Wycliffites.'"

The Lollards

Wyclif did not directly initiate the evangelical movement which emerged in England after his death—the movement then and now called the Lollards—but it is unlikely it would have taken root and grown to play a major role in the events of the 150 years prior to the Reformation had he not legitimated it.

Although the people who belonged to the Lollard movement had existed before Wyclif, the appearance of an esteemed Oxford theologian with political support at the highest levels who shared their central belief—that the medieval Church had become hopelessly corrupt and could only be reformed through the most radical measures—legitimated them and gave them confidence.

It now appears increasingly clear that the series of events that would eventually lead the Puritan party of the 1600s to cut off their king's head had begun more than 250 years earlier, when participants in the Peasant's Revolt of 1381 had killed their archbishop, shortly before Wyclif's death.

We have reports of some of the sermons which English evangelical preachers were delivering around the year 1400, and their contents tell us a great deal about the connection between evangelical religious experience and the demand for social justice that would characterize the English evangelical movements in succeeding centuries. This is what one contemporary person reports a Lollard preacher told his followers on the eve of the 1381 Peasants Revolt:

> And if we are all descended from one father and one mother, Adam and Eve, how can the lords say or prove that they are more lords than we are—save that they make us dig and till the ground so that they can squander what we produce?

> They are clad in velvet and satin, set off with squirrel fur, while we are dressed in poor cloth. They have wines and spices and fine bread, and we have only rye and spoilt flour and straw, and only water to drink.
>
> They have beautiful residences and manors, while we have the trouble and the work—always in the fields under rain and snow. But it is from us and our labor that everything comes with which they maintain their pomp....
>
> Good folks, things cannot go well in England nor ever shall, until all things are in common and there is neither villain nor noble, but all of us are of one condition.

Earlier historians have wanted to separate Wyclif and his theological writings from the political events which took place in the century following his death, but as one of Wyclif's successors on the Oxford faculty, Prof. Anne Hudson has shown with great skill and learning that is simply not possible. In the medieval world politics and religion were so intertwined that neither can be understood without understanding the other.

The Lollard movement survived for more than a century after Wyclif's death, but it did so not by engaging in political resistance, but by building a network of local communities of committed evangelical Christians throughout England. These small groups met regularly for Bible study and mutual support, much in the same way twentieth-century small groups have. In these groups ordinary people found respect and empowerment. Many learned to read in them. All were imbued with the words of the Gospels, especially those that support the principle of human rights.

Although the Lollards' goal was spiritual rather than political, their spiritual goals had powerful political implications, and they were not hesitant to acknowledge them. The preface to the Gospel of Matthew in the Lollard Bible acknowledges this quite candidly:

> Christian men ought much to travail night and day about the text of holy writ, and especially the gospel, in their mother tongue ... Every Christian person takes the state, the authority and the bond of God ... to be a disciple of holy writ and a true teacher thereof in all his life, upon pain of damnation ... But worldly clergy claim that holy writ in English will make Christian men to debate, and will suggest they rebel against their sovereign, and therefore should not be allowed among lay people.

In the Scriptures the ordinary people of fifteenth-century England found an independent source of authority, and they would not give it up despite the determined efforts of both religious and civil leaders to take it from them.

The ability of this network to survive and to engage in extensive publishing—including not only the Scriptures in English, but other evangelical books and pamphlets as well—laid the foundations for the combined political and religious events of the next 200 years in England, events that would ultimately impact the entire world as the principles of human rights, and the practices of democracy which are inherent in human rights, spread throughout the world.

The Hussites

Although Wyclif's ideas would have no immediate political impact in his native England they did have a major impact in the Czech nation, where they were taken by some of his students who had studied at Oxford.

As was the case in England at the time, the widespread and powerful discontent with clericalism which had emerged throughout the medieval Church also existed among the Czechs. It is estimated that by 1400 half of all the land in the Czech nation was owned by some Church institution, and Church leaders who benefited from this vast property often flaunted their wealth.

As a result there was a large constituency receptive to Wyclif's ideas when they were brought from England and taught in the Czech universities. One of Wyclif's students was especially active in transmitting Wyclif's beliefs to the Czech intellectual and religious community, spending the final 40 years of his life living there. The result would be a religious movement that would affect all Europe, and which would lay the foundations for the Lutheran Reformation a hundred years later.

The leader of the Czech movement was, John Hus, a Czech intellectual similar in many ways to Wyclif, but with a greater talent for popular leadership. Hus' great gifts simultaneously made him rector of Prague University, the spiritual leader of the common people, and an influential political leader—much in the same way that Bernard of Clairvaux had combined these roles 300 years earlier.

When this great leader was excommunicated and burned at the stake by a corrupt and divided papacy in 1414 it set off a furor in the Czech nation, and produced a national Church independent of the papacy a full century before this would take place elsewhere in Europe. But this bold step was soon retracted by the ruling nobility and the result was a long series of lay movements determined to preserve Hus' reforms.

One of these turned to military action and created an army that established a Christian commonwealth, but which was eventually defeated. Another became a nonviolent community, and although heavily persecuted for centuries it survived and became the present day Moravian Church.

The Legacy of the Medieval Evangelical Movements

The story of the medieval evangelical movements is above all a story of missed opportunities, and it can be read now by those who care about the Church only with a real sense of heartbreak. How differently things could have been! And how much healthier the Church would be today if other choices had been made in the medieval era.

But we do not live in the world that could have been, but in the world that our ancestors have left us, and the world we have inherited from them has been formed, to a far greater degree than we have realized in the past, by the medieval Church's failure to create a place in its structures for the evangelical movements.

This failure has left three major long-term impacts on the Christian tradition. The first is a view of orthodoxy that is almost exclusively doctrinal and negative. The second is an inadequate view of social justice in the Christian tradition. The third is the unexamined but widely shared assumption that the divide between the institutional Churches and the evangelical movements is unavoidable, irreversible and permanent.

Heresy

It has only been in the past century that the medieval movements have received the attention from historians which they obviously deserve. These new studies have been a great gain, not only for the Christian community but for our understanding of the medieval era, but the scholars involved have until recently continued the medieval tradition of regarding these movements as primarily characterized by their heretical doctrines. Many of the books and articles written by these scholars include the word "heresy" in their titles.

There is no question that doctrinal heresy occurred regularly in the medieval evangelical movements—sometimes serious error, other times less serious. But to focus on that fact in isolation ignores the equally evident fact that virtually everyone in the medieval period held beliefs or engaged in practices that by current standards would be considered heretical. There are many forms of heresy, and doctrinal deviation is only one of them. It is also heresy to exclude from confessional beliefs things that are essential to Christian faith. And surely it is heresy to condone and advocate practices that are contrary to the Gospel and the Christian tradition.

The medieval Church was hopelessly corrupt. The Council of Trent in its acts admits as much, and no one today would argue otherwise. To do so would require condoning and defending the actions of Church leaders engaged in rampant corruption of the most obvious kinds. This being so we must ask why we continue to call those who openly opposed these practices 'heretics', while continuing to regard those who defended them, or at least ignored them, as defenders of Christian orthodoxy?

Why is that those Christians, especially lay evangelical Christians, who criticized their corrupt bishops and popes are considered heretics, while the leaders they criticized are held to a much less stringent standard? Which was worse in the 1200s—the dualistic doctrines of the Cathari, or the 'orthodox' doctrines that allowed Church leaders to kill them? Which caused more harm—the eventually schismatic ecclesiology of the Waldensians or the Catholic clericalism that reduced all lay Christianity to passivity?

We have unconsciously adopted a view of heresy which blinds us to the fact that there has always been heresy in the Church, and always will be. Heresy is inevitable because the Church includes sinners among its numbers. What produces great harm is not doctrinal heresy itself—which tends to disappear when it is dealt with rationally, and when those who hold these mistaken beliefs are dealt with compassionately—but the practical heresy that allows persons in authority to intervene in the spiritual lives of less powerful persons with physical and emotional violence.

It is easy for educated persons to dismiss the beliefs of uneducated persons, but to do so educated persons must ignore our own heresies. The Church has always been riddled with heresy, and its leaders and intellectuals have often been among the worst offenders. Furthermore it has very often been our heresies that have led others into heresy, both by our actions and by our arrogance. Jesus makes it quite clear that the greatest heresy of all is the sin of the Pharisees—the temptation always faced by the good and powerful to view themselves as so holy and upright that they can pass judgment on others without themselves being judged.

It is widely recognized that heresy causes schism, but it is less often noted that schism just as surely causes heresy. Who of us as individuals can claim that we would never have fallen into erroneous beliefs if we had not been involved in and been accountable to an institutional Church that maintained the consensus Great Tradition? The present writer certainly could not make that claim.

And if that is true for individuals why should we not expect it to also be true for local Christian communities as well? And since schism only rarely takes place without the participation of both parties involved, it follows that when schism produces heresy everyone involved in creating that schism bears some responsibility for the heresy that occurs.

The great question that emerges from this study is this: Are the medieval evangelical movements a deviation from the Christian tradition or are they an essential part of it? Using the word heresy to describe these movements is to indicate that this important question has already been answered, and in the negative. But in fact it has yet to be asked in any serious way.

Social Justice

The story of the medieval evangelical movements begins with the Peace of God social justice movement, a movement which brought the entire Church—lay, clerical and monastic—into an inspiring act of joint political action. Five centuries later the medieval story ends with the Church's leadership almost unanimously allied with the ruling elites in a joint attempt to preserve the status quo against the rising middle and working class discontent that was present everywhere. Why did a story that began with such great hope and such great initial success end with such despair and with so many civil wars?

We cannot begin to answer that very important question until we recognize how profoundly the ideas of religious uniformity and political order were intertwined in the medieval world—and how that combination led people in these centuries to equate religious dissent with political chaos.

In the highly charged religious atmosphere of the medieval period doctrine mattered in a way that it does for only a few persons today. But it appears to have mattered much less to the medieval evangelicals than it did to the ruling elites who saw in these movements a grave threat to their power and privilege. One suspects for example that what mattered to Mark the gravedigger, who spent his life preaching the Cathari message to the common people of northern Italy in the 1100s, was not so much the details of Cathari doctrine—he was no theologian, and in fact was quite possibly illiterate—but that by joining the Cathari movement he was able to use his obviously considerable talents as a leader.

Had he remained in the institutional Church of the time he would forever have been a spectator, and a spectator to rituals developed and presided over by persons from a social class that assumed its members were entitled to oppress him and the other members of his social class. By joining the Cathari he brought on himself the stigma of being regarded a heretic, but he was rewarded by being able to serve his community, speaking a language they understood and engaging in rituals they could understand.

We can be horrified by the sectarian, dualistic and Pelagian beliefs which the Cathari held, while at the same time—given the new standards of social justice that have emerged in the Christian community in the twentieth century—look with great sympathy on the legitimate demands for social and political change which attracted persons by the thousands to this movement in the 1100s and 1200s.

It appears that what these people were looking for was not a new set of doctrines, but a new kind of Christianity that recognized their unique needs and which took their social condition seriously. And if these oppressed people concluded that if the social practices which the institutional Church supported were contrary to the Gospel, then likely the other doctrines taught by the Church were equally mistaken, who can blame them?

There is no heresy greater than believing the Christian faith can be reduced to a set of specific liturgical practices and codified doctrines, or that a concern for social justice has no essential place in the Church's life. To do so is to ignore vast portions of the Hebrew prophets and equally vast portions of the New Testament—above all this phrase in the

Lord's Prayer: "Thy kingdom come, thy will be done, on earth as it is in heaven."

But in the medieval period it was the 'heretics' who spoke out on behalf of social justice, and it was the orthodox institutional Churches which most frequently defended the unjust status quo. It was the heretical Cathari for example who were able to welcome the poor and marginalized into their communities in a way the orthodox Churches would not have been willing to do, or able to do.

The Christian community has now reached a virtually universal consensus that Christian belief requires a commitment to social justice. Anyone for example who taught that it is permissible for a Christian to own slaves would quickly be condemned in the strongest possible terms. But this view of slavery is a relatively recent development in Christian history. In the medieval era the vast majority of Christians believed owning slaves was perfectly legitimate. Popes and bishops and members of religious orders owned slaves. If members of the evangelical movements did not it was likely due to their being unable to afford them rather than to moral scruples.

And so we must be generous and charitable in judging our distant ancestors in the faith, but at the same time we must also acknowledge that it is the basic political stance of those who were called heretics in the medieval era—those who believed that human rights are inviolable, and that social justice is essential to being a Christian—which is now held almost universally throughout the Christian world.

The Great Divide

As the Waldensian story indicates, the medieval religious revival of the 1100s and 1200s not only brought new energy and vitality to the Christian community, it also divided it. For the remainder of the second millennium there would increasingly be two Christian Churches.

One segment of the Church has been focused on preserving the traditions of the past and maintaining the institutions formed in the past. It has been led by an increasingly professionalized hierarchy, one that has been faced with the constant temptation to increase its social and economic privileges at the expense of its pastoral duties.

The other segment of the Church has been formed by the enthusiastic lay movements which have sprung up everywhere in the second millennium. Their focus has been on restoring Christianity to its apostolic simplicity and integrity, and it has been largely led by charismatic individuals who have been faced with the constant temptation to put personal independence and local autonomy above the unity of the Church.

But despite their fierce and fundamental disagreements the institutional Churches and the evangelical movements have shared a fundamental belief. It is that one of them is right and the other wrong, and that therefore Christians must choose one or the other.

The evangelicals have held that only individual religious experience and personal piety matters, and that participation in the Church's rituals and doctrinal deliberations are non-essentials that can safely be ignored. The institutional Churches have held that only the rituals and doctrines inherited from the past matter, and that individual religious experience and personal piety are non-essentials that can safely be ignored.

This split inherited from our medieval past has left us with two competing and contradictory stories which are being told throughout the Christian community. One holds that the evangelical movements are heretical and always have been, and that they have contributed nothing to the Church except the disunity caused by their heretical beliefs and their refusal to submit to ecclesiastical authority. The other holds that the institutional church is heretical, and has been since the time of Constantine, and that it has contributed nothing to Christianity in the centuries since except persecution and corruption.

Both stories contain elements of truth, but in their simplest forms they are both contradicted by the historical record. There are of course examples of individual evangelicals adopting heretical views, and acting in ways that have brought disunity to the Church, but there are as many examples of bishops holding views that are now considered heretical, and whose resort to violence has often severely rended the Church's unity.

And there are numerous examples of institutional Church leaders allying themselves with the ruling classes and ignoring the needs of the poor, but there are equally as many examples of evangelical leaders adopting a selfish and individualistic pietism unconcerned with the poor, which has supported the economic and political status quo in order to enhance its members' personal status.

The Christian community is true to its founding traditions only when it combines personal religious experience and communal rituals, individual piety and carefully tested doctrine. Without these combinations heresies of all kinds are inevitable. The most certain of these are clericalism and individualism, the heresies that have most deeply and persistently wounded the Church, greatly diminishing its effectiveness and its service to the world, and causing great suffering among the world's poor.

The important story—the one which we in the Christian community most need to attend to at this point in our history—is the story of the conflict which has produced these two competing accounts of our past. We must compose a new and more truthful account of our history, but we cannot hope to do so until we together acknowledge the heresy embedded in both the old stories—the belief that these two parts of the Christian community can exist in isolation, that it is possible for the Church to be healthy and whole without the contributions of both its evangelical members and those who maintain its institutions.

Both are necessary, neither is sufficient.

SEVEN

From the Anabaptists to the Baptists

In the centuries following the Reformation there would be a flourishing of evangelical movements throughout the Christian world that would equal and in many ways exceeded the growth of monastic movements in the thousand years prior to the Reformation. These post-Reformation evangelical movements would have an impact on the development of western civilization that would be equally as significant.

THE THREE REFORMATIONS

In recent decades historians have come to see that three quite different Reformations took place in the 1500s. The first is the one commonly referred to as "the Reformation"—the one initiated by Luther and Calvin and adopted by northern European political leaders including Henry VIII. This reformation would eventually produce the group of Christian denominations now represented by the World Council of Churches.

But there would also be a Catholic Reformation. Although it took place in reaction to the Protestant Reformation and adopted many of its reforms it would take a quite different course. This reformation would eventually produce the Roman Catholic Church over which Pope John Paul II presided at the end of the twentieth century, a very different institution than the one Luther and the other Protestant reformers had rejected.

And there would also be a third reformation, the one now known to scholars as the Radical Reformation. It was produced by the thousands of independent Christian communities which sprang up across Europe

167

in the 1500s, apparently spontaneously. This movement had no single leader and only local institutional structures. It would eventually produce the independent evangelical and pentecostal-charismatic movements that proliferated in the twentieth century.

From its beginnings the Radical Reformation was characterized by its diversity. It was as though a great dam had broken and all the dissident individuals and groups which had accumulated behind the medieval Church's resistance to change had suddenly burst into the open, flooding across Europe.

George H. Williams, the great twentieth-century Harvard historian of Christianity has described this event in a ground-breaking work entitled *The Radical Reformation*. This book has not only established the existence of a third reformation alongside the Protestant and Catholic reformations, it gave this movement its name and provided an encyclopedic survey of its many forms. In the book's fifteen hundred pages we meet with an almost bewildering array of dissident groups—in Spain, in Italy, in Germany, in the Netherlands, in Switzerland, in Austria, in Bohemia, in Moravia, in England, in Poland and Lithuania, in Slovakia and Hungary.

The differences in doctrine and practices between the Radical Reformation communities are immense, ranging from unitarian to semi-monastic. At first they appear to share only a commitment to being neither Catholic nor Protestant, but in fact they shared two other fundamental characteristics. The first is that they were based on the personal commitments of the individuals who joined them, and the second is that they insisted on the right to form independent congregations, free from both civil and ecclesiastical control. For these reasons they have been called "Free Churches" by some twentieth-century historians.

Simply by insisting on the right to exist these groups would play an essential role in establishing two foundational principles upon which western civilization is now based—the fundamental freedom of the individual, and the right of free individuals to associate with one another in any way they choose. Neither of these rights existed before the Radical Reformation, and neither were recognized by the other two sixteenth-century reformations.

At the heart of the Radical Reformation was creating the congregation as an alternative to the parish. The parish was a geographical designation, and all Christians within its boundaries were automatically considered to be members of that parish. The congregation by contrast was formed by the personal choices of those who belonged to it. Like a monastery its membership was voluntary, and if no one chose to join there would be no congregation. It was created by the human person's capacity for intentional choice.

The governing elites in Europe at the time, both Protestant and Catholic, immediately recognized that granting this right would revolutionize Europe society—as in fact it did. A majority of the population supported their leaders, fearing that this radical innovation would produce an even greater social and political upheaval than the one caused by the Protestant Reformation and for that reason the new evangelical movements would be fiercely persecuted.

As a result of this persecution an internal chasm opened up across Europe that was wider in some ways than the one which separated Protestants and Catholics. What Protestants and Catholics were competing for was control of the diocesan churches which had been established in the medieval period. What the evangelical movements were struggling to achieve was the freedom to create religious associations outside the established diocesan structures.

THE SIXTEENTH-CENTURY ANABAPTISTS

Only a few of the independent evangelical groups that emerged from the Radical Reformation would survive, and even fewer would continue to grow in subsequent centuries. But those which did survive would make substantial contributions to the development of western civilization—not only its religious development, but its cultural and political development as well. Among these the movements now collectively known as the Anabaptists have a preeminent place.

The Zurich Anabaptists

On Saturday evening January 21, 1525, in Zurich, Switzerland, a Catholic priest knelt before a lay Christian in the home of another lay Christian and asked his lay colleague to baptize him. The priest took this radical step because he had come to believe that baptizing infants was contrary to the Gospel, and that the baptisms described in the New Testament always involved the conscious intention of adult believers. After he had been baptized as an intentional adult the priest, Fr. George Blaurock, in turn baptized the others present.

In a later account Fr. Blaurock made it clear that he and the other 15 persons present understood the momentous significance of what they were doing. "Fear began to come over them," he says, and "they were oppressed in their hearts." They all knew their action would cost them dearly, and indeed within a few years many of them including Blaurock would be dead—executed by the civil and religious authorities in their newly Protestant state.

Despite this severe opposition the movement requiring intentional adults to undergo a second baptism grew rapidly, first spreading into other areas of Switzerland then north and east into Germany and Austria. Five centuries later the descendants of this movement, both biological and spiritual, number in the hundreds of thousands and are arguably the oldest continually functioning lay evangelical community in existence.

Michael Sattler, OSB

What enabled this heavily persecuted movement to not only survive but also maintain its original vision and commitments was a steady stream of exceptional leaders who sacrificed their personal advantage to join this marginalized and heavily persecuted community. The founders of the Zurich movement, Conrad Grebel and Felix Manz, were the first but they were soon joined by another leader who gave up a privileged position in the institutional Church to join them in shaping the new Anabaptist movement.

This was Fr. Michael Sattler, OSB, prior of the Benedictine monastery of St. Peter, located just across the Swiss border in the Black Forest. The monastery which Sattler belonged to and which he helped administer was one of the oldest in Europe, with roots reaching back into the pre-Cluny medieval era. Like many of the older monasteries in Europe it had come to own vast tracts of land and its members lived in relative wealth.

We know nothing of Sattler's early life, only that by age 34 he had risen to the position of prior, second in command to the abbot. But in 1525, the same year the Zurich Anabaptists rebaptized each other, this young Benedictine prior emerged from obscurity to play a major role in the development of the Swiss Anabaptist movement.

This great transformation began when the monastery's tenant farmers began to complain about the increased financial demands being placed on them. Fundamental economic changes were reducing them to poverty, and Luther's recent dramatic break from the medieval political and religious structures had emboldened them to demand that their grievances be taken seriously. Throughout the early 1520s this unrest had built up until finally in 1525 it coalesced into a vast Peasants Revolt which swept across Germany, powered by a rich mixture of resentment, greed and a legitimate demand for justice.

At first the peasant armies were victorious, looting castles and monasteries throughout Germany, but when a peasant army came to the gates of St. Peter's it is reported that they were treated with hospitality. The monastery's abbot had fled, taking refuge in nearby Freiberg and leaving Fr. Sattler in charge, and the young prior rather than treating his tenants as enemies apparently listened to their complaints and engaged them in conversation.

Some of them had already joined the evangelical movement in a nearby town, where a charismatic pastor had been preaching the inadequacy of infant baptism for several years.

We do not know what transpired in these conversations, but we do know two things that happened afterwards. The first is that St. Peter's monastery was not looted, and the second is that soon afterwards Fr. Sattler left St. Peter's and joined the new Anabaptist community in Zurich. He asked to be rebaptized and soon emerged as a leader in this new evangelical community.

A year and a half after his great change in affiliation Sattler joined the movement's other leaders at a conference in a small town called Schleitheim where they adopted what was in effect a rule for their new movement. They called it a "confession." It is generally believed that Sattler, the most educated person in the movement's leadership at that point and the one with the greatest leadership experience, played the primary role in composing this document.

The document established a few simple principles which would guide the Swiss-origin Mennonite and Amish communities for the next 500 years. Its core vision was the formation of a network of self-governing Christian communities whose way of life would share several fundamental monastic principles:

- These new lay communities would set high standards for membership;
- They would choose their own leaders;
- They would be politically independent;
- Their members would be absolutely non-violent.

What would most distinguish these communities from their monastic predecessors was that they consisted of families, rather than celibate males. Sattler himself had married, joining his life to that of a former Beguine, and together they had cast their lot with the common people, where marriage is essential to survival.

A few days after the conference at Schleitheim Sattler was arrested, along with his wife and several other members of their small Anabaptist community. Sattler refused legal counsel at his trial, saying that to have accepted it would be to recognize the trial's legitimacy, which he denied since no civil court should have jurisdiction over religious belief.

Sattler's enraged accusers viewed him as a traitor to his social class—and in the aftermath of the Peasants Revolt in which an estimated 100,000 people had been killed, they also viewed him as a dangerous political dissident. They ordered him to be executed in an exceptionally gruesome way, even by the standards of the time, specifying extensive tortures before he was burned alive.

At his death one of Sattler's executioners taunted him, saying in effect, "You could have been one of the bosses. What are you doing here?" Sattler is reported to have replied, "This way is better." Two days later Sattler's wife was executed by drowning, rejecting an offer of clemency if only she would renounce her husband's beliefs. Several other members of their community were also condemned and executed.

Sattler's trial and death had a major impact on his contemporaries. Four independent accounts of his trial and execution have survived, all depicting him as a Christian martyr in the classical model. We do not know how his colleagues at St. Peter's monastery reacted to his death.

The Dutch Anabaptists

Another major Anabaptist movement would emerge in the Netherlands in this same period, but completely independent of it. The two groups shared many beliefs and practices, and would eventually share the same name, Mennonite, but the very different political, cultural and religious backgrounds from which they emerged, and the fact that they spoke different languages, ensured that there would be significant and permanent differences between them.

The Dutch Anabaptist's founder was a charismatic revival preacher, Melchior Hoffman, who traveled throughout North Germany and the Netherlands in the early 1530s. His message was strongly apocalyptic, focused on his belief that a divinely initiated new world was imminent. Many people in these unsettled times found this message attractive and he gained large numbers of followers—as well as determined opposition among those who found his message dangerous.

Hoffman would fade from the scene after he was jailed in the spring of 1533, but his apocalyptic message was taken up by some of his younger followers and acted on in a way that profoundly and negatively impacted the development of evangelical Christianity in Europe for the next century, and longer.

In the German city of Münster, just south across the Netherlands border, Hoffman's followers established an Anabaptist theocracy, forcing the city's inhabitants either to be rebaptized or to leave the city. As virtually always happens these young leaders soon lost all touch with reality, instituting polygamy and a primitive communism, both of which primarily benefited themselves. This tragic situation lasted for a year and a half, at the end of which the occupants of the city were facing starvation. It ended when one of them betrayed the city's defenses to the bishop's troops which had surrounded it.

To those looking on elsewhere in Europe the catastrophe in Münster proved beyond any question what many had long believed—that if people were granted religious liberty they would veer off into some terrible form of heresy which would eventually produce political chaos. To this day the iron cages in which the leaders of the Münster revolt were placed to die remain on display in the tower of the city's cathedral.

Menno Simons

After the Münster debacle the post-Reformation evangelical movement hung by a thread. In the Netherlands and Germany it produced not only severe political opposition, but an equally severe disillusionment within the Anabaptist community itself. It now appears likely that the Dutch Anabaptist movement would not have survived had not an unusually gifted leader once again appeared to guide it to a new stage of development.

This new leader was the Catholic pastor of a small parish in northeastern Netherlands, a priest named Menno. At this point in Dutch history many people had not adopted family names, and were known simply by their given name and their father's name. Menno was one such person. His father's name had been Simon, and so he was known as Menno Simonszoon, Simon's son. He is known to history as Menno Simons. Although Menno joined the Anabaptist movement a decade after it had been founded its largest surviving branch is named after him.

When Fr. Menno saw his parishioners return from Münster, defeated and broken, it produced a crisis of conscience. "The blood of these people, although misled, fell so hot upon my heart that I could not stand it," he later wrote. "These zealous children," as he called them, had willingly sacrificed their lives "for their doctrine and their faith."

What caused Menno the greatest pain was his awareness that he had been telling his parishioners about "the abominations of the papal system" but had done nothing to correct these abuses. "I continued in my comfortable life and acknowledged abominations simply in order that I might enjoy physical comfort and escape the Cross of Christ" he said.

"Pondering these things my conscience tormented me so that I could no longer endure it," he said. He finally realized that if he allowed himself to continue to be paralyzed by fear—not using "all my powers to direct the wandering flock who would gladly do their duty if they knew it"—he would endanger his eternal soul. "Oh, how shall their shed blood, shed in the midst of transgression, rise against me at the judgment of the Almighty and pronounce sentence against my poor, miserable soul!"

Menno finally decided to renounce all "worldly reputation, name and fame" and to submit to "stress and poverty under the heavy cross of Christ." One night in January 1536 he left his home, his profession, and his reputation to cast his lot with the despised Anabaptists. He requested adult baptism and became an underground evangelist for the new movement, both preaching to others and reproving those Anabaptists who had adopted the mistaken beliefs that had led to the Münster disaster.

A few years after becoming an Anabaptist Menno married and fathered several children. He lived most of his life with a price on his head but managed to survive until his death in 1561, twenty-five years after his great change in affiliation from Catholic priest to Anabaptist pastor.

Menno would become the de facto bishop of the Dutch Anabaptist community and succeeded in forming it into an institution that has survived to the present. He wrote prolifically, always stressing two things—the centrality of Christ and the absolute necessity of nonviolence—and that would characterize the tradition he founded. Although he had no hierarchical authority he governed effectively, with firmness and charity, and the fact that the majority of the communities which trace their origins to the sixteenth century Anabaptists now bear his name is entirely deserved.

The Hutterites

At the same time the Swiss Anabaptist movement was forming in the area around Zurich, and the Dutch Anabaptist movement was forming in the Netherlands, a third Anabaptist movement was forming in the Tyrolean region of Austria. This one was also led by a gifted leader, a layman named Jacob Hutter, and it would also survive to the present.

What distinguishes this movement from the other Anabaptist movements is its commitment to communal economic life. In this sense it is arguably the most monastic of the surviving Anabaptist movements. In all other respects the Hutterites resemble the more conservative Mennonite communities.

The Hutterite movement currently consists of nearly 500 colonies, three-fourths of them located in the prairie provinces of Canada and the remainder in South Dakota and Montana. Total membership is currently estimated at 40–50,000, the vast majority biological descendants of members of the original sixteenth century movement.

The Amish

After the original fervor of the 1500s the Anabaptist movement would become a movement of Baptists—those who delayed the baptism of their children until they were adolescents or young adults. In Holland these groups came to be called *Doopsgezind*, derived from the Dutch word for baptism, and in Switzerland they were referred to as *Taufer*, derived from the German word for baptism.

In the Netherlands the Dutch Baptists achieved gradual toleration until by the mid-1600s they were able to function more or less openly, although still with significant civil disabilities, which they shared with Catholics and Lutherans.

In Switzerland however the Swiss Baptists continued to be persecuted rather heavily throughout the 1600s, and when some of them participated in the Swiss Peasants Revolt of 1653 the Swiss civil authorities decided to make a final attempt to rid their nation of this troublesome minority. Having found that execution was counter-productive the Swiss government turned to deportation, and over the final decades of the 1600s they were largely successful to forcing all Swiss Baptists to leave the country.

Under the pressures of this intense persecution the Swiss Baptist community split into two antagonistic factions. One advocated accommodation and limited compromise in order to survive, the other a return to the strict standards of the original Schleitheim Confession. The stricter group was led by a young pastor named Jacob Amman, and his followers to this day are known as the Amish.

The Amish movement thrived in the early 1700s, both in Alsace where a local aristocrat protected them in exchange for their exceptional agricultural abilities, and in Pennsylvania where they were among the earliest dissident religious groups who emigrated there for religious toleration. In the nineteenth century the original Amish immigrants established colonies across the midwest United States and are now widely known for their counter-cultural lifestyle.

Those communities currently known as the Amish are however only a relatively small portion of the descendants of the original American Amish. A second less conservative group of Amish emerged in the nineteenth and early twentieth centuries, a group now known as Mennonites although their roots are in the Swiss Amish tradition rather than the Dutch Mennonite tradition. This more progressive Amish group has been active in foreign missions, international development, education and other institutional efforts.

The more conservative Old Order Amish have maintained the Swiss peasant culture which their immigrant forebears brought with them in the eighteenth century, and are virtually all physical descendants of the original immigrants. This conservative group has gained increasing attention in recent decades for its refusal to adopt modern technology.

It had a major impact on public opinion in 2006 when several young girls from one of its communities were murdered in Lancaster County, Pennsylvania and the Amish community to which they belonged responded immediately with acts of forgiveness.

From Persecution to Acceptance

The five century history of the Anabaptist movement has been marked by a gradual transition from fierce persecution in the sixteenth century to gradual acceptance and even admiration in the late twentieth century.

The fierce resistance these communities faced in the 1500s and 1600s came primarily from the pervasive fear in European society that religious liberty would result in political disorder. That fear was gradually dissipated by the process of democratization in the late 1700s and early 1800s, but it was replaced in the nineteenth and twentieth centuries by anger at these movements because their members refused military service.

The Anabaptist communities managed to survive these challenges to their existence by a combination of cultural practices based on their founders' original commitments. Primary among the characteristics that have enabled the Anabaptist communities to survive have been the following:

- They have created communities of non-violent families. When communities are formed by persons who prohibit military violence they are also required to develop create cultures that do not depend on violence of any other kind. As that process continues over multiple generations the effect on family life and community life is quite significant. It fundamentally changes relationships between men and women, between men and men, and between men and their children, especially their sons.

- They have remembered their martyr origins, and have accepted that maintaining the commitments made by the Anabaptist founders, especially the commitment to absolute non-violence, would mean they also would be rejected by their peers. The great Mennonite martyrology, *The Martyrs Mirror*, first published in 1660 and in print ever since in various translations and editions, has played a major role in maintaining this aspect of Anabaptist culture.

- They have migrated constantly in search of freedom to practice their religion and to avoid military service. These migrations have eventually brought the great majority of the Anabaptist-origin groups to North America, where the democratic culture and its political institutions have been most compatible with their religious commitments.

- They have found ways to be useful to their neighbors, first as scientific farmers and more recently as members of the service professions. Rather than competing, their commitment to nonviolence has required them to develop ways to cooperate and this has proven increasingly valuable as society and the economy have become more complex. The current educational level among those Anabaptist-origin communities which accept education is now considerably above the national average.

After World War II, and especially after the Cultural Revolution of the 1960s, the Anabaptist origin communities in North America have received a rapidly growing acceptance in the Christian community and as a result have been able to enter mainstream life in several significant ways. Primary among these has been the numerous institutions they have established, ranging from colleges and universities to foreign mission organizations and humanitarian service organizations.

Politically their greatest impact has been their role in establishing the right of Christians and other persons of conscience to refuse military service. This right is now widely accepted throughout the western world.

As a religious body they have formed the Mennonite World Conference which is now emerging as a major international confessional body. This in turn has made it possible for Mennonites to enter into ecumenical dialogue with a variety of other Christian traditions, most notably the Roman Catholic Church, where a robust international dialogue emerged under Pope John Paul II which has been continued by Pope Benedict XVI.

The Anabaptist Legacy

The legacy of the evangelical communities founded by the sixteenth-century Anabaptists can be summarized in two statements. The first is that self-governing communities of intentional lay Christians who live out their lives in the ordinary conditions of family and work can be created and sustained. The second is that it is possible for such communities to be absolutely non-violent. The 500 year history of the Mennonite, Amish and Hutterite communities furnishes rather convincing evidence for both assertions.

But at the same time this long history makes it equally clear that such communities cannot exist in isolation. Throughout their history the Anabaptist-origin communities have depended on other Christian communities in a variety of ways—politically, intellectually and spiritually. Furthermore their isolation from the wider Christian community has inevitably led them into some often serious deviations from the Great Tradition, most notably in a disposition to believe that Christian faith can be primarily based on the will-based actions of individuals.

Harold S. Bender, the great twentieth-century Mennonite historian and Church leader, opened a new era in our understanding of western Christianity with his presidential address to the American Society of Church History in 1944. Entitled "The Anabaptist Vision" this short essay has stimulated vast amounts of historical research in the decades since, much of which has substantiated his viewpoint and much of which has required his views to be modified. But in both cases the presence of the evangelical movements in the Reformation era and following has been established and recognized.

Bender and most other twentieth-century historians, both Mennonite and others, have assumed that the sixteenth-century Anabaptists were a radical break with medieval Christianity. This is reflected in the popular belief that "the Anabaptists threw everything out and started over again from scratch." But when the sixteenth-century Anabaptist movement is viewed against the background of the medieval era and its intense struggle by lay Christians to find ways to live fully intentional Christian lives, the emergence of the Anabaptists in the sixteenth century appears to have been more a consequence of medieval Christianity than a break from it.

What is needed now is to continue the process of historical research which Bender initiated in the 1930s and 40s with an effort to view Anabaptist and Mennonite history against its medieval background. The difficulties of doing so are great, but surely can be overcome by taking an ecumenical approach.

Mennonites and other post-Reformation evangelicals are understandably reluctant to take the lead in this process, given the still substantial prejudice against their predecessor movements. Other historians, both religious and secular, who have persisted in seeing these movements as heretical and dissident are equally reluctant to view them in a positive light. A truly ecumenical and scientific history however will require that the evangelical strand in Christian history be taken seriously, that it be acknowledged as an essential component of both Church history and the history of western civilization, and that it be allowed to speak on its own terms.

Doing so will challenge virtually all the positions that are now taken for granted. Secular historians will have to acknowledge that religious beliefs are part of western history—an often crucial part. Historians from the institutional Church traditions will have to acknowledge the often brutal and indefensible violence which their predecessors often adopted in their efforts to repress the evangelical movements. And evangelicals will have to acknowledge the often serious deviations from the great Christian tradition which their predecessor movements so often fell into.

This will be painful for everyone. No one will be able to say, "We were right, we have always been right." But surely that pain can be endured, and the reward for doing so will be a new era in which instead of trading insults the various Christian communities will begin to exchange the gifts their traditions have bequeathed to them—and will in turn be able to share these gifts with persons outside the Christian community.

The Seventeenth-Century Puritans

Although post-Reformation evangelical communities would first emerge in the 1500s in the German-speaking areas of Europe, they would ultimately have their greatest growth in the following century in the English-speaking world.

The political consequences of the evangelical demand to form voluntary congregations free from civil control became clearly evident in the English Civil War of 1640 to 1660. This epochal event, which shaped western civilization in some profound and enduring ways, was in addition to other things a conflict between those who wanted religion to remain part of the national civil establishment and those who wanted it to become a matter of individual choice.

In the end the English people would compromise. The established religion would be retained, but the right of voluntary association would also be permitted. The implications of this compromise soon became apparent in the English colonies in North America, where a large number of talented and educated evangelicals—'Puritans' as they were then called—settled in what is now New England and established there a new civil society based on a new political vision, which they eventually expressed in the phrase, 'No kings, no bishops'.

The Puritans as Evangelicals

To view the seventeenth-century English Puritan movement as one in the long series of lay evangelical movements which we have observed throughout Christian history will not meet with universal agreement. Many of the original Puritans would have insisted that their goal was not to separate from the established English Church but to reform it, and that is the way their story has often been told by their descendants.

But in fact all the major elements that had characterized the medieval evangelical movements were present in the English Puritan movement. Personal conversion is primary. There is a strong focus on forming voluntary associations. Priority is given to personal morality rather than doctrinal orthodoxy. And above all there is fierce antagonism between this group and the existing institutional Church.

Furthermore it is becoming increasingly clear that the Puritan movement which emerged in the late 1500s was descended from the Lollard movement which had existed in England for the previous 200 years. The similarities between the Lollard small groups which met in private homes for Bible study and education in the 1400s, and the Puritan groups meeting in homes in the 1500s, gradually becoming independent congregations in the 1600s, is too great to be accounted for by coincidence.

Furthermore the Puritans like the Lollards before them would place great stress on publishing the Scriptures in English, eventually producing the Geneva Bible on which the King James Bible would to a large extent be based.

But the Lollard movement was far from the only stream that fed into what would become English Puritanism. There was also the example of what was happening in Calvin's Geneva, where a theocracy based on

Scripture was being created, and where many of the early Puritans went as refugees during the early decades of the English Reformation.

And there was the example of the Dutch Anabaptists. The Netherlands and England were closely connected by religion, politics and economics throughout the 1500s and 1600s and the emergence of the adult baptism movement in the Netherlands was well known to English evangelicals. Dutch Mennonite businessmen lived in England and established their own churches there. Some of the more radical early Puritan groups had moved to Holland where they affiliated with the Mennonites, and in one case nearly merged with them.

It is clear that the Dutch Anabaptists influenced the English evangelical movement, but the exact extent is still unknown because this relationship has only begun to be studied by historians. What is known is that memories of the Münster debacle remained vividly alive in England for more than a hundred years, and that these memories played a major role in preventing English evangelicals from adopting the apocalyptic doctrines on which Münster had been based, as well as the practice of adult baptism with which Münster was linked in the popular mind.

What the Münster example did not change was the Puritan belief that Christians are required to translate their beliefs into appropriate political practices, and that widely shared belief would produce the English Civil War.

The English Civil War

What most distinguished the English Reformation from the other Protestant reform movements is the gradual pace at which it occurred, unfolding over a 300 year period stretching from John Wyclif's preaching and teaching in the 1380s to its final resolution in the great constitutional settlement of 1688.

What appears clear in retrospect is a uniquely English desire to avoid an exclusive commitment to any of the major options before it. But this desire to avoid a radical break in English society would end in 1640 when the actions of an obstinate and rather weak king were challenged by the rising demands of the English population, and a civil war ensued.

Over the next 20 years an almost bewildering array of political and religious parties would compete for the English peoples' allegiance. The fundamental political issue was whether to allow the nation's hereditary monarchs to rule without parliamentary involvement, or on the other hand whether to let the parliament rule without a strong and independent executive. And there was a third political issue—whether to allow the vast discrepancies in wealth and income distribution which had grown up in the medieval era to continue.

Religiously there were at least five major options. The first was to maintain the minimal Protestantism of Queen Elizabeth. A second option was to establish a theocratic republic on the Calvinist model. A third was the Anabaptist option, allowing complete religious freedom, in effect taking the decision out of the public realm and giving it to individuals. The Dutch model of combining limited religious toleration with an established state Church was a fourth option. The final option was to return to Roman obedience, a view held by only a small minority.

When forced to sort their way through this bewildering thicket of competing options the English people characteristically compromised. They established a mixed government in which the king and the parliament shared power, and which increasingly provided ways for the middle and working classes to improve their condition. Religiously they adopted the Dutch model, establishing a state-supported Church but tolerating independent congregations, even eventually allowing Catholic churches to be re-established.

Given the present belief that religion and politics exist in unrelated domains it has been difficult for historians to enter into a world where nearly everyone believed that a person's fundamental religious beliefs were inseparable from his or her political views. In this world religious change without equivalent political change was regarded as impossible. As a result the Civil War has been studied primarily as a political event, and most often by historians whose own political views strongly colored their interpretations. When historians of religion have studied these same events it has largely been from a confessional perspective.

But the great question the English Civil War poses is the way politics and religion were intertwined in this epochal event—and the ways in which the numerous religious movements that emerged within it affected one another. These questions are made all the more urgent by the fact that modern democracy emerged, at least to some major extent, from the complex mixture of the sacred and the secular which characterizes this great conflict.

[margin note: repeat often / more than / he knows / available]

For the present study the role of the evangelical movements in this process is of course of primary interest. Unfortunately this is a topic that has yet to receive the attention it clearly deserves. But whatever the results of further scholarly study it is difficult to imagine the English Civil War having taken the course which it did without the involvement of the English evangelical movements.

The leadership of the revolutionary party—the people who took the ultimately radical step of beheading their king—was overwhelmingly evangelical, consisting of people who made no secret of their commitment to evangelical religion. The same is true for many of the soldiers and officers who provided the revolutionary party with its military power. Above all it is true of the preachers who furnished the intellectual and theological rationale for this great revolution, and even more so is it true of the revolution's most passionate supporters throughout the nation.

The Civil War has been called a war of religion, and it is difficult to see how this can be denied. The war, whatever its other causes, clearly pitted the evangelicals in England against those who supported the established institutional Church. In the end neither side would win this struggle, and in a real sense both would be defeated. An established institutional Church would survive, but it would never again have an exclusive claim to legitimacy. Alongside it there would be a constantly growing array of independent evangelical movements, ranging from the Baptists to the Salvation Army, but despite this the evangelicals would never again play the role in shaping the political affairs of the nation which they had in the Civil War.

The loser once again was society as a whole, which was left with a divided religious community, one in which the Church's inherited institutions and its popular wing were at war with one another, both limited in their ability to provide the moral authority on which all healthy societies depend for their survival.

The New England Puritans

Arguably the most important impact of the English evangelical movement of the sixteenth and seventeenth centuries would be in North America, where in the decade prior to the Civil War thousands of English Puritans had migrated with the intention of forming a pure Church and a new society based on evangelical principles.

When these immigrants first came to Massachusetts Bay they were firmly committed to remaining within the English Church as a reforming body, but it quickly became apparent this was unrealistic, especially after civil war broke out in England. What emerged instead was a network of independent congregations which were increasingly antagonistic to the established Church of England. A complete break was obviously inevitable and it took place during the Civil War. Eventually the New England Puritans began calling themselves Congregationalists.

also theocratic

The impact which this extraordinary group of immigrants had on the subsequent development of American culture can hardly be overestimated. Although they were only one of many groups which migrated to North America in the 1600s and 1700s their combined religious and political motivation gave them an energy and self-confidence which no other immigrant group had. Their culture-forming impact is probably best indicated today by noting that the oldest of the prestigious Ivy League universities in the United States were founded by its members.

well put

The Quakers

Almost on a par with the New England Puritans in their influence on the early development of American society were the members of another English evangelical movement which emerged during the Civil War. Known to its members as the Society of Friends, it is now commonly referred to as the Quakers, originally a name of derision but now one that is highly respected. It was founded by an exceptional English layman named George Fox.

What most distinguished this movement from the other seventeenth-century English evangelical movements is its pacifism. Whereas the other English evangelicals, despite their many other disagreements, believed their success depended on using military force, the Quakers believed that the success of evangelical Christianity depended on inner change, which they promoted in a variety of innovative and effective ways.

The movement which Fox and the other early Quakers founded thrived in both England and America in the 1700s and 1800s. Probably its greatest contribution was in establishing Pennsylvania and the city of Philadelphia. Pennsylvania provided a home for numerous persecuted evangelical groups from continental Europe, including the Mennonites and Amish, and Philadelphia would provide a place where the uniquely

American contributions of numerous persons like Benjamin Franklin could be made. It is probably no accident that the United States as a political entity was created in Philadelphia

Although Quakers continue to be admired by other Christians for the exceptional examples of lay intentionality which its members provide, the movement's influence in the wider Christian community has been limited by its doctrinal rejection of all sacraments, including baptism and communion.

The English Evangelical Legacy

The evangelical impulse which has been apparent in European civilization throughout the second millennium comes into clear and recognizable focus in England in the 1600s, especially in its Civil War. We no longer have to wonder what the evangelical movements are all about—the sermons and pamphlets produced in this period tell us very clearly what evangelicals are thinking. And if there is any doubt about the authenticity of the sentiments expressed in these documents the Puritans' actions in the Civil War removes it.

The deep-seated and long-standing desire for economic and social justice which we have seen throughout medieval European history is given the clearest possible expression in statements by the Levellers, whose role in the early stages of the Civil War is a central one. The demand for independent congregations formed by the voluntary consent of their members and free from any kind of civil control is central to English evangelicalism and was a major factor in the Civil War.

The demand for religious institutions in which Christians from the middle and lower classes could worship in ways they were comfortable with and which were intelligible to them—another characteristic of all the medieval evangelical movements—is also demanded by the English evangelicals. Their hatred of practices imposed on them by the institutional Churches repeats the positions of all the previous evangelical movements.

And above all their commitment to the Scriptures marks the English evangelicals as part of the long tradition of European evangelical movements, extending at least as far back as the Waldensians of the late 1100s.

The legacy which the English evangelicals have left us is in many ways a hopeful one. At their best they have often been able to find ways to combine evangelical practices with institutional structure. And they have also often found ways to bridge the wide diversity of theological and doctrinal positions that have emerged in the post-Reformation period. It is likely no accident that the modern ecumenical movement originated among English speaking missionaries of the nineteenth century.

The question that must be asked now is why given this legacy the evangelical wing of English speaking Christianity and its institutional wing continue to move further and further apart, and into ever greater antagonism?

THE EIGHTEENTH-CENTURY PIETISTS

Within 200 years after the Reformation it was becoming obvious to many European Christians that the great changes this event had initiated were much more profound than any of the Protestant founders and their original supporters had imagined. Many of the problems the medieval era had bequeathed to the modern era had been solved, but a whole new set of difficulties had emerged to replace them, most notably severe theological disputes and the rationalism they inevitably engendered.

Very few wanted to return to the situation before the Reformation, but it was clear that the Reformation of the 1500s had initiated a process that was far from completed. It became increasingly clear by the 1700s that those living in the very different world the Reformation had produced were going to have to adapt their thinking and their institutions to this new reality.

Zinzendorf and the Moravians

One such person was a young German nobleman, Nicholas von Zinzendorf, born in 1700, the year the new century began. He had been sent to study at the university in Halle, an institution established by the German Lutheran reform movement called "Pietism" which had emerged at the end of the previous century. The movement had been named by its opponents because of its almost exclusive focus on personal piety.

This movement envisioned "little churches within the Church"—small groups that would meet for Bible study and mutual support. The goal of the groups was to instill a "religion of the heart" in their members, providing an alternative to the excessively intellectual approach to religion that frequently prevailed in the German churches after the Reformation.

Count Zinzendorf was thoroughly converted by his teachers at Halle, and after graduating returned to his ancestral estate in eastern Germany determined to live an intentional Christian life as a wealthy landowner. He formed a pietist movement on his estate and began publishing literature which supported pietist doctrines.

The major turn in Zinzendorf's career occurred when he invited a group of religious refugees from one of the pre-Reformation Hussite movements in the nearby Czech nation to establish a village on his estate. He soon became deeply involved in their affairs, eventually becoming their bishop. Under his leadership the Moravians, as they came to be known, would send out the first Protestant missionaries.

Today the successor denomination to this evangelical movement is the Moravian Church in North America with some 80,000 members, and the much larger churches which Moravian missionaries founded in Asia and Africa, now numbering some 600,000 members.

Wesley and the Methodists

Perhaps the greatest permanent impact which Count Zinzendorf's leadership would have came from the influence his movement had on John Wesley, the Anglican priest who founded the Methodists.

Wesley was the product of the English Puritan revolution of the previous century. His grandfather had been a pastor in one of the independent congregations which had formed in that era, but his father had taken the opposite position, becoming an Anglican pastor and a firm advocate of the conservative reaction which emerged after the revolution, joining the party that stressed the continuity of the post-Reformation English Church with its pre-Reformation predecessors.

Wesley's father once wrote that he lamented that "after the destruction of the monasteries" nothing had been created to take their place. "None who had but looked into our own church history can be ignorant how highly instrumental such bodies of men as these were to . . . planting and propagating Christianity amongst our forefathers," he said. But he added that he believed the new societies which were being formed in the eighteenth-century English Church—especially the Society for the Promotion of Christian Knowledge (SPCK) and the Society for the Propagation of the Gospel (SPG)—would assume the role once played by the pre-Reformation monasteries.

As a young man John Wesley was heavily influenced by these new voluntary associations in which lay people played a major role, and he volunteered to go to the newly established English colony in Georgia as a missionary pastor for the SPG. His career as a missionary was short and unsuccessful, but on his voyage to the New World he encountered a group of Moravians from Count Zinzendorf's movement who were also bound for Georgia and their example would have a profound impact on him.

The small sailing ship in which they were traveling encountered some severe storms en route, one of which put the boat in danger of sinking. Wesley and the other passengers were terrified, but the Moravians were able to draw on a deep confidence in divine providence which made a permanent impression on the young pastor.

After returning to England Wesley visited the Moravian colony on Count Zinzendorf's estate. He was especially impressed by the large orphanage which had been established there, which housed some 650 children and provided schooling for some 3,000 more. He was also impressed by the colony's large publishing operation, and by the orderly way in which the community was organized as a network of small groups.

Although Wesley would eventually end his relationship with the Moravians over some doctrinal issues, their example would continue to exert a strong influence on the new movement which would emerge in England under his leadership. A modern Methodist historian has described the movement in its founding years as "a combination of influences—Anglican, Methodist, and Moravian."

What is significant for the present study is the way the Wesleyan movement provided an institutional structure for those lay Christians seeking a way to live more intentional Christian lives than had previously been possible in any of the European churches. In the beginning Wesley and his colleagues saw their movement as a part of the English Church—like the SPCK and the SPG.

The widespread desire throughout the English speaking world for some way to combine institutional Church membership and intentional Christian practice is clearly evident in the rapid growth of Methodism.

Within only 20 years after its founding in the early 1740s it had grown to 10,000 members, spread across England, Wales and Ireland. Within another 20 years its membership had tripled to 30,000, and in another 20 years it again more than doubled to 70,000.

The first Methodist evangelists were sent to what is now the United States in 1772, and the movement would grow there even more rapidly there than in England, gaining some 80,000 members in its first 20 years. Some 250 years later the World Methodist Council would include 76 independent denominations in 132 nations with a combined membership of about 75 million.

The Great Awakening in America

More than 30 years before the first Methodist evangelists came to the North American colonies an early revival preacher closely associated with the Wesleyan movement had already been there, bringing one of the major Methodist innovations to America. This innovation was sermons preached in the open fields which attracted crowds in the thousands and which virtually always produced large numbers of conversions to a pietist version of Christian faith.

This first evangelist was an Anglican priest named George Whitefield whose speaking voice was legendary at the time, said to be able to wake the dead. Whitefield's impact on the newly developing American culture would be major and permanent. He would inaugurate the tradition of revival preaching in North America, and would play a key role in establishing pietism as the prevailing theology in American evangelicalism.

The vast crowds which Whitefield drew wherever he preached, and the message he proclaimed democratized American religion in a profound way. That process in turn played a major role in producing popular support for the American independence movement in the 1760s and 1770s, and that movement in turn eventually led to the establishment of a successful democratic government in the United States.

Whitefield's preaching would also lay the foundations for the American Baptist movement. The role of the revival in the development of American culture can hardly be overemphasized, and the role of the Baptist Churches in the revival movement also cannot be overemphasized. Here all the elements of classical evangelicalism were present—the focus on individual experience, the primacy of the emotions, the freedom from past tradition and practice, and the autonomy of the local community.

The revival movement was also perfectly adapted to the needs of people living on the raw frontiers of America, places where they had come with expectations and cultural traditions developed in Europe, but where the infrastructure those expectations and traditions had taken for granted did not exist. Frontier Americans had little choice but to regard themselves as free individuals. There were no institutions to rely on, unless they created them.

Revivalism was based on this experience. In the revival service the emphasis was almost entirely on the believer and only slightly if at all on the Church. If there was any mention of the Church in the typical revival sermon it was likely to be a negative one, and the radically congregational Baptist ecclesiology was ideally suited to institutionalize this experience.

Today there are some 110 million members of Baptist congregations living in virtually every nation in the world. About 40 million live in the United States, where in many regions they are the dominant religious institution.

NINETEENTH- AND TWENTIETH-CENTURY INTENTIONALITY

Once the right to form voluntary religious associations was established in the English-speaking world an almost explosive growth of evangelical institutions took place, including a proliferation of new denominations, numerous mission societies, associations for the abolition of slavery and other social evils, hundreds of schools, colleges, and seminaries, numerous publishing organizations, and numerous charitable organizations.

In the year 1800 the evangelical movement was just emerging from centuries of vigorous persecution. Two hundred years later evangelical Christianity would be a major part of the institutional Church in North America, and there would be evangelical churches spread throughout the world. One evangelical organization claims that some 10% of the world population is now part of the evangelical community, and that this community's rate of growth is more than 3 times the rate of world population growth, and that the evangelical movement is currently growing at more than double the rate for all Christian Churches combined.

It is very clear that the long-standing attempt by the institutional Churches to prevent an independent evangelical movement from forming has failed. But it is equally clear that the merger of pietism and evangelicalism has changed the evangelical movement from its earlier focus on lay intentionality to something significantly different

The Triumph of Pietism

The freedom which the evangelical movement gradually won for itself understandably led its leaders to adopt a new theology which was compatible with its practices. Although there have been evangelicals who have opposed this gradual evolution, an essentially new theology has been created by American evangelicals in which tradition of all kinds has been replaced by individual religious experience.

Scripture is highly honored in this theology, but in the end it has become clear that any group of believers, or any single believer, is entirely free to interpret Scripture according to his or her personal experience. As the evangelical movement has matured it has become increasingly difficult for any believer to question another believer's experience on the basis of either Scripture or doctrine.

Everyone of course prefers belonging to worshipping communities whose members all hold the same beliefs, but given human nature this has proven impossible. All religious communities have had to find ways to deal with disagreements, often profound ones. The evangelical community has done so by allowing the option of forming new congregations and new denominations, and this option has been frequently adopted by dissident groups.

From this point of view the Church as an institution obviously has a secondary role. Since the Church is created by the voluntary association of its members, and since their decision to affiliate with a particular local church is based on personal religious experiences, individual religious experience becomes the primary event, and the Church becomes a secondary product of that event.

The sacraments, which had been at the center of Christianity until the Reformation, are frequently reduced to symbolic actions in which the individual believer's intention is primary. And since the believer's personal intentions are primary, sermons which deal with individual choices have taken the central role in Christian worship. Philosophy and theology often come to be regarded as non-essential and even dangerous by some, since they limit the autonomy of the individual.

In many ways the pietist movement which George Whitefield inaugurated in America in the first half of the eighteenth century was a return to the medieval revivalist movement led by St. Bernard of Clairvaux. His also was a movement from the intellect to the emotions, and from the conscious will to the unconscious heart. But there was this significant difference: Bernard had been deeply involved in the affairs of the institutional Church, and regarded his movement as a way to reform it, not replace it.

That also had been the pietists' original motivation, but as the revival movement matured in America it increasingly moved the evangelical movement toward a viewpoint which emphasized the primacy of the individual. When the traumas of the first post-Reformation centuries were combined with the immense personal challenges of frontier life in America it was easy for American Christians to conclude that the only option was to form local communities which consisted of redeemed individuals living in an unredeemed world.

By the mid-1700s the medieval ideal of a Christian empire had effectively been abandoned by nearly everyone, both Protestant and Catholic, with the result that Christian believers increasingly saw themselves as political aliens living in a world that was not only unredeemed, but unredeemable. As a result they increasingly retreated into various kinds of personal piety, leaving the management of civil affairs and the development of culture to their more secular neighbors.

The ultimate consequence was that the evangelical movements would move from the intentionality which had characterized the medieval and immediate post-Reformation movements toward a more purely emotional stance. Increasingly the defining question for evangelicals would become "How do I feel?" and less and less, "How can we follow Christ more faithfully?"

Evangelical Intentionality

There would be frequent attempts in the nineteenth and twentieth centuries to form intentional evangelical communities which were more communal in their outlook and more rigorous in their demands than the older evangelical communities, which in many cases had become the institutional churches in their areas.

The most visible of these new efforts at Christian intentionality were the semi-monastic communities which appeared in the nineteenth century. One of the most successful and probably the best known was the Shakers. Other nineteenth century intentional communities were the Amana Colony in Iowa, and the Oneida Community in New York. In many ways these communities were the evangelical equivalent of monasteries, and they were well known in the late nineteenth century, attracting significant membership. The buildings which these communities constructed are now preserved as museums in several cases, but none has survived as a community of believers.

In the twentieth century there were several attempts in England and Scotland to found intentional communities, most notably the Iona Community in Scotland. Only a few of these efforts have survived beyond the first or second generations. In the United States the Reba Place Fellowship was a Mennonite attempt to establish a non-celibate monastic community, but it too has not been able to maintain its founding vision beyond the first generation of members. The Bruderhof is non-celibate monastic group founded in Germany in the 1930s which at one time affiliated with the Hutterites.

At the beginning of the twenty-first century a group of young evangelical Christians largely from Eastern University in Philadelphia formed a "New Monasticism" movement which has attracted considerable attention in the evangelical world, but it will be several decades before its eventual success or failure is known.

In addition to these intentional communities there have been a larger group of what can be called communities of intentionality—various groups of evangelical Christians who have set out to live lives of more intentional discipleship.

Catholic Lay Intentionality

The emergence of lay-initiated evangelical movements in the nineteenth and twentieth centuries would not be confined to the Protestant Churches, although their impact would be greatest there. In Europe the Catholic Action movement would offer new opportunities for lay Catholics to participate in politics as Christians, and in North America the Catholic Charities movement provided opportunities for lay Catholics to participate in the Church's service to society.

Furthermore the Second Vatican Council of the 1960s which profoundly reformed the Roman Catholic Church created the potential for an institutional space for the laity which had never before existed. The result has been the emergence of numerous lay movements referred to as "ecclesial movements." Two of the largest and initially most successful have been Italian movements, the Community of Sant'Egidio and Foccolare.

In the United States the Catholic Worker movement has created a growing and largely successful network of local communities which are led by lay Catholics. They are evangelical in their outlook and theology while maintaining positive relationships with the rest of the Catholic community.

Pope John Paul II, whose efforts in helping to create and in guiding the Polish lay political movement Solidarity had a major impact on late twentieth century events, was a strong supporter of the post-Vatican II lay Catholic movements. In the final decade of his historic papacy John Paul II urged lay Christians to make creating "a civilization of love" their goal for the Third Millennium, telling them that only the laity acting together as part of the Church could bring this great objective into reality.

EIGHT

The Evangelical Legacy

Surveying the 2,000-year history of evangelical intentionality reveals four major developments that appear to be its permanent legacy to the Christian community as a whole.

- The first is that intentional evangelical communities have appeared in every century of Christianity, and in every place where the Christian faith has taken root. It now appears clear that the evangelical impulse is an integral part of the Christian tradition, not a departure from it.

- The second is the evidence that evangelical intentionality releases substantial new energy into the Christian community, resulting in increased evangelism, new institutions of many kinds, new forms of compassion and organized charity, and fundamental political changes throughout society.

- The third is the evidence that when the impulse toward greater evangelical intentionality is not provided with an appropriate place in the Church's institutions a crisis occurs, producing dissension, doctrinal deviation and personal suffering among the believers involved.

- The final legacy is the unfortunate history of animosity between the evangelical movements and the institutional churches, now so long established that it is taken for granted by both segments of the Church.

The challenge now faced by all Christians is to acknowledge this legacy and to act on it in appropriate ways.

THE EVANGELICAL IMPULSE

The Gospel is like a seed, which when planted must grow. And like every seed the Gospel carries within itself specific purposes, in the same way that biological seeds contain a DNA code. The seed must realize the goal encoded in its DNA or it will die, and in the same way the Christian Church must realize the purpose for which it was founded or it too will die.

If a seed carries in its DNA the intent to produce a tree it will either produce a tree or it will die. If the seed achieves its purpose the tree will grow taller or shorter depending on the nutrients available in the soil in which it has been planted and on the rainfall it receives, but either the seed will produce a tree or else it will produce nothing.

And the tree which that seed produces, despite its differences from other trees, will have certain fundamental features—roots and a trunk, branches and leaves. In the same way the Gospel inevitably produces some version of the Church. Its visible appearance will vary greatly, depending on where it is located and whether the conditions for its growth are favorable or unfavorable, but like a tree it will always have certain fundamental features.

It will have roots—a set of traditions and practices which connect it to the past, which feed it, and which anchor it to the real world. It will also have a trunk—a culture, sustained by appropriate institutions, which connects its branches to their roots, and to each other. And it will have branches—the arms which constantly reach out from the trunk, seeking to realize the Church's potential in new and previously untried ways.

All this is essential, but if a tree has only roots and a trunk and branches it will die, and in the same way if the Church does not produce life at the end of its branches it too will die. The purpose of the Church is to produce life, and in the same way that a tree produces life by giving life to its leaves, the Church produces life by forming individual Christians.

A tree's leaves are the place where it takes energy from the sun and uses that energy to transform the nutrients its roots have drawn from the soil and which its trunk has transmitted to its branches into actual life by means of a process scientists call photosynthesis. In the same way the Church remains alive to the extent that new life is constantly being produced in the lives of individual believers.

This process is referred to in many ways—as conversion, as a new birth, as simply becoming a Christian or being a good Catholic, as receiving the gift of the Holy Spirit, and numerous others. But regardless of how this process is named, in the end it can only be explained by attributing it to the Holy Spirit, whose role in the Church's life is almost exactly analogous to the sun's role in photosynthesis.

This impulse to promote new and better lives in its individual members is essential to the Church's existence and constitutes what can be called the evangelical impulse, a force that is a constant throughout Christian history.

But the history recounted in this book also bears witness to another equally important fact—that only when the individual leaves are attached to healthy branches, and the branches are attached to a healthy trunk, and when the trunk in turn is attached to a strong root system which is fed by sufficient water and by soil containing essential nutrients, do the individual leaves remain healthy and life giving.

The Three Options

This universal evangelical impulse has been realized in a great variety of ways, almost as great as the number of individuals involved, much in the same way that seeds from a given tree will produce many new trees, each unique and yet each alike. But despite this diversity it is possible to identify three major options which have appeared throughout the 2,000 years of Church history.

The most popular since the time when Christianity became the dominant religion in western societies has been nominal Christianity. This involves affiliating with the Church in some way and attending Christian services occasionally, but otherwise living ones life much as it would have been lived if that person had not been a Christian. Such persons regard their faith as a religion, having to do primarily with the spiritual, and their basic commitment is to the existing structures of society and to their place in it.

A second option has been what might be called a Christian-in-progress—persons who recognize their lives are in at least certain respects contrary to the Christian gospel but who regard full compliance with the

Christian ideal as presently unattainable, often because of family ties or civic or economic responsibilities. Such persons maintain the hope that becoming fully Christian can be reached at some point in the future, at least in some greater measure, and if not by themselves then by their descendents, but they do not hope to attain it in their own lives.

The persons in these two groups have constituted the vast majority of Christians throughout history. They form what can be called the great center—the persons who bear and rear children, and who provide the physical goods on which human life depends. They are the hard-working dependable people who make human civilization possible by constructing highways and maintaining plumbing systems, and who maintain the civic order on which everyone depends. They are the people who do the essential work of actually connecting the past to the future. It is persons from these groups who form the institutional Church.

But there will always be a third group of Christians—persons who want to go all the way, whatever the cost, people who want to live as the apostles and the early Christians did, completely committed to following Jesus in daily life, without compromise of any kind. These are the people whose story has been told in this book, and as we have seen they have very often been the ones who have invented the future. They are the prophetic minority.

The cost of making a radical commitment to Christian discipleship has kept the numbers in this third group relatively small, but their impact on society has been vastly disproportionate to their numbers because as we have seen in the events described in this book, their commitments have been so strong.

Communities of intentional evangelical Christians have formed in all twenty centuries of Christian history. Of course not all evangelicals either in the past or the present have been intentional. Many persons have been evangelicals for the same reason other Christians have affiliated with the institutions they belong to—because that is what their family traditions or their cultural traditions expected—but when Christians have voluntarily chosen to live with greater intentionality the vast majority have formed evangelical communities.

That pattern has continued into the twentieth century, and appears almost certain to continue for the foreseeable future. The reason for this seems rather obvious. The institutional Churches have been created to serve the needs of the great majority of Christians who are not highly intentional about their faith. As a result intentional Christians will almost inevitably find these structures inhibiting rather than supportive. The commitments of highly intentional Christians require that they create structures and institutions appropriate to their heightened commitments, and only the evangelical option provides them with the ability to do so.

The Intentional Evangelical Beliefs

The evangelical communities that intentional Christians have formed over the centuries have varied in numerous ways, often quite substantially, but there are several fundamental beliefs the great majority has shared:

- They equate being a Christian with having experienced a conscious adult conversion, and they make this a condition of membership. There is the assumption that individual believers can make direct contact with the divine without any mediating agent, and that a sudden and often dramatic appearance of the Spirit can occur in the life of any individual at any time.

- Their communities are initiated by lay people, they are led by lay people, and they remain committed to the belief that all baptized Christians share equally in the mission of the Church. Leadership tends to be based on charismatic gifts rather than ordination, and their communities are frequently named after the individual who founded the movement.

- There is a strong emphasis on the individual, as opposed to the institution which that person is affiliated with or the civil society he or she lives in. This produces a strong aversion to hierarchy, and an equally strong demand for self-government. As a result the evangelical communities tend to view themselves as movements rather than institutions.

- They proselytize very actively, and often experience rapid growth in their early decades. The evangelical communities are distinguished from other Christian communities by their exceptional devotion to evangelism.

- They tend to be highly critical of the institutional Churches, especially their sacraments and their hierarchical leadership. They typically believe a catastrophic fall of the Church occurred at some point, most commonly in the fourth century when the Emperor Constantine became a Christian, and they tend to believe their particular movement is restoring Christianity to its original form.

- They are deeply devoted to Scripture, making its study central to their spirituality and regarding it as their supreme authority. Because of this they place great emphasis on preaching, making it central to their worship.

- They are oriented toward practice rather than doctrine. They have a strong tendency to adopt rigorous ethical systems, combining this with a belief that the human will is strong enough to comply with the demands of these ethical systems.

- They are socially egalitarian, challenging all pyramidal social structures, both religious and political. They are frequently open to women's gifts, and are almost always welcoming to the poor and marginalized.

- They demand both freedom of conscience and freedom of assembly, and are political dissidents in the great majority of cases. They tend to reject coercive physical violence, both personal and governmental, frequently refusing to serve in the military. They also often refuse to swear oaths. They are frequently viewed by the prevailing cultures and by other Christians as a dangerous threat to civil order, and as a result have often been suppressed and heavily persecuted.

What is important to note is that many of these beliefs—especially the political ones which were considered so dangerous when they were first introduced—have frequently come to be accepted as integral parts of western civilization. It is also important to note that all these beliefs were regarded by the evangelical communities which held them as a unitary whole, so that the political positions they adopted were regarded as applying their more fundamental religious commitments to public issues.

THE EVANGELICAL ACCOMPLISHMENT

These evangelical beliefs have made it possible for the members of the communities which have adopted them to do many things that would not have been possible otherwise. On the whole the substantial contributions made by the evangelical communities over the centuries have been greatly under-valued by both secular and Church historians.

Evangelization

Wherever and whenever we encounter evangelicals, from the first century to the twenty-first, we find them preaching. We find them first preaching in the synagogues and in the Jerusalem Temple, until they are expelled. Then we find them traveling throughout the Roman Empire, preaching wherever people will listen to them. In the centuries following we find them preaching to the indigenous peoples of northern Europe, once again wherever and whenever they can gather a crowd.

In the medieval era we find them preaching in the churches—until they are expelled from the Church's pulpits, and then we find them preaching in the streets and the marketplaces, in the fields and in homes, in jails and taverns. After the Reformation we find them preaching to huge crowds in the open fields.

And wherever and whenever we find these Christians preaching we hear the same simple, powerful message:

- God's love and care for the individual is infinite.
- God is willing to forgive even the most horrible sins.
- God desires that every person, regardless of status, live in comfort and security.
- God can heal even the most serious illness or mental disturbance.

It has been these evangelical preachers who have opened the Church's doors to everyone—rich and poor, slave and free, women and men, children and the elderly, every ethnic group, every tribe, every social class. They continue to do so in steadily increasing numbers in the present, throughout the world.

The vast majority of persons who enter the Christian community from outside it now do so through the efforts of evangelical Christians. This fact requires members of the institutional Churches to ask who would make membership in the Christian community possible for those now outside its boundaries if the members of the evangelical Churches did not do so?

And it forces all members of the western societies to ask what would have happened had the Christian community not evolved in a way that included persons from all social groups and all economic classes? Would our civilization have come to hold the egalitarian values which now characterize it?

Biblical Study

The role which Scripture has played in forming the evangelical tradition over the past 800 years can hardly be stressed too strongly. Beginning with the Waldensians in the late 1100s and continuing to the present, the almost passionate commitment of evangelicals to making the Scriptures available to everyone, translated into the languages they actually speak and understand, has been a formative event in the development of both western Christianity and western civilization as a whole.

This part of the evangelical contribution is especially obvious in the English Lollard movement of the late 1300s and 1400s, and in the Brethren of the Common Life and the Beguines of the same period in Holland and Belgium. The Protestant reformers Luther and Calvin continued this tradition, as did the Dutch Anabaptists of the 1600s and the English Puritans of the 1600s and 1700s. It has been a major feature of evangelical missionary activity in the twentieth century.

This devotion to the Scriptures has had an impact far outside the religious realm. Above all the increase in literacy which this development has produced, and the empowerment of the Christian laity that resulted from it, has played a major role in the development of western civilization. The fact that the first book printed with movable type in Europe was an edition of the Bible is an indication of the role which the demand for affordable copies of the Christian Scriptures has played in the development of the western publishing industry.

The evangelical movements' great concern to correctly understand the Scriptures has affected all Christians, making Biblical scholarship an important part of all Christianity in the west. Even those Christians opposed to the evangelical movement have come to study Scripture more carefully than they would have otherwise in order to debate with their opponents. The result has been an almost explosive growth in Biblical scholarship in the twentieth century, at both the academic and popular levels.

It is very hard to imagine any of these developments taking place without the determination of the evangelical movements—despite fierce resistance from the institutional Churches—to make the Scriptures central to popular piety and Christian practice.

Education

In one of the documents which have survived from the Catholic Inquisition of the 1500s we find a Franciscan priest questioning an Anabaptist pastor. The pastor has been arrested for leading an unauthorized evangelical congregation and faces death as a result. The Franciscan priest's responsibility is to produce a judicial record that will justify the execution of his Anabaptist counterpart.

"You were nothing but a poor weaver and candle maker before you went around preaching and rebaptizing out here," the Franciscan friar says to the pastor, with great contempt. He proudly notes that in contrast to the uneducated pastor he is a graduate of the University of Louvain. The pastor responds by quoting Scripture, reminding the friar that Jesus had thanked the Father for revealing the truth to "babes" and hiding it from "the wise of the world."

This answer infuriates the Franciscan. The very idea that God might have revealed the truth to "weavers at the loom" and to "bellows menders" and "scissors grinders" and other members of the "riff-raff", while concealing it from "us ecclesiastics who have studied from our youth, night and day" was to him proof of the Anabaptist's dangerous doctrines.

"Before you are rebaptized you can't tell A from B, but as soon as you are rebaptized you can read and write," he angrily tells the pastor. Surely he says, this is proof that the devil is behind the movement you lead. But the pastor patiently explains that it is the "grace which God grants our simple converts when we diligently teach them to read" which makes their education possible.

Throughout history virtually every evangelical movement has offered the same opportunities for education to poor people, people who otherwise would have remained illiterate.

A prominent Chinese scholar once told the author that he had received his primary education from two evangelical women from the

United States who came to his village in rural China early in the twentieth century, devoting their lives to learning the regional dialect and teaching the village children, including himself, to read. Needless to say he was profoundly grateful to these women, and considered himself a member of their religion, although his understanding of Christian doctrine was minimal.

Today this process continues throughout the world where thousands of evangelical Christians, both indigenous and those sent from other nations, are patiently engaged in educating the poorest of the poor.

Institutions

Even though the evangelical movements have typically placed the individual before the communal they have in fact created large numbers of institutions, many of them now important parts of the institutional Church.

At the beginning of every form of Christianity, wherever and whenever it has come into being, stands the same foundational evangelical experience—some particular person has encountered Christ in some particular way at some particular time and place, and has acted on that encounter. As a result of this encounter these persons have begun to interact with others who have had the same experience, and in these interactions they have encountered yet another form of new empowerment.

When these communities have assembled for worship—for song and prayer and the reading and exploration of Scripture, and to eat the meal Christ taught his followers to share each time they gathered—they have experienced Christ being present among them, physically as well as spiritually.

This experience has in turn always led to the formation of institutions. First congregations are formed, then schools and charitable organizations. Soon missionaries and evangelists are being sent out, and institutions created to support them. Publishing and broadcast programs are established, also maintained by appropriate institutions. Finally regional, national and eventually international federations are formed.

Although evangelical theology places little emphasis on the role of institutions, evangelicals have quite likely produced more institutions per capita than the Churches in the institutional tradition. The evangelical institutions tend to be smaller and more voluntary than those in the institutional tradition, but what they lack in size or authority is often made up for in vitality and in the commitment of their members. This is especially the case in regard to evangelism.

Social Justice

The role which evangelicals have played in making social justice and compassion a major component of western civilization is also vastly under-appreciated, both by present day evangelicals and by historians, secular and religious.

Throughout this survey we have encountered the intentional evangelical movements' concern for the poor and marginalized. Indeed a great many of these movements were founded by poor people who were also politically oppressed and culturally marginalized—beginning with the original Christian community in Jerusalem.

The second Christian millennium opened with the Peace of God movement, an event that is quintessentially evangelical and at the same time completely devoted to social justice. We have seen this same passion for social justice in the English Lollards, in the Czech Hussites, and in the Anabaptist movements which emerged at the time of the Reformation. Concern for social justice would also play a major role in the English Civil War in the 1600s and in the evangelical communities that developed during that era, especially the Quakers.

In the late 1700s and early 1800s it would be evangelical Christians in England who frequently took the lead in abolishing slavery. William Wilberforce, an English evangelical and political leader, would introduce the first bill in the British Parliament to abolish slavery. A former slave ship captain who was converted and became an evangelical Anglican pastor—the author of the popular hymn *Amazing Grace*—would also play a major role in eventually enacting this great monument to human rights. American evangelicals would play a similar and equally significant role in the United States.

In the late nineteenth and early twentieth century evangelical Christians were in the forefront of political reform in the United States. An evangelical Christian, William Jennings Bryan played a major role in forming the present Democratic Party and in enacting several measures that have been essential to its eventual success, including the direct election of senators and the establishment of an income tax.

The Civil Rights Movement of the 1960s was led by a Baptist pastor, Dr. Martin Luther King, Jr., and will always stand as a monument to the major role which social justice has played in the African American Churches, which tend to be overwhelmingly evangelical in their origins.

Democracy

Equally significant—and equally ignored by most historians, both secular and religious—has been the role which evangelical Christians have played in the development of democracy. Just as the monastic movement introduced the ideas of elected leadership and elected representative government into western societies in the pre-Reformation period, the evangelical movements have been the pioneers in recent centuries in introducing the equally important concept of human rights into western politics.

The exact impact which evangelical beliefs requiring religious liberty and freedom of association have had on the development of democratic societies in Europe and North America is not known at this point because it has yet to be studied by historians, but evangelical beliefs have surely played a significant role, and they may well turn out to have played the major role once this aspect of our history receives the scholarly attention it deserves.

Nearly everyone would agree that the freedom to express dissent is an essential characteristic of democracy. But such freedom did not exist in the Roman period, and it did not exist in medieval Europe—at least not for any significant number of people. All human societies were pyramidal until recent centuries, and no pyramidal society can survive if it tolerates dissent. It was this assumption on which all the pre-modern attempts to coerce religious belief were based, including the Inquisition.

This pattern remained in effect until recently because most people will put up with a great deal of injustice rather than pay the heavy price required to confront it. Only a few highly motivated people will risk their lives and the well being of their families to challenge deeply entrenched social and political structures. Had not a significant number of people in Western Europe been willing to do so over a period of centuries it is very difficult to image democracy having become the dominant paradigm.

Throughout western history evangelical Christians have been at the forefront of those willing to make these great sacrifices. Notable among them is Roger Williams, the seventeenth-century English evangelical Anglican pastor who founded the state of Rhode Island, the first full democracy in North America. Although William's statue now stands in the rotunda of the U.S. Capitol, recognized as the earliest of the founders of American democracy, there has been a surprising and unexplainable lack of scholarly study of his contribution to the development of democracy in the United States.

Lay Intentionality

The prominent role which baptism has had in many of the intentional movements is striking and surely significant. This is particularly the case with the Anabaptist movements of the sixteenth century and their successor communities, and with the Baptist movement that began in the eighteenth century. It was also a feature of many pre-Reformation evangelical movements.

It is clear that for many intentional Christians, perhaps a majority, baptism was something that mattered, an act that meant something, an act that was so significant that believers should be willing to die to make sure it was done correctly.

It was clear to a great many medieval evangelicals that baptism had to be an intentional act. And since only mature adults are capable of intentionality, they held that baptism should be reserved for adults who freely chose it and who were willing to live accordingly, including the willingness to sacrifice their lives if necessary to uphold the commitments baptism represents.

For many intentional Christians the institutional Churches' willingness to baptize infants was proof that these Churches had transformed the Christian Gospel from something costly, as it had been at the beginning, into something so easy it was little more than a promise to conform to the customs of the prevailing society. And when baptism came to be mandated by law, as it had been throughout Europe in the medieval era, this only added to these earnest Christians' sense of betrayal.

Many medieval evangelicals knew that the medieval monastics had a tradition of describing their monastic vows as a second baptism, and these lay Christians demanded that they too be given an equivalent opportunity to make a full adult commitment to the Christian faith. Surely this long tradition of voluntary adult commitment played a role in bringing the possibility of greater intentionality into not only the Christian Churches, but into western society as a whole.

We are increasingly coming to understand that being intentional is more than simply making a choice, or having the intent to seek some particular goal. Full-intentionality, we are seeing, involves a prior step—the conscious choice to make a conscious choice. Each day every human makes dozens of choices, some small and some large, but only a few are intentional in the sense that we are conscious of making these choices, and even fewer are intentional in the sense that we have chosen to consciously weigh our choices, and have accepted our full human freedom to choose whatever we wish, regardless of the cost.

Many people, both religious and secular, are now coming to see that our increasingly complex and affluent way of life requires greater intentionality, and that as a result we must become more intentional about being intentional. Surely the witness of the religious communities which have been practicing this discipline for many centuries has played a role in this development, and can contribute to its continuation.

Individualism

It is now clear that the evangelical impulse has played a major role in history, releasing great energy and producing important new innovations, but it is also now clear that it has left a legacy of individualism that needs to be acknowledged.

The intentional communities' emphasis on the individual and on his or her potential not only energizes the members of those communities, it also inevitably presents them with the temptation to privilege their personal condition so highly that they ignore the collective historical experience of the believing community. The result is that rather than transforming believers into people progressively more devoted to the common good, this movement has unfortunately often transformed them into people primarily focused on their own welfare.

St. Paul's conversion has often been regarded by the evangelical movements as a paradigm of conversion, occurring as it did in a direct encounter with the divine, and because it unleashed the power of the Christian missionary movement. But what is often forgotten is that if after his conversion Paul would not have gone to great lengths to hold himself accountable to the larger Church—then gathered around the person of St. Peter in Jerusalem—his energy and the energies of the missionary movement he founded would have been destructive to the Church, rather than being extraordinarily constructive as they were.

Furthermore for every person who has met Christ in the dramatic way Paul did there have been many others who have encountered Christ in the same profound way through the Church's worship and in its institutional life. How can we know Christ unless we first know that Christ exists, and how can we know that Christ exists except through the Church? Was this not how Paul came to know the person he had met on the road—first from those who were already believers challenging him, and then later from their taking him into their company?

The evangelical emphasis on individual conversion is essential to a vital Christian faith. But when this emphasis is not combined with an equally strong awareness that genuine conversion always takes place over time, and that it virtually always takes place within the Church, a serious deformation of the faith takes place. Rather than relying on those who have already been converted and whose faith has been tested over time, the inclination is to focus on individual experience and to reject all those who disagree.

But without other believers how can we distinguish between what is an authentic personal experience of the divine, and what is an aberration, an idiosyncratic deviation from the tradition? And what does it mean for our relationship with others to make personal experience primary— especially at the levels of culture, politics and morality?

American society has been formed to a major extent by evangelical Christian beliefs and much of that influence has been positive. But the excessive individualism which has developed in American society must be confronted if we are to continue to develop as a democratic society, and be replaced by the ancient Christian doctrine of the common good. Surely only the evangelical community can provide some of the leadership in doing so.

THE EVANGELICAL CRISIS

Whenever the Gospel is proclaimed without providing some means for ordinary persons to put its message into practice we must expect great frustration to result. That frustration will increase in direct proportion to the level of commitment of the people involved. If highly committed

Christians are not offered some way to act on their commitments a serious crisis will inevitably occur.

This is caused by an inherent human impulse toward consistency—a drive to act on the beliefs that one holds. If for example a person makes acquiring money the ultimate goal in his or her life that person will eventually become quite frustrated if she or he does not acquire some money. The same is true of anything else which has been chosen as the ultimate value in one's life.

Certainly it is true for those who have chosen Christian faith as the ultimate value in their life, especially since a major element in Christian faith is the belief that one's life must be consistent with his or her professed beliefs. Nothing is so severely condemned in the Gospels as hypocrisy.

The ultimate source of the evangelical crisis is the Evangel itself—the story told in the four Christian Gospels. In this story individuals again and again encounter Christ, directly and unmediated. As a result they are converted, changed in fundamental ways, including physically. They are filled with a new Spirit, given a new kind of energy and a mental clarity they had never known before—and that experience must be acted on.

The First Evangelical Crises

The first major evangelical crisis occurred when persecution ended, and for the first time it became possible for persons with only minimal commitment to enter the Church.

This crisis was resolved through the monastic movement and by its institutionalization, embodied in the Rule of St. Benedict. This in turn enabled non-celibate Christians, including members of the ruling elite, to participate in the monastic movement by endowing monasteries, by sending their children to be educated there, and by choosing to live in the vicinity of monastic establishments where they could participate regularly in their liturgical and sacramental life.

A second major evangelical crisis occurred in the 1100s and 1200s, when the success of the monastic movement made it clear to people throughout Europe that Christian beliefs offered very practical benefits to those willing to base their lives on these beliefs. What caused this second crisis was a steadily increasing sense that the benefits of the monastic way did not require the traditional monastic practices. From the 1200s until this crisis was finally resolved in the Protestant Reformation, we find group after group in Europe struggling to establish a way for non-monastic Christians to live at higher levels of commitment than ordinary parish membership made possible.

Although theological dissent appeared from time to time that was not the defining characteristic of this group of people. Indeed, on the whole the persons involved were quite content with Christian doctrine as they had received it. Their discontent came from the fact that they had no way to put into practice what they were being taught by the Church. Either the Christian message could no longer be proclaimed or something had to be done to apply it, since the Gospel itself proclaims rather dire consequences for those who fail to put its teachings into practice.

The third major evangelical crisis was produced by the Protestant Reformation. As the political ramifications of this great revolution became apparent, national and local governments acted to prevent or at least to limit the social chaos which a revolution of this magnitude inevitably produced. This was achieved by doing what the various European national governments had sought to do for several centuries—to nationalize the Church in their territories.

This in turn produced yet another crisis for intentional Christians. The monasteries were no longer open in the Protestant nations, and the parish churches remained very much like their pre-Reformation predecessors, with the exception that the priest or pastor was now expected to be married. No new institutions had been created to provide for non-celibate intentional communities.

As a result people, especially in the Germanic areas, began to create such institutions. This produced the Radical Reformation and—as with the medieval evangelical movements—there is both bewildering diversity, and at the same time a common thread in this movement. Indeed, the diversity comes to a large extent from the common thread, which is that the individual now has complete authority over his or her actions as a Christian.

No longer would intentional Christians be prevented from acting on their commitments by government coercion. Now intentional Christians would be prevented from doing so by their very freedom. They could do anything they wished, but how were they to know what they were doing was the right thing to do? Rather than resistance they experienced paralysis.

This crisis would have its greatest impact in English-speaking North America, where the evangelical rejection of state-controlled Protestantism was most thorough. Whereas in Europe the evangelical communities, monastic and Protestant, were never more than a tiny portion of the population, there are now areas of the United States, especially in the South, where evangelicalism is the dominant religion. Probably 25–30% of all North American Christians are evangelical and it is the most rapidly growing segment of the Church in the United States.

The New Evangelical Crisis

The Christian community is now experiencing a fourth major evangelical crisis as it enters the third Christian millennium. This crisis equally involves the evangelical community and the institutional Churches, and profoundly challenges the existing intentional Christian communities.

Despite its anti-institutional bias the evangelical movement in North America has produced numerous institutions, some quite powerful, which now must be maintained. This has forced the evangelical community to move rather far from its roots in many cases, and to borrow techniques and practices from the institutions it once rejected. And although the evangelical movement originated as a protest against the control of the Church by the State it has now become so strong numerically it has been forced to accept political responsibility.

Both developments have raised questions, and quite profound ones, about the relationship between the individual believer and the various institutions—religious, political, economic, and social—on which all humans depend. These are questions that did not exist so long as evangelicals were marginal, but which cannot be avoided now that the evangelical community has taken a leadership role in the Protestant community.

The decline of much state-supported Protestantism into an increasingly enervated civil religion has often left Protestant Christians with little choice other than the evangelical movement if they wish their faith to consist of more than occasional attendance at religious services where the message proclaimed is frequently a generic religiosity only loosely connected to the historic Christian tradition.

But evangelical Christianity for its part often has no real mission for its lay members—other than convincing other persons to become evangelical Christians. But the Scriptures, to which evangelicals are so strongly dedicated, seem rather clearly to envision a kingdom on earth where God's will is done, as it is in heaven. There are of course endless opportunities for disagreement on how this goal of a kingdom on earth is to be realized, but the goal itself is so central to the Gospel that it cannot be ignored.

In the Catholic community the strong affirmation of the role of the laity adopted by the Second Vatican Council has raised new expectations without yet being translated into any adequate institutional form. The new ecclesial movements are clearly steps in this direction, but none has yet reached the scale needed to give the Catholic laity the ability to carry out the culture-transforming work Vatican II has assigned them, and none has yet taken American cultural form.

Among the older intentional evangelical communities, including the Mennonites, Quakers and others, there is a growing awareness that they have become so strongly acculturated they have little to offer that distinguishes them from other evangelical and Protestant denominations.

What is clear from history is that the evangelical impulse cannot be suppressed or ignored. Every attempt to do so in the past has failed, and the only result has been to drive the evangelical impulse underground, where it has produced schism after schism, and the heresies which schisms always produce.

Meeting at the River

Our story began at the Lake of Galilee, with two brothers fishing. It has ended with a highly institutionalized global religious movement, spread across the globe. What has happened in these 2,000 years has now made things possible that could not have been even imagined when this process began.

Hundreds of millions of people have been involved in this story, each in a unique and important way. The vast majority have acted out their commitment to Christ by affiliating with one of the Christian religious institutions established over the centuries. But another segment of the Christian community—the one whose story has been recounted in this book—has acted on its commitment to Christ by making maximum use of the human capacity for intentional action.

Only a relatively few persons in history have chosen to pattern their lives on intentional choices, and an even smaller number of communities have formed based on intentional choices, but when such communities have formed they have had immense impacts. Even the institutional Churches have been profoundly shaped by the movements formed by intentional Christians, both the members of celibate monastic orders and the non-celibate evangelical communities.

As the third millennium of Christian history opens it is clear that the future of Christian intentionality is in the lay evangelical movements. The great question for many centuries has been whether the evangelical movements, especially the highly intentional lay communities, are a deviation from the Christian tradition or whether they are an essential part of it. Events in the twentieth century appear to have answered that question rather unequivocally. Given the growth of evangelical Christianity throughout the world how can it be doubted that these movements are an integral part of the Christian tradition?

The challenge which now faces the Christian community as a whole is to repair the animosity which almost from the beginning of Christianity has existed between the institutional Churches and the evangelical communities. How can we hope to move forward unless we acknowledge the mutual recrimination which has built up over the centuries? How can the Church realize its immense potential for good if we do not replace the animosity of the past with a new relationship that recognizes both the institutional and the evangelical as equally essential components of the Christian tradition?

That will require finding ways to incorporate the evangelical impulse into the Church's permanent structures—ways that allow the Church's intentional evangelicals to live in mutually productive relationships to the institutional Churches.

GLARING ACROSS THE RIVER

Perhaps the most striking finding that emerges from this study is the intense and enduring dislike which institutional and intentional Christians have had for each other over the centuries, and the often violent and emotional outbursts which this mutual disdain has produced.

This mutual hostility is most visible in the frequent attempts by institutional Christians to suppress the intentional evangelical movements, executing their members and outlawing their assemblies. But it has been equally present in the actions and attitudes of evangelical Christians who have frequently declared that the institutional Churches' leaders are the anti-Christ predicted in the Revelation of St. John, and that the institutions themselves are the "whore of Babylon" referred in that book of Scripture.

What causes this intense hatred—no other word is strong enough? And why has it been a constant in a religious community dedicated to the belief that theirs is a religion of love? There is hardly any question Christians can ask as we enter the new millennium that is more important.

Why?

When we ask why the institutional Churches have so consistently rejected the evangelical movements and sought to suppress them, a variety of possible answers emerge.

Is it because the evangelical movements, and especially the more intentional ones, have adopted higher standards of Christian conduct than the institutional Churches? Is it because intentional Christians virtually always challenge the status quo, demanding fundamental and often difficult changes in the institutions of the Church? Is it because they almost always raise difficult political questions? Is it because they nearly always eventually adopt doctrinal positions outside the Great Tradition? Is it simply because they are wrong?

And if we ask why the independent lay movements have consistently believed that the institutional Churches have betrayed the Christian tradition an equally varied set of possible reasons emerges.

Is it because intentional Christians believe their high ethical standards are required for all Christians? Is it because they are natural rebels, inclined to opposition whenever possible? Is it because they are so committed to individual freedom they cannot tolerate any limit on personal autonomy for the sake of the institution? Is it because they regard the institutional Church's focus on doctrine as an impediment to evangelism, and an effort to impose elitist control on other Christians? Is it because the institutional Churches have in fact become apostate?

In the end none of these conjectures is able to explain the persistence of this animosity, nor its intensity. There is clearly something fundamental and emotional taking place here, something which our present ways of thinking make it difficult for us to see and understand.

Whatever the reason the Christian community has inherited a profound division as we enter the third millennium. One group is committed above all to the institutional integrity of the Church—its unity, its doctrines, its fidelity to past tradition, its sacraments, its institutional authority. A second group is committed above all to the conversion of individuals—to their interior experiences of the divine, to living lives based on that experience and developing beliefs based on it, and to their freedom to worship in ways that reflect their experience.

These two groups rarely speak to each other, much less worship together or engage in serious dialogue about their differences. It is as though they stand on the opposite banks of a river, glaring across the river at each other and justifying themselves by carefully noting the defects in the beliefs and practices of those on the other side.

This division separates not only traditions and denominations but individual parishes and congregations. Attend any Christian worship service anywhere in the world and you will likely find persons whose commitments vary widely. Some will be there because of family tradition, some from habit, some because they are seekers, and some will be there from such deep conviction they would willingly suffer martyrdom.

Those Christians who are especially committed will be inclined to view less committed Christians as insincere, sometimes to the point of questioning whether they are actually Christians. For their part those Christians whose commitments are less fervent will be inclined to view more highly committed believers as unnecessarily fervent, often to the point of regarding them as fanatics.

But surely it is now clear that the lesson of history is that the Church must provide places for persons across this entire continuum, from the least committed to the most intentional. This is true at the level of the local congregation, it is true at the denominational level, and it is true at the international level. Just as Jesus made a place in his life for everyone, from the worst sinner to the most faithful saint, and from the strongest human to the weakest child, so everyone belongs in the Church.

When that reality is ignored, as it often has been, the result has always been one of two equally debilitating dualisms. When the institutional Churches' exclusive concern becomes creating places where people of minimal commitment can worship in comfort it eventually produces a Church divided into two sharply distinguished groups—one a passive pay-pray-and-obey laity, and the other an increasingly self-absorbed and eventually corrupt clerical establishment.

And when the independent evangelical communities confine themselves to creating places where individuals with high levels of commitment can be comfortable it has virtually always produced a doctrinal individualism in which anyone can believe anything they want and still claim to be a Christian. This eventually produces such great doctrinal and institutional chaos that in the end no one believes anything.

Both of these dualisms are now widespread in the Churches, and are routinely defended by pointing out the defects of those who hold the opposite one. As this process continues the Christian faith inevitably degenerates into a generic religiosity that has little to do with the real life of real people in the real world. This has already taken place in both Catholic and Protestant Europe, and the same process is now well underway in the Americas.

This process affects not only religious belief and the established religious institutions. What people believe shapes their behavior in all aspects of life, and what people in one segment of society believe affects everyone else in that society. When the Christian community is divided, as it now is, it becomes a force that divides society, rather than becoming a reconciling force as it could be and was intended to be by its founder.

What Can Be Done

The binary beliefs just described are increasingly being questioned by the majority of Christian leaders, both pastoral and theological, as well as by the Christian laity.

The solid and steady growth of the ecumenical movement throughout the twentieth century is convincing evidence that the Christian community as a whole is searching for a way to live out its beliefs in ways which incorporate the traditions of the past but which also move us beyond its rancorous divisions. The fluid movement of the laity from one denomination to another is equally compelling evidence of this change.

We are increasingly coming to realize that we all drink from a single river, a river of grace, and that we would not exist if this river did not exist. It supplies us with an invisible yet completely real stream of energy that flows through human history and into every human life, making every human community and every human family and every human life possible, in every second of every day. If this river were suddenly to cease flowing the entire physical universe would collapse into a single particle of nothingness, and all biological life everywhere would come to an end in a split second, like a candle blown out.

As a result of this growing realization actions that would have been completely impractical only a decade or two ago are now realistic possibilities. These include three specific actions which the Christian community could take, which if persisted in would heal the great division between the institutional and the intentional communities which now cripples us. Two of them have already begun. The third is new but well within the realm of practical possibility.

Dialogue

Of all the major developments in Christianity in the twentieth century the most significant is quite likely the emergence of ecumenical dialogue. Although this was virtually unheard of when the twentieth century began, by the end of the century it had become an established part of Church life.

Virtually all the institutional Churches are now engaged in serious on-going high level dialogues with each other. Many of these formal dialogues have already produced significant results—above all the international agreement between the Lutheran and Roman Catholic Churches declaring that the doctrine of salvation by grace alone is no longer a Church-dividing issue.

However this great movement has only begun to include the evangelical communities. In large part this is due to the very different ways the evangelical churches and the institutional churches are organized. The institutional churches are able to appoint delegations to speak on their behalf in formal dialogues with similar delegations from other institutional Churches, but the evangelical communities lack this ability and so thus far have largely been excluded from the ecumenical process.

However there have been important exceptions to this pattern and their recent success furnishes solid grounds for hope that the evangelical communities, including the most independent ones, can be included in the process of ecumenical dialogue in the near future.

The oldest of the dialogues between an institutional Church and one of the independent Christian communities is the formal dialogue that has been underway for several years between the Pentecostal Churches and the Roman Catholic Church. The great majority of the Pentecostal congregations throughout the world are independent, but an internationally respected group of Pentecostal pastors have initiated a formal dialogue with the Roman Catholic Church at the Vatican level and this dialogue has now produced a series of reports that indicate a good deal of mutual respect between these two previously estranged segments of the Christian community.

There have also been several efforts to organize a dialogue between Catholics and Baptists. A formal dialogue has developed at the international level, involving the Baptist World Alliance and the Vatican, and less formal dialogues have emerged at local and regional levels.

In 1998 a surprisingly successful dialogue between the Mennonite World Conference and the Vatican has also emerged. The report of its first five-year series of annual dialogues is entitled *Called Together to Be Peacemakers* and reports a surprising level of agreement on issues that were thought to involve virtually irreconcilable differences when the dialogue began.

Associated with this dialogue but separate from it has been a unique form of ecumenical dialogue called Bridgefolk. This is a voluntary association of Mennonites and Catholics who meet annually for conferences open to anyone, at which serious discussion of the issues which divide these two traditions takes place. Although it has no official status in either denomination it has attracted numerous leaders from both, as well as more than 200 lay Christians.

What this recent history indicates is that if the independent evangelical and pentecostal-charismatic Churches and the institutional Churches are willing to abandon the long-held assumption that their estrangement is inevitable and permanent it is entirely possible for them to find ways to join in truly Christian dialogue—one based on charity, on a willingness to face past sins and ask forgiveness for them, and one which looks to the future with hope rather than to the past with anger.

This study of Christian intentionality appears to indicate rather clearly that our task as Christians in the third millennium is not to continue the battles of the past, but to find ways to replace the animosity between the evangelical communities and the institutional Churches which we have inherited from the past with new forms of respect and cooperation.

Doing so will require great effort, and a willingness to accept the gifts that can only come to us from the Holy Spirit. But it will release immense new amounts of energy and innovation that will empower the Churches as institutions and enable their members to grow and to serve the world in new ways—a goal all Christians share, and which none of them can achieve alone.

Studying History Together

One of the first things the Mennonite Catholic dialogue revealed is that both communities have very different views of the past, and that these views are a major factor in their estrangement.

In the final report of the international dialogue, jointly published by the Vatican and the Mennonite World Conference in 2003, the first section was entitled "Considering History Together." Several parts of this section deserve to be quoted since the experience of those involved in this dialogue has a wide relevance.

> Both our traditions have had their selective ways of looking at history. . . . We sometimes restricted our views of the history of Christianity to those aspects that seemed to be most in agreement with the self-definition of our respective ecclesial communities.
>
> The experience of studying the history of the church together and of re-reading it in an atmosphere of openness has been invaluable. It has helped us gain a broader view of the history of the Christian tradition. We have been reminded that we share at least fifteen centuries of common Christian history. The early church and the church of the Middle Ages were, and continue to be, the common ground for both our traditions.
>
> We have also discovered that the subsequent centuries of separation have spelled a loss to both of us. Re-reading the past together helps us to regain and restore certain aspects of our ecclesial experience that we may have undervalued or even discounted due to centuries of separation and antagonism.
>
> Our common re-reading of the history of the church will hopefully contribute to the development of a common interpretation of the past. This can lead to a shared new memory and understanding. In turn, a shared new memory can free us from the prison of the past.
>
> On this basis both Catholics and Mennonites hear the challenge to become architects of a future more in conformity with Christ's instructions when he said: "I give you a new commandment, that you love one another. Just as I have loved you, you also should love one another. By this everyone will know that you are my disciples, if you have love for one another" (*Jn* 13:34–35). Given this commandment, Christians can take responsibility for the past. They can name the errors in their history, repent of them, and work to correct them.
>
> We need to be aware that we have developed significant aspects of our self-understandings and theologies in contexts where we have often tried to prove that we are right and they are wrong. We need tools of historical research that help us to see both what we have in common as well as to responsibly address the differences that separate us.

Early on members of the informally constituted Mennonite Catholic Theological Colloquium organized two scholarly conferences which brought together experts from both the Mennonite and Catholic communities to jointly confront the persecution of the sixteenth century Anabaptists by the institutional Churches, especially the Catholic Church.

Based on this experience it is clear that immense opportunities await those scholars willing to engage in historical research in an ecumenical context, especially research into the previously ignored roles which both the lay evangelical movements and the monastic movements have played in Christian history.

Creating a Space for Lay Intentionality

Great as the two opportunities just described are, there is a third and possibly even greater opportunity open to us. It is the opportunity to ask together—in an ecumenical context and against the background of a shared history—a question that has never really been asked in previous Church history. It is this: *How can we create a productive and positive place in the Church's permanent structures for its lay members who have been called to lives of greater Christian intentionality?*

Again and again in the pages of this study we have encountered the immense tragedies which have occurred because such a place did not exist, but despite this the Christian community as a whole has never asked in any serious or sustained way how these tragedies can be avoided, or how the energy that produces them can be turned to more productive uses. It is clear that there is a great vacuum in the Church's institutions, and it is clear that it must be dealt with. The question is how.

We can surely best begin to confront this challenge by remembering that the Church exists to serve the world, not primarily its own members. The principle which Jesus enunciated when he said that "those who seek to save their lives will lose them" has proven to be as true as the law of gravity, and those who have ignored it have paid a price as severe as those who have chosen to ignore the law of gravity.

The second thing that can guide us is to recognize that without the laity's full and enthusiastic participation the Church can never hope to serve the world. The laity comprises some 99% of the Church's members, a fact that speaks for itself. This fact does not require us to ignore the essential leadership which the Church's ordained and professional members provide, but it does require us to think in new ways about the relationship between the Church's lay members and its pastoral leaders.

A third thing that must be confronted is the role of sexuality in Christian faith. The tradition of clerical and monastic celibacy played a major role in dividing the laity from its pastoral leadership during the first 1,500 years of Christian history, and it continues to play that role in the Roman Catholic community. And even though the Protestant Churches have abandoned required celibacy, the legacy of the pre-Reformation tradition still remains in many forms.

The role of sexuality in dividing the lay evangelical movements from the institutional Churches can hardly be overemphasized. Always hanging over all lay Christians, and especially over the most intentional lay Christians, has been the question, "If you were really good Christians wouldn't you be celibate like the bishops and priests and the monks and the nuns?" Behind this lies St. Paul's negative attitudes toward sexuality, epitomized in his opinion that marriage can only be accepted for Christians in those cases where it is "better to marry than to burn" with lust.

But why must we fear sexuality? Why cannot it be celebrated as the major form of embodied love in human experience? Pope John Paul has taken a major step in this direction with his "theology of the body" and a dialogue between celibate members of the monastic communities and married members of the lay evangelical movements would likely yield great progress in this area—progress which is essential if the divide between the intentional movements and the Catholic Church is ever to be healed.

Surely the way forward is for all Christians to ask, "How can we serve the world" and surely offering the world a more realistic view of human sexuality—one which avoids both the current excesses of promiscuity, and the previous excesses of viewing sexuality as inherently evil—would be a gift of great value.

Ultimately we must ask what it means to be an intentional Christian in the new millennium? That is the fundamental issue, and we cannot hope to create new structures for Christian intentionality until we have confronted it. This is a great issue, one that no single person or any single community can hope to deal with alone.

It raises immense questions like what it means to be a Christian in the new millennium, with its conditions of democratization and globalization? What does it mean to be intentional in a world that offers human persons opportunities that had never before existed in their society? What does it mean to be a Christian in a world that has been fundamentally shaped by 2,000 years of Christian existence? And what does it mean to be an intentional Christian in this new world?

We will answer these questions only by being intentional about doing so, and we will we find answers only by being in conversation with other intentional Christians, and by learning from our common history.

MEETING IN THE RIVER

We have been living beside the river of grace, some on one side and some on the other. We have watched the river from one side or the other, drunk from it, bathed in it, occasionally launched our boats on it. We have built castles and cities along its banks, and farmed the land it waters. We have accepted its gifts and most often taken it for granted.

What we have rarely done is to cross the river to visit those who live on the other bank. We have been aware that others live there but we have noticed that they live differently than we do and we have found that frightening, a threat to our beliefs that the way we are living is the only proper way. The result is that the river which feeds us has also divided us.

Obviously the Christian community cannot be united if we continue to choose sides in this way, and the only way we can avoid choosing sides is to choose to live in the river. This means allowing the river to take us where it is destined to flow, coming ashore from time to time, sometimes on one bank and at other times on the other. Jesus called his first followers to be "fishers of men" and we can only hope to continue their mission if we too leave the safety of the shore and launch into the waters around us.

That will require institutional Christians to recognize that in the beginning all Christians were evangelicals and all were lay persons. They had to be evangelical because without the evangelical spirit they simply could not have survived. And they had to do so as lay persons. The twelve apostles had been chosen and trained by Jesus himself, but they were not priests, just as he had not been. They were something new in religious history—the models for the Christian pastor, leaders who serve rather than command and who are defined by their responsibilities rather than their authority.

And these first Christians had to live intentionally. There was no other reason for them to be Christians, other than their decision to say "Yes" to Jesus' invitation to follow him. There was no social or political reward for saying "Yes", no promise of anything in this life other than opposition and persecution. They said "Yes" because they chose to, and they continued to say "Yes" throughout their lifetimes because they chose to do so.

But in the same way evangelical Christians will be required to recognize that the founders of Christianity immediately created a new institution. They were a movement but they were a movement determined to succeed long term and they realized that meant organizing so that the story they had been entrusted with would continue to be told, and told accurately, and the power they had received would continue to be passed on to future generations.

The early Church's success in forming a unified international community whose leaders cooperated and supported one another was essential for it success and its survival. Unity was not a luxury during these centuries, it was absolutely crucial. Everything depended on it, especially evangelization. Competing Christian missionaries of the kind which have been sent into the world in the years since the Reformation would have been unthinkable to the early Christians.

The connection between the institutional and the evangelical was a very close one in the early centuries of the Church—really two sides of the same coin—but this connection has gradually weakened over the centuries until now the institutional Churches and the evangelical Churches have come to act and think almost as though they are two separate religions. Both have suffered tremendously as a result, but it is those outside the Church who have suffered the most.

This virtual war between the Church's two sides is not sustainable. It must come to an end, and it can end only when the institutional Churches make places in their structures for the Churches' evangelical members—and when the Church's evangelicals recognize their need for accountability and structure, needs which can only be filled by the institutional Church.

The world is filled with problems, great and small. All are causing immense human suffering. All can be solved, if not immediately then eventually. But they can only be solved by joint action, involving everyone affected. The Christian Church has a unique ability to bring people together, but it can only do so when it is united. If it does not use that ability it becomes one of the problems causing suffering, not a healing and reconciling force..

The history summarized in this study is long and varied, and has involved millions of people living throughout the world, at very different times and in very different situations. But despite its diversity this story's lessons can be summarized in three simple sentences:

> *The Church needs its evangelicals.*
> *The evangelicals need their Church.*
> *The world needs both.*

Chapter 1: "Follow Me"

The quotation from Dag Hammarskjöld's *Markings* appears on p. 205 of the 1964 English edition.

Chapter 2: From Anthony to Benedict

St. Anthony: There are numerous editions and translations of Archbishop Athanasius' *Life of St. Anthony.* The most recent scholarly edition is by Robert C. Gregg, published in 1980 by Paulist Press in the Classics of Western Spirituality series. David Brakke's *Athanasius and Asceticism*, published by The Johns Hopkins University Press in 1995, contains a detailed and carefully researched account of the background to this book. Although Anthony is the name used in most popular literature, he is referred to as Antony in the scholarly literature.

The Other Monks: Among the many collections of stories regarding the early Egyptian monks Helen Waddell's *The Desert Fathers*, first published in 1936, remains a classic. The recent scholarly study by the Jesuit scholar William Harmless, *Desert Christians: An Introduction to the Literature of Early Monasticism*, published by the Oxford University Press in 2004, is encyclopedic in extent and rich in detail.

From Monk to Monastery: A scholarly edition of the biography of St. Pachomius was published by Cistercian Publications in 1980, with an introduction by the translator Armand Veilleux. It is entitled *The Life of Saint Pachomius and his*

Disciples, and is number 45 in the Cistercian Studies Series. James E. Goehring's *The Letter of Ammon and Pachomian Monasticism,* published by Walter de Gruyter in 1986, provides an excellent window into the fourth-century Egyptian monastic movement.

The Impact of Egyptian Monasticism: The insightful phrase "the prophecy of behavior" is from Susan Harvey. It is quoted in James E. Goehring, *Ascetics, Society and the Desert: Studies in Early Egyptian Monasticism,* published by Trinity Press in 1999, p.34.

Greek Monasticism: The paragraphs on early monasticism in the eastern Mediterranean are based on Adrian Fortescue's article, "Eastern Monasticism" in the 1911 *Catholic Encyclopedia.*

Italy: St. Augustine's account of his encounter with Athanasius' *Life of St. Anthony* is in Book VIII of his *Confessions,* paragraphs 13 through 20. The best modern English translation is by Henry Chadwick, published by Oxford University Press in 1991.

St. Benedict: The primary source for St. Benedict's life and work is his *Rule.* There is an outstanding modern translation with a book-length historical introduction, produced by the Benedictine monks of Saint John's Abbey in Collegeville, MN and published by their Liturgical Press in 1981. The monks of Saint John's also published a translation of Gregory the Great's biography of Benedict in 1949, entitled *The Life and Miracles of St. Benedict.*

Chapter 3: From Martin of Tours to Cluny

The New People: William H. McNeill introduced the existence of the Steppe Civilzation to English-speaking readers with *Europe's Steppe Frontier, 1500–1800,* published by the University of Chicago Press in 1964. The French scholar René Grousset produced a more comprehensive account in *The Empire of the Steppes: A History of Central Asia,* translated and published by Rutgers University Press in 1970. J. M. Wallace-Hadrill's *The Barbarian West, 400–1000,* published by Blackwell in 1996, connects the Lombards, Franks and Visigoths to this story. Michael Richter's *The Formation of the Medieval West: Studies in the Oral Culture of the Barbarians,* published by St. Martin's Press in 1994 provides helpful detail about the cultures of the northern European tribes. James B. Minahan's *One Europe, Many Nations: A Historical Dictionary of European National Groups,* published by Greenwood Press in 2000, documents the continued existence of many of the northern European tribes. Jean Décarreaux's book, translated as *Monks and Civilization: From the Barbarian Invasions to the Reign of Charlemagne,* published by George Allen & Unwin in 1964, documents the role of the monastic movement in the cultural transition of the northern tribes in the first millennium.

Among the many histories of the northern European tribes which have been produced in the twentieth century, the work of Nora Chadwick on the Celts is particularly important. See especially *The Celts,* published by Penguin Books in 1971, and reissued with an introduction by Barry Cunliffe in 1997. Other works include Herwig Wolfram's *History of the Goths,* published in German in 1979 and reissued in revised form in an English translation by the University of California Press in 1988. An excellent illustrated summary of recent archeology is available in Simon James' *The World of the Celts,* published by Thames and Hudson in 1993.

The New Religion: The story of the conversion of the northern tribes to Christianity is told by Richard Fletcher in *The Barbarian Conversion: From Paganism to Christianity,* published by the University of California Press in 1999.

Martin of Tours: The basic source of information on the life of Martin of Tours is the contemporary biography written by Sulpitius Severus. A translation is available online. A modern biography by the French scholar Régine Pernoud, *Martin of Tours: Soldier, Bishop, and Saint* was translated into English and published by Ignatius Press in 2006.

Columban: The basic source of information on the life of Columban is the contemporary biography written by the monk Jonas. It was translated into English and published in 1895 in Philadelphia. A scholarly edition of his sermons with English translations was published by the Dublin Institute for Advanced Studies in 1957, edited by G. S. M. Walker and entitled *Sancti Comumbani Opera.* The monastic rule of St. Columban is included in the Saint John's Abbey edition of the *Rule of St. Benedict.* J. M. Wallace-Hadrill's translation of *The Fourth Book of the Chronicle of Fredegar,* published by Thomas Nelson in 1960, contains a good deal of contemporary evidence regarding Columban. Gregory of Tour's *The History of the Franks,* written in the late 500s, is a delightful description of life in France at the time Columban lived there. It was translated and published in the Penguin Classics series in 1974. The only modern biography of Columban was written by George Metlake nearly a century ago and published as *The Life and Writings of St. Columban.* It was recently reprinted by Kessinger Publishing. Columban's influence on western literature is described in a series of scholarly essays edited by Michael Lapidge entitled *Columbanus: Studies in the Latin Writings* and published by Boydell Press in 1997.

Charlemagne: The most recent biography of Charlemagne is a small volume by Roger Collins entitled *Charlemagne* and published by the University of Toronto Press in 1998. There are two contemporary biographies, one by Einhard who served in Charlemagne's court, and a second by a monk known as Notker the Stammerer. They were translated and published in a single volume in the Penguin Classics series in 1969. Patrick J. Geary's *Before France and Germany: The Creation and Transformation of the Merovingian World*, published by Oxford University Press in 1988, tells the story of Charlemagne's rise to power out of the chaos of the times. A recent popular work, *Becoming Charlemagne: Europe, Baghdad, and the Empires of A.D. 800* by Jeff Sypeck, published by HarperCollins in 2006, provides an entertaining window into the international relations of Charlemagne's era.

Cluny: There is a recent popular account of the Abbey of Cluny by Edwin Mullins entitled *Cluny: In Search of God's Lost Empire,* published by BlueBridge in 2006. It contains a full bibliography.

Chapter 4: From Bernard of Clairvaux to Martin Luther

Bernard of Clairvaux: There are excellent articles on the Cistercians in both the 1911 *Catholic Encylopedia* and the 1967 *New Catholic Encylopedia.* The primary source for Bernard of Clairvaux is his voluminous writings. A selection was published by Paulist Press in 1987 in the Classics of Western Spirituality series, entitled *Bernard of Clairvaux: Selected Works,* translated and edited by G.R. Evans with an introduction by the Benedictine scholar Jean Leclercq. G. R. Evans has also published a scholarly introduction to Bernard's life entitled *Bernard of Clairvaux* and published by Oxford University Press in 2000. The documents quoted in the text are: Bernard's *Apology,* translated by David Burr and available online; his *Sermons on the Song of Songs,* translated by G. R. Evans in the Classics of Western Spirituality volume; his *Apologia for the Second Crusade,* translated by James Brundage and available online; and his *In Praise of the New Knighthood,* translated by Conrad Greenia and available online. The passage relating to the treatment of dissident evangelicals is from G.R. Evans' biography, pp. 109–13. The quotation from Fr. Leclercq is in his "Introduction" to the Classics of Western Spirituality volume, p. 41.

Francis of Assisi: This summary of Francis' life is based on Adrian House's excellent biography, *Francis of Assisi: A Revolutionary Life,* published in the United States by HiddenSpring in 2000. It in turn is based to a large extent on an earlier biography by the mayor of Assisi, Arnaldo Fortini, whose book *Francis of Assisi* was translated into English and published by Crossroads in 1981. Other recent biographies include Lawrence S. Cunningham's *Francis of Assisi: Performing the Gospel Life,* published by Eerdmans in 2004; and Ivan Gobry's *Saint Francis of Assisi,* translated from the French and published by Ignatius Press in 2006. Francis' own writings were published in the Classics of Western Spirituality series in 1982, entitled *Francis and Clare: The Complete Works.* The C.S. Lewis quotation is from his 1936 book, *The Allegory of Love: A Study in Medieval Tradition,* and is quoted in House's biography on p. 13. The quotation from Pope Innocent III is taken from Fortini's biography, and is quoted in House, p. 52. The quotations from House regarding the power of Francis' preaching are on pp. 111–12.

The Mendicant Era: This summary of the Mendicant movement is based on C. H. Lawrence's *The Friars: The Impact of the Early Mendicant Movement on Western Society,* published by Longman in 1994. The quotation from Prof. Lawrence regarding the role of the mendicants relative to the secular clergy is from pp. 220–21. The volume *Early Dominicans: Selected Writings,* published in the Classics of Western Spirituality series in 1982, provides solid background on the early development of the Dominican order.

Three Medieval Lives: The section on Peter Orseolo is based on the article by C. M. Aherene in the *New Catholic Encyclopedia;* the article "St. Peter Urseolus" in the 1911 *Catholic Encyclopedia;* and the article in Butler's *Lives of the Saints.* The section on Angela of Foligno is based on *Angela of Foligno: Complete Works,* published in the Classics of Western Spirituality series in 1993, with an Introduction by the translator, Paul Lachance, OFM. The section on Walter Hilton is based on *Walter Hilton: The Scale of Perfection,* published in the Classics of Western Spirituality series in 1991, translated from Middle English with an "Introduction" by John P. H. Clark and Rosemary Dorward. The quotation at the conclusion of the section on Hilton is from the article by J. Walsh in the *New Catholic Encyclopedia.*

Martin Luther: There is a voluminous literature on Luther, which has been very ably summarized in the long article on Luther in *Encyclopedia Britannica.* The quotations from Luther are both from this article. The first is from his *De votes monasticis* of 1521. The second is from a biographical note written in 1545 and included in his preface to his collected works.

Chapter 5: The Legacy of Monasticism

Monasticism and the Future: The call for a 'new Benedict' was voiced by the philosopher Alasdair MacIntyre in his 1984 book *After Virtue: A Study in Moral Theory,* published by the University of Notre Dame Press, p. 263.

Chapter 6: From Jerusalem to the Millennium

The Montanists: The most important scholarly study of Montanism has appeared in works dealing with Tertullian. Chief among them is the biography by Timothy David Barnes, *Tertullian: A Historical and Literary Study,* published by Oxford University Press in 1971, with a second edition in 1985. David Rankin's *Tertullian and the Church,* published by Cambridge University Press in 1995, makes the parallels of Montanism to the twentieth-century Charismatic movement quite clear. Christine Trevett's *Montanism: Gender, Authority and the New Prophecy,* published by Cambridge University Press in 1996, is a friendly treatment by a Quaker scholar. William Tabbernee, *Montanist Inscriptions and Testimonia: Epigraphic Sources Illustrating the History of Montanism,* published by Mercer University Press in 1997, contains a wealth of archeological evidence.

The Donatists: The description of the Donatists is based on D. Faul's articles "Donatism" and "Donatus" in the 1967 *New Catholic Encyclopedia.* W. H. C. Frend's *The Donatist Church: A Movement of Protest in Roman North Africa,* published by Oxford University Press in 1952, first recognized the centrality of social justice in forming the Donatist movement. Augustine's interactions with the Donatists are described by Peter Brown in chapter 19 of *Augustine of Hippo: A Biography,* published by the University of California Press in 1967. Augustine's letters, translated and published in various sources, furnish indispensable but biased information about this movement.

Eustathius of Sebaste: This section is based on the relevant articles in the 1911 *Catholic Encyclopedia* and the 1967 *New Catholic Encyclopedia.*

The Priscillianists: Henry Chadwick's *Priscillian of Avila: The Occult and the Charismatic in the Early Church,* published by the Oxford University Press in 1976, is the primary source for this section. The canons of the Council of Sargossa in 380 condemning the Priscillianists are on p. 14. A more recent study by Virginia Burris, *The Making of a Heretic: Gender, Authority, and the Priscillianist Controversy* was published by the University of California Press in 1995.

The Paulicians: The essential source for this movement is Nina G. Garsoïon's *The Paulician Heresy A Study of the Origin and Development of Paulicianism in Armenia and the Eastern Provinces of the Byzantine Empire,* published by Mouton in 1967. She brought to her research a command of the relevant languages that is unmatched.

The Legacy of First Millennium Evangelical Intentionality: The impact of. Augustine's support of the use of government coercion to resolve religious disputes is described in great detail in chapter 1 of Frederick H. Russell's *The Just War in the Middle Ages,* published by the Cambridge University Press in 1975.

CHAPTER 7: FROM THE PEACE OF GOD TO THE REFORMATION

The Medieval Religious Revival: Unfortunately there is no single work which deals with this exceptionally important development. There are two works which describe the sudden emergence of European civilization in the period immediately following the year 1000. They are R. W. Southern's *The Making of the Middle Ages,* published by Yale University Press in 1953, and R. I. Moore's *The First European Revolution, c. 970–1215,* published by Blackwell in 2000.

The Peace of God: The primary historian of this event is Prof. Richard Landes. With Thomas Head he edited a volume of essays, *The Peace of God: Social Violence and Religious Response in France around the Year 1000,* published by Cornell University Press in 1992. He has written several subsequent essays, which are available online. The one quoted at the conclusion of this section is entitled, "Peace of God: *Pax Dei*". There is also important information in chapter 1 of Moore's *First European Revolution,* cited above; the contemporary historian quoted is Radulfus Glaber, whose remarks appear on p. 9.

The Patarines: The best description of this movement is in the works of R. I. Moore: *The First European Revolution,* already cited; and chapter 3 of *The Origins of European Dissent,* published by Blackwell in 1985.

The Eastern Dualist Movements: The basic source is Walter L. Wakefield and Austin P. Evans' *Heresies of the High Middle Ages: Selected Sources Translated and Annotated,* published by Columbia University Press in 1969. Malcolm Lambert's *The Cathars,* published by Blackwell in 1998, contains a detailed account of the movement. Joseph R. Strayer's *The Albigensian Crusades,* first published in 1971, was reissued with an epilogue by Carol Lansing by the University of Michigan Press in 1992. The story from Toulouse is in C. H. Lawrence's *The Friars,* cited above, p. 192.

The Waldensians: There are two outstanding recent histories of the Waldensians: Euan Cameron's *Waldenses: Rejections of Holy Church in Medieval Europe,* published by Blackwell in 2000; and Gabriel Audisio's *The Waldensian Dissent: Persecution and Survival c.1170–c.1570,* published by Cambridge University Press in 1999.

Other Early Lay Movements: These sections are based on the relevant articles in the 1967 *New Catholic Encyclopedia;* and from Lawrence's *Friars,* pp. 113–14.

The Beguines: There is an outstanding recent history of the Beguines: Walter Simons' *Cities of Ladies: Beguine Communities in the Medieval Low Countries, 1220–1565,* published by the University of Pennsylvania Press in 2003. The passage quoted is on p. 35. Two other recent works have also described the significant role women played in the early intentional movements: Jane Tibbetts Schulenburg's *Forgetful of Their Sex: Female Sanctity and Society, ca. 500–1100,* published by the University of Chicago Press in 1998; and *Women Preachers and Prophets through Two Millennia of Christianity,* edited by Beverly Mayne Kienzle and Pamela J. Walker, and published by the University of California Press in 1998.

The Devotio Moderno: The best source is the volume in the Classics of Western Spirituality series, *Devotio Moderno: Basic Writings,* which contains a long introduction by the translator, John van Engen. The basic characteristics of this movement are described on pp. 13–18; the concluding quotation is from p. 23. There is an earlier work by Albert Hyma, *The Brethren of the Common Life,* published by Eerdmans in 1950, and reprinted by Wipf & Stock.

Wyclif, the Lollards and the Hussites: The primary source for this section is Prof. Anne Hudson's *The Premature Reformation: Wycliffite Texts and Lollard History,* published by Oxford University Press in 1988. Her summary statement of Wyclif's significance appears on p. 60. The passage from a Lollard sermon is quoted from Norman Cohn, *Pursuit of the Millennium: Revolutionary Millenarians and Mystical Anarchists of the Middle Ages,* published by Oxford University Press in 1970, p.199. The passage from the Geneva Bible is quoted from Hudson's *Premature Reformation,* p. 276, with language modernized.

Chapter 8: From the Anabaptists to the Baptists

The Three Reformations: George Hunston Williams' seminal book, *The Radical Reformation,* has been published in three editions. The first was published by Westminster in 1962, followed by a Spanish edition, and a revised English edition published by Truman State University Press in 1992.

The Sixteenth-Century Anabaptists: The best current sources for the history of the early Anabaptists are the works of C. Arnold Snyder: *The Life and Thought of Michael Sattler,* published by Herald Press in 1984 as No. 26 in the Studies in Anabaptist and Mennonite History series; *Anabaptist History and Theology: An Introduction,* published by Pandora Press in 1995; and *Following in the Footseps of Christ: The Anabaptist Tradition,* published by Orbis in 2004 in the Traditions of Christian Spirituality Series.

The story of the Amish is told by Steven M. Nolt, *A History of the Amish,* published by Good Books in 1992. An account of the Amish community's response to the shooting of their children is available in Donald B. Kraybill, Steven M. Nolt and David L. Weaver-Zercher, *Amish Grace: How Forgiveness Transcended Tragedy*, published by Jossey-Bass/Wiley in 2007.

Harold S. Bender's seminal essay, "The Anabaptist Vision" inspired a collection of essays by his colleagues and students, *The Recovery of the Anabaptist Vision; A Sixtieth Anniversary Tribute to Harold S. Bender,* published by Herald Press in 1957; and a second collection, *Anabaptist Visions for the New Millennium : A Search for Identity,* published by Pandora Press in 2000. The present book has its origins in the author's undergraduate days at Goshen College in the early 1960s when Dean Bender was still living.

The Seventeenth-Century Puritans: The essential work on the Lollards is Anne Hudson's *Premature Reformation,* cited above. The history of sixteenth-century Puritanism is recounted in Patrick Collinson's *The Elizabethan Puritan Movement,* published by Oxford University Press in 1990. An important set of essays relating the events of the English Civil War to the religious currents of the times, *Radical Religion in the English Revolution,* was edited by J. F. McGregor and B. Reay and published by Oxford University Press in 1984.

The Eighteenth-Century Pietists: The crisis produced by the mutual persecution of Christians by Christians in the early centuries of the Reformation is described in an important work by Brad Gregory, *Salvation at Stake: Christian Martyrdom in Early Modern Europe,* published by Harvard University Press in 1999.

The rise of the Methodist movement in seventeenth-century England, and its relationship to the Moravian movement, is told in two recent works: Richard P. Heitzenrater's *Wesley and the People Called Methodists,* published by Abingdon in 1995; and Stephen Tomkins' *John Wesley: A Biography,* published by Eerdmans in 2003. The quotation from Wesley's father appears on p. 30 of Heitzenrater's book.

The Great Awakening in America: The basic source is a collection of documents edited by Alan Heimert and Perry Miller, *The Great Awakening: Documents Illustrating the Crisis and Its Consequences,* published by Bobbs-Merrill in 1967. Heimert also wrote an extensive analysis of this movement and its relation to political events of the era, *Religion and the American Mind, From the Great Awakening to the Revolution;* published by Harvard University Press in 1966. Edwin Scott Gaustad's *The Great Awakening in New England,* published by Harper in 1957, remains of value. Nathan O. Hatch's *The Democratization of American Christianity,* published by Yale University Press in 1989, describes the role of revivalism in shaping America's democratic culture in the nineteenth century.

The role of both the Great Awakening of the 1740s and the Second Great Awakening of the early 1800s in the emergence of the American Baptist movement is documented in *The Diary of Isaac Backus,* edited by William G. McLoughlin, published in 3 volumes by Brown University Press in 1979. Backus was a major figure in the founding of the American Baptist churches and his faithfully kept diary provides an insightful window into the human factors which produced this group of churches.

Evangelical Intentionality: The recent movements of lay intentionality are described by Jonathan Wilson-Hartgrove in *New Monasticism: What It Has to Say to Todays Church,* published by Brazos in 2008. His first book, *To Baghdad and Beyond: How I Got Born Again in Babylon,* published by Cascade Books in 2005, is an important autographical account by one of the leaders in this new movement. The present book was initiated by the author's contacts with this group of intentional Christians, and especially Jonathan Wilson-Hartgrove.

Catholic Lay Intentionality: Mark and Louise Zwick's *The Catholic Worker Movement: Intellectual and Spiritual Origins,* published by Paulist Press in 2005, is written by a married couple who have devoted their lives to creating a Catholic Worker House in Houston, TX.

A complete collection of John Paul's statements on the Civilization of Love has been published online at *www.CivilizationOfLove.net.*

Chapter 9: The Legacy of Evangelical Intentionality

The Evangelical Accomplishment: The Inquisition record quoted in the "Education" sub-section appears in the 15th edition of *Martyrs Mirror,* published by Herald Press in 1987, pp. 774–75. The full title is *The Bloody Theater, Or, Martyrs' Mirror: Compiled from Various Authentic Chronicles, Memorials, and Testimonies by Thieleman J. van Braght ; translated from the original Dutch or Holland language from the edition of 1660 by Joseph F. Sohm.*

The evangelical contribution to social justice is summarized by Jim Wallis in his 2008 book, *The Great Awakening: Reviving Faith and Politics in a Post-Religious Right America,* published by HarperOne, pp. 17–24. There is a detailed study of the role of American evangelicals in the abolition of slavery in the United States in Bertram Wyatt-Brown, *Lewis Tappan and the Evangelical War Against Slavery,* published by Case Western Reserve University Press in 1969.

For the author's views on Roger Williams's role in the development of American democracy see his essay, "Democracy, Nonviolence and the American Experience" in *Nonviolent America: History through the Eyes of Peace,* edited by Louise Hawkley and James C. Juhnke, published by Bethel College (Kansas) in 1993.

CHAPTER 10: MEETING AT THE RIVER

Information regarding the International Pentecostal Catholic and Baptist Catholic dialogues is available on the Vatican website, *Vatican.va.*

The report of the International Mennonite Catholic Dialogue is available online at *Bridgefolk.net,* which includes a great deal of additional information about this dialogue, both on the international and North American levels.

INDEX

A

Acts of the Apostles xiv, 4, 105, 109, 112
African American Churches 207
Albigensians 124, 138, 140, 142, 235
Alexandria 3, 6
Alsace 176
Amana Colony 194
Amazing Grace 206
Ambrose of Milan, St. 14, 121, 137
America 185, 190–93, 210, 219
American Baptists 190, 238
American Society of Church History 179
Amish ix, 175–79, 185, 237
Amman, Jacob 176
The Anabaptist Vision 179, 237
Anabaptists 169–79, 204, 206, 208, 237
    Dutch 172–75, 182, 203
    and education 204
    Hutterian 175
    legacy of 178–9
    and medieval Christianity 179
    Swiss 170–72, 175
ancient world 9, 10, 19–21
Angela of Foligno 72–75, 77–78, 233
Anglican 188–9, 206
Anthony of the Desert, St. xvi, 4–6, 14–17, 20, 31–32, 34, 144, 229–30
Antioch 13, 122
apocalyptic movements 173, 236

Apostles xv, 4, 90, 105–12, 146, 153, 199, 225
apostolic tradition 110, 112, 123, 141
Aquinas, Thomas, St. 70, 92
Archbishop of Canterbury 156
Ariald of Milan 136–37
Arians 33
Armenia 122, 124, 138, 235
art 53, 59
Assisi 58, 60, 63, 65, 73, 75, 233
Assyrian Christians 122
Athanasius of Alexandria, St. 6, 20, 229
    Life of St. Anthony 6, 14, 20, 229–30
Audisio, Gabriel 236
Augustine of Hippo, St. 14–16, 33, 56, 116, 140, 143, 230, 234
    and Donatists 115–17, 125–26, 234
    and just war doctrine 56, 116, 235
Augustinian canons 67
Augustinian friars 75, 81–82
Austria 146, 168, 170, 175
Avars 27

B

Backus, Isaac 238
baptism 106, 119, 123, 139, 169–70, 175, 186, 208–9
    adult 123–24, 139, 169–70, 174–75, 182, 208–9
    infant 118, 123, 139, 169, 171, 208
    rebaptizing 170, 204, 208

M

Machiavelli, Niccolò 78
MacIntyre, Alasdair 99, 234
Magyrs 27
Manicheans 14, 138, 140
manual labor 91, 151
Manz, Felix 170
Map, Walter 145–46
Mark the gravedigger 163
Martin of Tours, St. 31–34, 121, 231
martyrs xviii, 12, 42, 44, 90, 112, 114–
    16, 121, 123, 137, 140, 172, 177,
    218, 237
Martyrs Mirror 177, 239
Mary, St. 106, 139, 148
Massachusetts Bay 185
McNeill, William H. 230
medieval era 78, 80, 102, 160, 164, 179,
    183, 187, 202, 208
medieval plague epidemic 79
medieval religious revival 59, 128–30,
    136, 143–44, 164, 193, 235
Mediterranean world 8–9, 12, 23, 26,
    37–38, 117
mendicant movement 50, 66–71,
    81–83, 92, 233
    academic studies 68–70, 81–82
    orders 67–69, 71, 83, 97
    preaching 67, 69–70
Menno Simons 173–75
Mennonite Catholic Dialogue ix, x,
    221–23, 239
Mennonite Catholic Theological
    Colloquium 223
Mennonite World Conference 178,
    221–22
merchants 69–70, 95, 137, 144
Messiah xii, 107–8
Methodists 123, 188–90, 237–38
Metlake, George 231
middle class 58, 69, 95, 133, 137, 147,
    155–56, 162, 183, 186
Milan 14, 16, 33, 135–38
military 27, 44–45, 47–48, 56, 58, 79,
    88, 93, 125, 134, 184
    coercion of religious belief by 48, 79,
    125, 134

military (*continued*)
    non-participation in xix, 33–34, 44,
    96, 113, 147–48, 177–78, 185,
    201
    power of 21, 93, 128, 184
    soldiers *see* soldiers
Minahan, James B. 230
miracles 37–38, 73, 106–7, 230
missionaries xiii, xix, 17, 31, 35, 43, 65,
    68, 71, 87, 117, 138, 187–89, 191,
    203, 205, 209, 226
monasticism ix, xvi, xxi, 1, 3, 6–8, 12–
    16, 21, 36, 79, 86, 88, 101–2, 167,
    175, 188–89, 207, 211, 231, 234
    and democracy 93–94
    eastern 13, 118, 230
    Egyptian *see* Egyptian monastic
        movement
    and evangelical communities 169,
    194, 212
    first millennium 1, 8, 12–18, 20–26,
    31–32, 35–36, 38, 41, 132
    and the future 98–99
    and institutional Church xx, 8, 38
    and intentionality 88–89
    and the laity 70, 76, 94–96
    legacy of 86–89, 93, 96, 98–99
    medieval 47, 78, 87
    monasteries 3, 4, 7, 13, 33–35,
    51–52, 73, 133, 170
    monastic life 11–13, 16–20, 35, 38,
    49, 70, 88, 90, 92, 94–95
    monks 3–7, 72, 231
    and the ordering of time 89–90
    political impact of 8, 21, 36, 43, 45,
    48–49
    post-Reformation 86
    and work 91
money 4, 60, 109, 130, 144, 211
Montanism 111–13, 117, 234
Montanus 111
Montpellier, Guy de 148
Moore, R. I. 235
morality 30, 153, 181, 201, 210
Moravia 168
Moravians 160, 187–89, 237
Moses 56, 90
Moses the Black 6